Staged News

A VOLUME IN THE SERIES

*Journalism and Democracy*

EDITED BY

*Kathy Roberts Forde and Sid Bedingfield*

# STAGED NEWS

THE
FEDERAL
THEATRE
PROJECT'S
LIVING
NEWSPAPERS
IN NEW YORK

## JORDANA COX

UNIVERSITY OF MASSACHUSETTS PRESS
*Amherst and Boston*

ISBN 978-1-62534-679-7 (paper); 680-3 (hardcover)

Designed by Deste Roosa
Set in Alternate Gothic ATF and Adobe Garamond Pro
Printed and bound by Books International, Inc.

Cover design by adam b. bohannon
Cover photo: Harry Shaw, from the Federal Theatre Project Production Notebook from Seattle
production of *Power,* box 1058, Federal Theatre Project collection, 1932–1943, Library of Congress.

Library of Congress Cataloging-in-Publication Data
Names: Cox, Jordana, 1986– author.
Title: Staged news : the Federal Theatre Project's Living Newspapers in New
York / Jordana Cox.
Description: Amherst : University of Massachusetts Press, [2023] | Series:
Journalism and democracy | Includes bibliographical references and
index.
Identifiers: LCCN 2022024380 (print) | LCCN 2022024381 (ebook) | ISBN
9781625346803 (hardcover) | ISBN 9781625346797 (paperback) | ISBN
9781613769591 (ebook) | ISBN 9781613769607 (ebook)
Subjects: LCSH: Federal Theatre Project (New York, N.Y.)—History. | Living
newspaper—History and criticism. | Theater—New York (State)—New
York—History—20th century.
Classification: LCC PN3307.U6 C68 2023  (print) | LCC PN3307.U6  (ebook) |
DDC 792/.022—dc23
LC record available at https://lccn.loc.gov/2022024380
LC ebook record available at https://lccn.loc.gov/2022024381

British Library Cataloguing-in-Publication Data
A catalog record for this book is available from the British Library.

A portion of chapter two was published in a previous form as "The Phantom Public, the
Living Newspaper: Reanimating the Public in the Federal Theatre Project's *1935* (New York,
1936)," *Theatre Survey* 58, no. 3 (2017): 300–325. Reproduced with permission of the Cambridge
University Press. A portion of chapter three was published in a previous form as "The
Loudspeaker and the Little Man: Mass Media and Democratic Participation in the Federal
Theatre Project's One-Third of a Nation," *Journal for the History of Rhetoric* 23, no. 2 (2020): 121–
147. Reproduced with permission.

# CONTENTS

# PREFACE

My grandfather Hersz Szajnfarber was a news enthusiast. He survived the Holocaust, brought his family to Montreal, and after two decades in a textile dyehouse, spent his retirement glued to CNN, taking brief breaks to swim and eat. At the dinner table, when my family came back to visit, he would hold forth on current affairs, focusing especially on politics and economics. When the conversation became too grim or esoteric, my grandmother Angie would remind him of his audience, quieting him with a wave of her hand and a brusque "Anyway . . ." I usually welcomed my grandmother's interjections— they often came with offers of more food—but I also wished I could keep up with my grandfather, and match his appetite for news. Listening to my grandfather, I came to believe that news stories encoded fundamental truths about the world—reminders of who was in power, evidence of what was possible, and warnings of war and catastrophe. My grandfather showed me that keeping up with the news was not only an abstract civic obligation; it was also a practice of kinship and survival in a country that would never quite feel like home.

In college I took courses that I thought would help me decode the news like my grandfather. I studied politics, international relations, and theories of democratic citizenship—the stuff, as I understood it, of "hard news." Rather than demystifying current affairs, however, my studies only revealed complexity. And instead of bringing me closer to my grandfather, they confirmed the chasm of difference in our histories, habits, and perspectives. These differences prompted introspection. I started thinking about what it was like to take in the news, how I made sense of what I read, saw, and heard, and how I determined what the news was asking of me. I became curious about the *experience of consuming* news and how it was shaped by journalistic labor and imagination.

Ultimately I found a path for this inquiry in a long-standing love of theater. During my graduate studies in theater and drama, I learned about a group of theater-makers who shared my preoccupation with news, as well as my curiosity about the experience of consuming it. Under the auspices of the United States Federal Theatre Project, a Depression-era employment initiative, an assemblage of artists, craftspeople, and journalists in New York worked together to adapt news for the stage. Their productions were unusual: part newspaper, part public gathering, part artwork. And while theater scholars had aptly contextualized these so-called "Living Newspapers" in the culture and politics of the New Deal, they were also, as the name suggests, experiments in news-making. The creators of Living Newspaper played with light, color, form, sound, the narrative possibilities of time and space, and the palpable presence of performers and spectators to convey current events in new and surprising ways. When information was overwhelming and abundant, Living Newspapers could direct their spectators' care and attention. Living Newspapers explored new ways to make news, and new ways to take it in.

Early in my research, as I explored the Library of Congress's online collection, I found a photo (featured on the cover of this book) that captured these possibilities, as well as some important limitations. It was taken by WPA photographer Harry Shaw, and appeared in lobby displays for a 1937 Living Newspaper called *Power*. The photo did not seem to reference a specific scene but rather to capture a broad journalistic vision, what I call in this book "staged news."

The promise of staged news emerges somewhere between the photo's background and foreground. In the background are columns of stock market figures—information in overwhelming abundance, at least to the non-expert. In the foreground, however, is a human figure, offering a reassuring guide. He sits easily in a chair, and shows the viewer where to look. When I look at this image, I find myself oscillating between relief and suspicion. I am drawn in by the promise of guidance, but I am wary of the figure's authority, the "look" of information, and the presentation of wonder; I am concerned with what this self-proclaimed guide might be missing—and what this absence might ask of its viewer.

*Staged News* seeks to carry both of these orientations in its account of journalistic experimentation. It interrogates the disparate forms of experience and expertise that FTP workers brought to their reporting. It recovers the ambitiousness and uncertainty of news workers who were seeking to challenge professional norms while stabilizing their working conditions. It traces a body of work that was often strident and clunky, but nonetheless prompted reflection and action. It shows how, even in professional institutions profoundly shaped by racism and sexism, powerful critiques emerged from the margins. Situating Living Newspapers amid the shifting field of 1930s journalism, *Staged News* recounts an unusual history—one with still-prescient implications for news production and consumption. As important, it offers an optic for seeing how news is put together, consumed, interpreted—how it shapes personal lives, relationships, families, and identities, as I learned early on from my grandfather—and how it might work differently and more inclusively.

# ACKNOWLEDGMENTS

Like most Living Newspapers, this book reflects the time, energy, and insight of a huge number of people. I would like to acknowledge the integrity, expertise, and collegiality of the University of Massachusetts Press team: in particular, Matt Becker, Rachael DeShano, and Sally Nichols. Amanda Heller provided erudite and meticulous copy editing, and Jessica Hinds-Bond expertly assembled the index. I am honored to be part of the Journalism and Democracy series that Sid Bedingfield and Kathy Roberts Ford have so thoughtfully conceived, and I greatly appreciate their attentive engagement. I received invaluable comments from two anonymous reviewers, to whom I am especially grateful.

This project began under the guidance of exceptional mentors: Kate Bosher, Harvey Young, and especially Bob Hariman, Tracy C. Davis, and Susan Manning. Several of my friends and colleagues at Northwestern University have become profound sources of inspiration and support, in particular Dawn Brandes, David Calder, Faye Gleisser, Elliot Heilman, Lisa Kelly, Laura Lodewyck, Ruth Martin, Anndrea Mathers, Liz McCabe, Nick Miller, Dwayne Overton-Mann, Aileen Robinson, and Tara Rodman.

I received generative support and feedback from my colleagues at the University of Florida's Center for the Humanities and the Public Sphere: Tim Blanton, Bonnie Effros, Sarah Harms, and my supervisor, Sophia K. Acord. At the University of Richmond, the Faculty Humanities Seminar challenged and sharpened my thinking about what theater, history, and rhetoric can do in the world. I also benefited tremendously from conversations with Paul Achter, Tim Barney, Nicole Maurantonio, Robin Mundle, Rob Nelson, Patrice Rankine, Nicole Sackley, and Eric Yellin. Mari Lee Mifsud quickly became a formidable mentor, whose rigorous care and intellect are an ongoing source of inspiration. My UR Writing Group, Eva Hageman, Lauren Tilton, and Caroline Weist, infused the writing process with joy and curiosity.

My colleagues at the University of Waterloo offer insight and inspiration. Rob Danisch and Kim Hong Nguyen have asked thoughtful questions that deepened my research. Greg Campbell, Ceylan Enver, Ian Milligan, and especially Aynur Kadir (subsequently at the University of British Columbia), Sarah Klein, and Shana MacDonald, have been crucial sources of support. Colleen Kim Daniher (University of Laurier), Kim Lopez, Johonna McCants-Turner, and Nicole Nolette have sustained me through the final push of writing, as did Rebecca Schwartz-Bishir. My students have asked sharp questions and energized much of this research. I am especially grateful to my research assistants, Janelle Gunaratnam, Prithvi Nair, Jasmine Rajaballey, and especially Rachel Lazare.

Beyond the places where I have worked and studied, I am deeply indebted to interlocutors at the Evanston Workshop; the Radcliffe Seminar in Theater, Media, and Publics; the Mellon Institute on Research, Pedagogy, Activism; the Federal Theatre Project Conference at the Université Toulouse–Jean Jaurès, as well as the American Society for Theatre Research, the American Studies Association, and the Rhetoric Society of America. Some of the content in this book appeared in articles published by *Theatre Survey* (2017) and the *Journal for the History of Rhetoric* (2020), and benefited greatly from editors Nick Ridout and Ned O'Gorman, respectively, as well as four anonymous peer reviewers and *Theatre Survey* copy editor Michael Gnat.

My archival research has received funding from the Northwestern University School of Communication, the Social Sciences and Humanities Research Council of Canada, and the University of Waterloo. This book would not have been possible without the labor and expertise of archivists at the Federal Theatre Project Music Collection (especially Walter Zvonchenko); the National Archives and Records Administration; the George Mason Special Collections; University of Oregon Special Collections; New York University Tamiment Library and Robert F. Wagner Archives; and the Associated Press archives (especially Francesca Pitaro).

I have benefited enormously from opportunities to witness Living Newspapers at Jackalope Theatre (Annual Living Newspaper Festival), the Illinois Humanities Council (*Shelter/Chicago*) and the Green Mill (*Paper Machete*), and the Royal Court Theatre (*Living Newspaper: A Counter Narrative*). Special thanks to Anoushka Warden and to Vicky Featherstone for speaking to me at length about her work, as well as Ri Tornello, who sourced materials at Target Margin Theatre. I am also profoundly grateful to the teachers and mentors who taught me about theater and performance long before I learned about Living Newspapers, including Natalie Stern, Marti Maraden, Paul Griffin, Jan Irwin, Lise Ann Johnson, and Arthur Milner.

I am grateful to colleagues and friends who shared their expertise in the form of guidance, resources, or careful readings, including Kate Dossett, Lindsay Goss, Elizabeth Osborne, Marlis Schweitzer, Elliott Turley, and Ann Folino White.

My family's contributions to this book are too numerous to count. The Chermels, Golds, Coxes, and Shainfarbers gave me soft places to land at stressful moments. Ann Cox offered encouragement, and Riva Gold shared insights into professional journalism. Wallace Hersch has provided me with a steady supply of unadulterated joy, and I owe a special debt of gratitude to Emily Dirks, who has helped to care for him so I could write. Zach Cox and Amy

Killoran are a constant source of love, commiseration, and celebration. My parents, John and Lily Cox, model intellectual engagement, and their love is what gives me the courage to write. Kevin Carey, my favorite person, makes everything possible.

I dedicate this book to my family and to the friends who read the messiest drafts, asked the biggest questions, and nudged me over the finish line too many times to count: Kevin Carey, Faye Gleisser, Anndrea Mathers, Dwayne Overton-Mann, Aileen Robinson, and Tara Rodman. Thank you for your love and curiosity.

# A NOTE ON TERMINOLOGY

Federal Theatre Project workers and historians have used a variety of names to describe the group of theater-makers and journalists I discuss in this book, including the Living Newspaper, the New York Living Newspaper Unit, and the Living Newspaper Division. I use "New York Living Newspaper" (NYLN) or "the Unit" to disambiguate the New York team from other groups of artists creating Living Newspapers within and across other FTP units. Similarly, I capitalize "Living Newspaper" in order to distinguish the FTP's distinctive take on the form from precedents and variations abroad.

The NYLN employed a large staff with a variety of work backgrounds and skills. Many of them, from seamstresses to actors to public relations agents, fell well outside the parameters of "professional journalism." Therefore I use the term "news-making" to encompass the NYLN's work, and "news-makers" as a broad work/professional designation. The latter nods to and broadens the term used by Hanno Hardt and Bonnie Brennen in their pathbreaking volume, *Newsworkers: Toward a History of the Rank and File.*

Staged News

# THEATER, NEWS, AND JOURNALISTIC IMAGINATION

Not many people can say that a job in theater is their professional safety net, but journalist Morris Watson could. Born in Joplin, Missouri, in 1901, Watson started reporting when he was just twenty-two, beginning at the *Omaha World Herald* before moving on to the *Denver Post,* the *Chicago Herald,* and then the *Chicago Examiner.* He went on to work for the Associated Press, first in Chicago and then in New York. He was in his own words "a newspaperman" through and through. Watson was also, however, an active labor organizer, and in 1935, one year after he became vice president of the newly formed American Newspaper Guild, he was fired from his job at the AP. Suddenly jobless in the depths of the Great Depression, Watson, like many Americans, turned to President Franklin D. Roosevelt's Works Progress Administration, a stimulus and relief program.

Among the WPA's many infrastructural and cultural initiatives was the Federal Theatre Project. Under the FTP's auspices, Watson would join nearly thirteen thousand Americans across the country who earned their paychecks by making free or low-cost theater. Watson's assignment, however, was unique. He was appointed the managing producer of the New York Living Newspaper unit. A team of journalists and theater-makers supported by a range of other craftspeople and professionals, the NYLN identified issues that urgently affected Americans, from affordable housing to public utilities. They sourced statistics, quotes, and legislative excerpts, and brought their reporting to the stage in sweeping dramatic narratives. In the Manhattan offices of the NYLN, Watson had found his way back to the newsroom, but in service to a very different kind of news.

The NYLN was short-lived but significant. Between 1935 and 1939, the NYLN would create six Living Newspaper productions: *Ethiopia* (staged for a small invited audience, 1936); *The Events of 1935* (Biltmore Theatre, 1936); *Injunction Granted!* (Biltmore Theatre, 1936); *Triple-A Plowed Under* (Biltmore Theatre, 1936), *Power* (Ritz Theatre, 1937), and *One-Third of a Nation* (Adelphi Theatre, 1938). The NYLN was the Federal Theatre Project's most prolific producer of Living Newspapers; in fact, it was the only unit dedicated entirely to the form. And while its productions garnered large audiences, and in some cases critical praise, they also drew suspicions of propaganda, especially from Roosevelt's more conservative critics. Within a few years, the Dies Committee in the US Congress, a precursor to the House Un-American Activities Committee, was holding hearings with FTP staff, whom it accused of disseminating communist propaganda both onstage and behind the scenes. When the Dies Committee formed in 1938, the NYLN was staging its most popular production, *One-Third of a Nation,* which ran for ten months, drew over 200,000 spectators in New York, and inspired adaptations in Cincinnati, Detroit, Hartford, Washington, New Orleans, Philadelphia, Portland, and Seattle. On June 30, 1939, Congress dismantled the FTP, and with it the NYLN. A new Living Newspaper about health care was in development, but without the infrastructure of the WPA, it would close after only a short commercial run the following year.

Nearly a century after the FTP ended, a small cohort of artists have continued to explore the Living Newspaper form. In doing so, many invite their audiences to consider what was lost. Chicago's Jackalope Theatre, for example, has described its annual Living Newspaper Festival as an "homage." The Metropolitan Theatre in New York presented a Living Newspaper triptych in "jubilant celebration of these social dramas created by the WPA." London's Royal Court Theatre advertised its "living newspapers for our times" in bold red typography, evoking Red Decade design.[1] These contemporary living newspapers are much more than tributes; they have reimagined, and at times critiqued, their antecedents. Yet they are also tinged with nostalgia, all asking, in some way, how artists and producers might re-create the conditions in which Living Newspapers thrived.

Though indebted to the energy and intellect behind these and other contemporary adaptations, this book aims neither to rehabilitate the NYLN's work nor to lament its loss.[2] Instead it seeks to recuperate and continue an inquiry that has been sidelined in Living Newspaper historiography: a sustained series of efforts to reimagine the news. The phrase "staged news" attempts to capture this goal. In the most literal sense, it describes what happened when journalists worked for the FTP; in a more conceptual sense, it offers an optic for seeing how news-makers artfully assemble observations, sensations, and narrative for public witnessing.

My argument is that in making news for the stage, the New York Living Newspaper sought not only to relay current events, but also to draw attention to the ideas and techniques that mainstream newspapers used to elicit Americans' care and attention. In doing so, Living Newspapers cultivated *journalistic imagination,* a capacity to perceive, reflect on, and revise the processes through which people and issues are deemed *newsworthy.* Living Newspapers cast a spotlight on norms that were coalescing in print journalism and offered a compelling—though imperfect—alternative.[3]

This alternative was collaborative, self-conscious, and dynamic. Living Newspapers espoused a commitment to rigorous truth-telling while experimenting with who news was for and what it could do. Living Newspapers, however, were neither universal nor transcendent; journalistic imagination is shaped by social, cultural, and material conditions. Most significantly, perhaps, the NYLN reflected the expansive coalitions of the Popular Front and also its systematic inattention to race and racism. Living Newspapers reimagined news, but they would reiterate what the African American scholar Richard Iton calls "the solidarity blues."[4]

This book's central claim, that Living Newspapers were in fact a form of *news*, might sound too obvious to need saying. The word, after all, is in the name. Yet Living Newspapers are strikingly absent from histories of journalism.[5] One reason for this might be that the history of journalism as an academic field in the United States is relatively new. The historian John Nerone dates it to the early twentieth century, and the self-proclaimed "oldest peer-reviewed journal of mass media history in the United States" dates back only to 1974.[6]

Even setting aside the relative newness of journalism history, however, Living Newspapers make for an unusual case study. They resist powerful journalistic norms or, more specifically, distinctions: between objectivity and bias, bearing witness and taking action, propaganda and democratic communication, public interest and exclusion. Moreover, they are works of theater—an unconventional medium for scholars who usually attend to mass media and material archives, and a cultural discourse that bears embarrassing associations with manipulation, trickery, and deceit.[7]

All of these possibilities, however, are speculative. And none of them explain why, just as journalism historians have tended to ignore Living Newspapers, theater historians have tended to sideline the journalists who helped create them. Perhaps lurking behind the mutual hesitation is uncertainty about what theater and journalism might actually have to offer each other, whether in the past or in the future. To characterize the problem in broad strokes, journalism is supposed to be lean, accurate, informative, while theater is—reputedly— excessive, deceptive, and distracting. The tension resonates in the words "Living Newspaper," albeit with slightly different connotations. The "living," as that which is animate, messy, and in the flesh, implies that the newspaper is at best dull—and at worst, dead.

Together, however, the words are hopeful. Perhaps, "living newspaper" suggests, the theater and the newspaper might supplement and transform each other. At the NYLN, the suggestion was often just that: a glimmer of possibility in an often clunky repertoire and its polarizing politics. ("Are they any good?" a professor asked incredulously when I proposed studying Living Newspapers in graduate school.) Less concerned, however, with artistic assessments than with cultural history, this book argues that the possibility of mutual transformation was foundational to the form.

Consider an article Watson penned for the leftist *New Theatre Review* after less than a year at the Unit's helm.[8] Trying to articulate what, exactly, he and his staff were up to, he titled it simply "The Living Newspaper." The article was tentative but full of excitement. Watson explained how the NYLN came about and described a recent production. As the article neared its conclusion, he attempted to summarize the Living Newspaper as a whole: "A literally rough estimate of it at the moment would be: 'Combine the newspaper and the theatre and to hell with the traditions of both.'"[9] Watson's terse imperative, a call to "combine the newspaper and the theatre," implied a novel experiment. His rejection of what came before—"to hell with the traditions of both"!—invoked a daring avant-garde. Though Watson's description was, by his own account, a "rough estimate," the work he described was undeniably ambitious. It implied nothing less than a radical inquiry in journalistic practice.

*Staged News* aims to excavate this inquiry, and in doing so, to explain how the NYLN conceived the work of news-making at a moment when news-making was in profound transition. In this chapter I introduce two seemingly disparate histories: the first is about how the newspaper was contested and defined in the interwar United States; the second is about how conventions of theatrical reporting moved across Revolutionary Russia, the Weimar Republic, and the United States in the 1920s. After tracing these two histories, I offer a way to see and interpret their connections, theorizing what I call "journalistic imagination" in the NYLN's repertoire.

## PRINT JOURNALISM IN TRANSITION: DEFINITIONS AND CONTESTATIONS IN THE INTERWAR PERIOD

The 1920s and 1930s were a pivotal period in the history of mass communication; indeed, it was toward the end of this period that the neologisms "mass media" and "mass communication" entered popular use.[10] In the wake of World War I,

Americans were reckoning with the effects of the nation's first systematic, mass-mediated propaganda campaign—a campaign that had sent over 115,000 Americans to their deaths. At the same time, the economic boom of the 1920s gave some Americans, predominantly though disproportionately white people with disposable income, unprecedented access to new media and technologies. By 1929, over 80 percent of Americans were watching newsreels, and 40.3 percent of families owned a radio set.[11] After the stock market crashed in 1929 and the Great Depression ensued, news and communication workers would be among the 15 million Americans who lost their jobs. But many would feel compelled to bear witness to the suffering around them and record, photograph, or write about what they saw. What William Stott calls the "documentary movement" coalesced around "the presentation or representation of actual fact in a way that makes it credible and vivid to people at the time." At the heart of this movement was "documented fact," which Stott characterized as "the mainstay of all journalism."[12] Social-scientific case studies like Clinch Calkins's *Some Folks Won't Work* (1930), documentary photo initiatives like the ones sponsored by the Farm Security Administration and Office of War Information (1935–1944), and documentary films like *The Plow That Broke the Plains* (1936) all adapted journalistic sensibilities. Documentary impulses would gain momentum under Franklin Delano Roosevelt, whose New Deal–funded initiatives included a nationwide photography project under the Farm Security Administration.[13] A canny communicator himself, Roosevelt addressed the nation more than any other president before him, exploiting the new possibilities of radio in his weekly "fireside chats."[14]

Amid these developments in mass communication, newspapers remained popular if no longer hegemonic. Even during the Great Depression, the average household subscribed to at least one newspaper.[15] News workers, however, including reporters, rewrite staff, and editors, would vigorously debate the meaning and parameters of their work.[16] Although there were many developments that shaped these debates across the 1920s and 1930s, five interrelated areas were especially instrumental: (1) new media and technology; (2) professionalization and institutionalization; (3) objectivity as a professional standard; (4) commercialization and corporatization; and (5) the rise of press criticism. These developments, though by no means an exhaustive history, were especially influential on NYLN's engagement with journalism.

### NEW MEDIA AND TECHNOLOGY

New media and technology expanded, challenged, and changed the work of print journalists, particularly those employed by newspapers. Reporting had gotten faster and more expansive since the late nineteenth century, when journalists began to use typewriters, pneumatic tubes, and telephones. The telephone, a newsroom fixture by 1920, also created a new role in "rewrite" staff, who would take calls from reporters and synthesize their findings. Meanwhile, as radio entered its "golden age" in the 1930s, it also "emerged as a competitor to both morning and evening newspapers."[17] In 1935 the United Press and the International News Service (two of the AP's competitors) sold their services to radio networks, bolstering radio's capacity to deliver breaking news.[18]

Developments in photography, too, were dramatically transforming newspaper work. Illustrations and photos had appeared in news publications since the 1880s, but sparingly. Starting at the turn of the century, however, "the halftone, the roll-film camera, the flash, and improved printing presses" made photos more accessible to publications. In the early decades of the twentieth century, it was mostly advertisers in tabloids and magazines, especially women's magazines, that took advantage of these developments. By the 1930s, however, mainstream newspapers were following suit. Over the course of the decade, Gallup surveys would find major dailies almost doubling their weekly photo outputs.[19] Cameras could now capture candid, vivid images, and starting in 1935, with the AP's launch of its Wirephoto service, they could reach newsrooms faster than ever before, as the very events they documented were unfolding.[20] Meanwhile, magazines continued to popularize photojournalism: of special significance was *Life,* which *Time* publisher Henry Luce bought in 1936, and transformed into the first American pictorial.[21] In her institutional history of *Life,* the historian Sheila Webb cites a reader's admiring observation that the magazine attracted its millions of readers by giving "the sense of living more abundantly."[22] At its best, this reader implied, photojournalism could infuse everyday life with richness and meaning.

While many readers and news-makers saw photojournalism as a means of vivid storytelling, others were anxious about its rise. Among some print journalists, photos were no more than a supplement to the written word, or worse, a vestige of yellow journalism that pandered to undiscerning readers. Just as the photograph was claiming space in new newspapers, however, photographers were claiming status in the newsroom. As the media historian Will Mari observes, the 1930s saw designated spaces and departments, and reporters began to acknowledge—in some cases perhaps begrudgingly—that photographers were indeed "newspaper men." Star reporters collaborated with photographers on major assignments, and lower-level reporters, especially those in money-strapped Depression-era newsrooms, were tasked with taking their own photos.[23] New media, and particularly new photographic technologies, changed the material conditions of news work, and they raised ideological questions about its value. Technologies of circulation, in conjunction with the documentary movement, brought about a cultural shift, leading many Americans to identify "seeing" with "knowing," including in the news.[24] As photojournalism rose to new heights of popularity in the 1930s, it asked newspaper journalists to grapple with the limits and possibilities of the printed word.

PROFESSIONALIZATION AND INSTITUTIONALIZATION

The 1920s and 1930s saw important developments in institutions and training, and subsequently a growing sense of shared professional identity among journalists. As the journalism scholar Michael Schudson explains, the 1920s saw many journalists identifying as a professional class for the first time.[25] They were bolstered by several decades of institutional growth, including the first university courses in the 1860s, followed by dedicated programs and departments in the early twentieth century, the Society of Professional Journalists in 1909, and the launch of the Pulitzer Prize in 1917. Serious journalists, moreover, felt pressure to define themselves against new and troubling alternatives: propagandists, public relations professionals, and tabloid journalists. In April 1923, 107 newspaper editors gathered to address a recent article denigrating the newspaper in the *Atlantic Monthly*.[26] They would form a professional organization, the American Society of Newspaper Editors (ASNE), and publish a code of ethics.

The so-called "Canons of Journalism" articulated a shared purpose for newspapers: "to communicate to the human race what its members do, feel and think." The mission was ambitious and entailed responsibilities. Thus, the Canons asserted seven principles: (1) responsibility; (2) freedom of the press; (3) independence; (4) sincerity, truthfulness, accuracy; (5) impartiality; (6) fair play; (7) decency. The code was widely adopted. A 1930 AP guide for filing editors invoked "the principles which have commanded universal respect for the service," including "impartiality and accuracy," balance and independence from special interests, and "an unbiased and fearless recording of actualities."[27] Thus, by the 1930s, the largest US wire service was not only reiterating the Canons of Journalism but also crediting them with "commanding universal respect." Although journalists and editors would contest the applications of these principles, they remained powerful throughout the 1930s; indeed, in 1926 the Society for Professional Journalists adopted it, and in 1938 the ASNE restated them without revision.[28]

The ASNE also advanced conversations about journalism training. By the 1930s, over fifty institutions taught journalism, and attention was turning to standardization. The ASNE's Committee on Schools vigorously debated what aspiring journalists needed and what kind of knowledge their craft required. At the heart of these debates were long-standing questions about the nature of journalistic expertise. In 1930, writes the journalism historian Jean Folkerts, an ASNE report described tensions between editors who "frankly want the departments of journalism to be trade schools" and those who wanted students to acquire a "broader background" that introduced them to "manifold relationships of men to society."[29] Debates about education reflected changes in the field: the modern newsroom was increasingly large, stratified, and streamlined, with specialists needed not only for different beats but also for different components of news production. A 1937 study by the media sociologist Alfred McClung Lee observed that the modern newsroom looked like "an automobile manufacturer's assembly line."[30] Meanwhile, popular films and plays were still portraying journalists in solitary, obsessive pursuit of the story that only they could tell. It is no surprise that journalists grappled with questions about divisions of labor and knowledge throughout the interwar period.

The most visible forums for these debates were profoundly exclusionary. The historian Fred Carroll observes that white journalists seldom recognized their Black counterparts as professionals despite the fact that they tended to be college graduates.[31] Thus it is no surprise that the ASNE, for instance, excluded the largely weekly Black newspapers, and by extension Black editors, by limiting membership to papers with daily circulation. As a result of "arbitrary rules of circulation," Mari notes, it would not be until 1965 that the ASNE would accept the *Chicago Daily Defender*'s John Sengstacke as its first Black member.[32] Black women's absence from the organization is especially striking, given significant journalistic leadership from the likes of Sadie Warren, publisher of the *New Amsterdam News* from 1926 to 1936, and Marvel Cooke, who did editorial work at the NAACP's journal *The Crisis* as well as writing her own column.[33] Within Black news organizations too, however, women were underrepresented. Throughout the twentieth century, D'Weston Haywood has argued, leaders in the Black press aligned racial advancement with Black masculinity. Black women journalists were rarer than their male counterparts, were paid less, and were often relegated to the "women's pages."[34] There, however, they made significant contributions. As the historian Kim Gallon argues, women's page editors like Thelma E. Berlack, Bertha Perry Rhodes, and Julia Bumry Jones addressed a "northern, urban workforce" of "domestics, factory workers and teachers" growing amidst the Great Migration.[35]

White women were involved much earlier than Black men and women in the ASNE, but in limited numbers. Despite the overrepresentation of men in the newsroom, cultural and demographic, women were gradually becoming more visible. The 1920s saw the number of woman reporters and editors double; 1936 marked the publication of Ishbel Ross's *Ladies of the Press: The Story of Women in Journalism by an Insider;* and first lady Eleanor Roosevelt allowed only women to cover her press conferences, meaning that dailies and wire services required women on staff.[36] As the historian Paul Alfred Pratte notes, however, "the ASNE treated women idiosyncratically, if they were even treated at all." Alice Fox Pitts, a working journalist trained at Columbia, served in executive administrative roles from 1931 to 1963; Zell Hart Deming, who published the *Tribune Chronicle* in Warren, Ohio, was the first recorded woman member. Even once they were admitted to the ASNE, however, women faced rampant sexism and stereotyping in professional discussions.[37] This was a reflection of newsroom culture, in which mostly male editors were habituated to bawdy jokes and angry tirades. "Handling groups of men," Ross wrote, was an occupational hazard for any woman working on a major assignment. It was a "ticklish matter, although it has been done repeatedly with success."[38] White women and women of color made significant contributions to 1930s journalism, but only by navigating gendered and racialized norms of professionalism.

### OBJECTIVITY AS A JOURNALISTIC STANDARD

Bolstered by professional institutions and the models of professionalism they privileged, objectivity became the "chief occupational value of American journalism" by the 1920s. While journalists had pursued various forms of impartiality, neutrality, and independence in the past, the articulation of these values by the ASNE enshrined objectivity in mainstream journalistic standards. As Michael Schudson observes, it was only when journalists identified as a distinctive professional class that they could define objectivity as a "self-conscious articulation of rules with moral force."[39] Professional journalists seeking legitimacy in mainstream publications would now seek to disentangle their reporting from their political commitments.

Yet "at the very moment that journalists claimed objectivity as their ideal," Schudson writes, "they also recognized its limits." By way of example, he points to the rise in the 1930s of "interpretive journalism," which sought to contextualize and explain complex issues.[40] Thus, while objectivity reigned as a norm, so too did columnists like Heywood Broun, Walter Lippmann, Dorothy Thompson, and Walter Winchell. Columnists' accounts were often factual and well researched but by no means impartial. Indeed their first-person perspective was the basis of their appeal. Although editors tended to disapprove of columnists' "cult of personality," publishers knew they sold papers.[41] Star columnists could earn significantly more than rank-and-file reporters.[42]

While celebrity allowed some journalists to transcend the expectations of objectivity, for others—especially white women and Black journalists—objectivity was another yet pretense for exclusion. There were some notable exceptions: Lorena Hickock made a name for herself at the AP and developed a friendship with Eleanor Roosevelt by way of an interview; Genevieve Forbes

Herrick worked for the *Chicago Tribune*. But white women tended to find significant assignments where impartiality was seemingly less in demand, in venues like tabloids and occasionally, as in Dorothy Thompson's case, in columns. This was a legacy of the nineteenth century, when white women's route to publication had often entailed emotionally charged first-person testimonial. They were crucial to the rise of yellow journalism but were also denigrated as "stunt reporters," "sob sisters," and "pity platoons."[43] Thus, as journalistic standards consolidated around impartiality, women journalists faced a paradox. The journalism scholars Deborah Chambers, Linda Steiner, and Carole Fleming explain, "Those who refused to accept restrictions on what they could write about and who were not suitably feminine at work were branded as personally deviant, while those who accepted the limitations imposed on them and allowed themselves to be treated as feminine were professionally marginalized."[44] This paradox held fast in the 1920s and 1930s, and the rise of objectivity often impeded the integration of white women journalists into mainstream journalism. White women either had to sacrifice respectability in order to professionalize or had to sacrifice professionalism in order to maintain respectable womanhood. It is no surprise, then, that white women were underrepresented in commercial newsrooms.

Journalists of color also wrestled with the limits and possibilities of objectivity. In his history of African American journalism, for example, Fred Carroll notes that "white press critics accused Black journalists of violating the news industry's faith in objectivity by exaggerating racial wrongs and needlessly inflaming racial relations—an unpardonable lapse of professional integrity that most white journalists believed black reporters could never overcome."[45] What such critics missed was, in many cases, Black journalists' nuanced negotiations of objectivity with lived experience. As the historian Gerald Horne recounts, Claude Barnett founded the Associated Negro Press in 1919 as "something along the line of today's Associated Press." In keeping with the Canons of Journalism, the ANP advised writers, "Do not editorialize" but "tell both sides of the story." But Barnett recognized that the reigning standards posed challenges, both theoretical and practical, especially to Black journalists. "We," he acknowledged, "no more than the white papers try to [but] cannot always adhere strictly to an ideal of journalistic ethics." Black news-makers negotiated a tension between "the dissemination of news and the fight against injustice," all the while struggling to compete with white papers for advertisers.[46] It is provocative to consider how the Canons of Journalism might have gained complexity and nuance had Black editors been formally included in their composition.

## CORPORATIZATION AND CONGLOMERATION

If professional institutions and journalistic standards were raising questions about who made news and how, corporatization and conglomeration were drawing attention to who *owned* the news and dictated its interests. Corporate publishing moguls, including William Randolph Hearst and Joseph Pulitzer, had been vying for publications and readers since the 1890s. And though Pulitzer died in 1911, it was the fall of his *New York World* twenty years later that "finally convinced publishers that the Depression was real," writes David Welky.[47] Hearst, though deep in debt, weathered the Depression, as did Joseph Medill Patterson and Robert R. McCormick.

Smaller local and independent papers fared worse, continuing a trend that had already begun before the crash. The number of dailies in the United States," Welky observes, "declined from 2,514 in 1917 to 2,268 in 1930." By the mid-1930s, Hearst owned one-seventh of the daily papers that remained and one-quarter of the Sunday papers. His conglomerates and others took over local papers or ran them out of business. They were less inclined than individually owned dailies to cover local issues and perspectives, and relied instead on syndicated columns, press releases, and wire services like the AP. Hearst himself maintained close editorial control.[48]

The consolidation of newspapers under magnates like Hearst was troubling to many journalists, in part because it meant fewer perspectives and less original reporting. But there were other concerns too. Hearst's *New York Journal* was infamous for its "yellow journalism" techniques; sensational depictions of violence, scandal, and sexual innuendo had driven up circulation but compromised standards of propriety and accuracy. Moreover, with the exception of Patterson, Hearst and his peers were overwhelmingly conservative. Many had initially supported President Herbert Hoover until the continuing Depression and his controlling rapport with the press strained the relationship. And though Hearst and his colleagues were taken with Roosevelt at first, they opposed his expansive approach to social welfare. Under the auspices of their professional organization, the American Newspaper Publishers Association (ANPA), they would challenge New Deal labor reforms. By the time Roosevelt was up for reelection in 1936, McCormick and Hearst were publishing venomous editorials and accusing Roosevelt of communist sympathies.[49]

Between the conservative bent of Hearst, McCormick, and others, the eradication of local papers, and the homogenization of news coverage, it is no surprise that conglomerates and their executives drew the ire of critics, especially on the left. One of the most prominent among them was George Seldes, lionized by some as the "father of American press criticism." In 1928

Seldes resigned from his reporting job at the *Chicago Tribune* and spent the following decade exposing corruption and censorship, with a focus on the press. His 1938 book *Lords of the Press,* dedicated to the American Newspaper Guild "and others interested in a free press," adapted muckraking techniques to expose the machinations of the ANPA. In the following decade, he and his wife, Helen Larkin Seldes, would publish a media criticism newsletter, *In Fact.* While Seldes's work was pathbreaking, he was not alone. As the historian Helen Fordham observes, he worked alongside other critics who challenged the press from within, and often worked with tips from fellow reporters.[50] Press criticism surged in the 1930s, from inside the mainstream press and outside it.

### CRITIQUES OF THE PRESS AND MASS CULTURE

A groundswell of press criticism and cultural critique drew attention to the social and political implications of the newspaper's many transitions. As with the other changes I have described, this phenomenon acquired new prominence and inflection in the interwar period, and especially in the 1930s, though it had been developing over several decades. Crucial forerunners of this practice, though rarely acknowledged as such by white counterparts, were African American journalists, who had developed an extensive tradition of press criticism as a means of survival. Because Black journalists worked at the margins of a white and racist mainstream, their reporting was often inextricable from commentary on white reporting. As a result, while white news workers and even some white historians have tended to distinguish press criticism from reporting, Black news workers revealed how the two concepts were often entangled. Most canonically, perhaps, in her groundbreaking 1892 pamphlet *Southern Horrors: Lynch Law in All Its Phases,* Ida B. Wells revealed southern white newspapers' complicity in lynching and condemned newspapers across the nation for associating Blackness with violence and criminality.[51] In the twentieth century, the tradition of Black press criticism and journalism would grow with the founding of Black publications like the *Chicago Defender* (1905), the *New Amsterdam News (1909)* and the *Pittsburgh Courier* (1910). In *The Crisis,* editor W. E. B. Du Bois regularly presented excerpts from white newspapers and exposed their racial biases.[52] By the time the Harlem Renaissance was underway, the intertwined traditions of Black journalism and press criticism were well established, galvanized by reporting on the Great Migration.[53] With Black journalism at its peak popularity, millions of Black readers were not only consuming news but also considering what white newspapers were getting wrong, and what news could and should be.

In a more limited way, often ignoring the impact of race and racism, white newspapers and magazines had also turned attention to the shortcomings and possibilities of news. To some extent, the Progressive Era tradition of muckraking had catalyzed this self-consciousness. Starting at the turn of the twentieth century, muckrakers repeatedly exposed what other journalists and publishers had missed, studiously ignored, or covered up. In his 1906 book *The Jungle,* for instance, Upton Sinclair criticized the press for its antipathy toward unions and subsequent misrepresentation of corruption in the American meatpacking industry. *The Brass Check*, which he published in 1919, trained its focus exclusively on journalistic corruption, with Hearst as a central figure.[54]

By the 1930s, muckraking had been in decline for about a decade. Some had come to see it as overly sensationalist and commercial; even Ida Tarbell, widely remembered as one of the movement's originators, insisted in her autobiography that she did not like the label. "The truth of the matter," she proclaimed, "was that the muckraking school was stupid. It had lost the passion for facts in a passion for subscriptions."[55] Communication scholar Helen Fordham adds two other possible reasons for muckraking's decline. The first was the corporatization of news outlets, which made publishers more hostile to reporting that antagonized corporations. The other was World War I, which turned public sentiment against "unpatriotic" revelations of America's shortcomings.[56]

The development of public opinion research, however, took press criticism in new directions. Here, journalist and researcher Walter Lippmann played a crucial role. In 1920 he authored *A Test of News* with Charles Merz, one of his fellow editors at *The New Republic.* The study analyzed thousands of *New York Times* articles covering the Russian Revolution and concluded that the coverage was neither neutral nor accurate. Two years later Lippmann published *Public Opinion,* "generally recognized as the first important scientific study of news content."[57] Interpreting the findings from *A Test of News,* it argued that when the news failed to provide adequate information, citizens embraced stereotypes, prejudices, and "stored up images," which made them susceptible to manipulation. The development of empirical opinion research soon followed with the rise of opinion polling. Sociologists surveyed roughly thirty thousand residents of a small Connecticut city and in 1929 reported their findings in *Middletown: A Study in American Culture.* Eight years later they would publish a follow-up study, called *Middletown in Transition.* In 1935, George Gallup founded the American Institute of Public Opinion and surveyed Americans about their view on "relief and recovery."[58]

Opinion polling was instrumental not only in the formation of public opinion but also in the very idea of an "average" American and the culture such a person shaped and inhabited. Social statistics, as the historian Sarah Igo argues in *The Averaged American,* revealed "knowledge regimes and intellectual frameworks that allowed Americans to relate in new ways to 'the public.'"[59]

For editors and publishers, the rhetoric of "average Americans" was powerful: it informed market decisions about readers and circulation; it reinforced the idea of a singular public interest championed in the Canons of Journalism; and it supported norms around what kind of language was readable and accessible.

At the same time, critiques of mass culture were emerging from Marxist philosophers, writers, and artists. Theodor Adorno and Max Horkheimer, who fled Hitler's Germany in the mid-1930s, proposed that mass culture, writ large, was fundamentally dehumanizing. Newspapers, radio, and newsreels were complicit in the circulation of a culture that numbed citizens to serious threats, including the rise of fascism.[60] As the American studies scholar Laura Browder has shown, a cohort of radical Depression-era writers expressed similar anxieties. In James T. Farrell's Studs Lonigan trilogy, Studs skulks around pool halls and mindlessly gazes at comics and tabloids. In Horace McCoy's *They Shoot Horses, Don't They?* Robert Syverten kills his partner after a grueling dance marathon, sensationalized by the newspaper. In his *USA* trilogy, John Dos Passos critiqued the claims of journalists, mass media, and media owners to tell a singular truth about American history. McCoy, Farrell, and Dos Passos, of course, were also participants in mass culture themselves. And as Browder points out, some of their contemporaries saw new possibilities in mass culture: Clifford Odets praised film as a "genuine art-form for the masses of people"; Langston Hughes used jazz—infamously maligned by Adorno—to "promulgate a radical interpretation of African American history."[61] Where some saw hopelessness in mass culture, other saw possibilities for new social formation.

The news was hotly contested throughout the 1920s and 1930s. By professionalizing, institutionalizing, engaging in press criticism, and arguing with others in their field and beyond, news-makers were attentive to journalism's limits and possibilities. Journalists, educators, publishers, artists, and readers struggled to define who owned the news, who made the news, and who read it.

Amid the varied perspectives they offered, one recurring theme was *self-consciousness:* explicit attention to questions of journalism's definition and purpose. Living Newspapers made a powerful contribution to debates about news because they responded to this self-consciousness: in the theater, a space of witnessing, they drew attention to often abstract social formations that the news invoked and addressed; they asked if and how citizens and publics could come to know themselves and how they could communicate with one another. Just as importantly, they drew attention to the act of reporting: a culturally and historically specific practice, as James Carey describes it, of "rendering reality."[62] For this they drew on a lineage that lay outside the United States, outside print media, and well outside predominant models of objectivity.

## THEATRICAL REPORTING:
### REFRAMING LIVING NEWSPAPERS' ORIGINS AND INFLUENCES

To identify Living Newspapers with a single point of origin, or even a single lineage, would be to ignore the complex ways that performance moves across time and space. By definition, performance revises existing embodied practices. As the performance scholar Richard Schechner has famously written, performance is "restored behavior," enacted "never for the first time."[63] History too is a kind of restored behavior; it is always inflected by stories already told, by commitments and orientations that determine what historians can perceive. The theater scholar Stuart Cosgrove noted these limitations even as he offered an expansive history of living newspapers, beginning with Revolutionary Russia and the Weimar Republic before pointing to variations across Japan and Czechoslovakia, the UK, and the United States.[64] News and journalism have inspired performances around the world, and only occasionally under the English moniker "living newspaper."

Among the Living Newspaper's many antecedents and variations however—some, no doubt, yet to be studied—three are especially worth revisiting in the context of staged news at the FTP. The Blue Blouse movement of post-Revolutionary Russia and the German stage directors Bertolt Brecht and Erwin Piscator made demonstrable impacts on FTP artists. They did so in part as pioneers in "documentary theater" and "propaganda theater," traditions that emphasize Living Newspapers' use of primary source materials and leftist messages, respectively. Yet Blue Blouse, Brecht, and Piscator might also be understood in a tradition of theatrical reporting, one that continually sought to dramatize the present in urgent and provocative ways.

Theatrical reporting rejected illusion. Instead it espoused material realities that could be apprehended with the senses. In this respect, Blue Blouse, Brecht, and Piscator were indebted to myriad avant-garde artists, but especially to the Russian actor, director, and theorist Vsevelod Meyerhold. Whereas his teacher, Konstantin Stanislavsky, pioneered theatrical realism, Meyerhold had little interest in verisimilitude. Stanislavsky cultivated an acting system (the "Method") with careful attention to psychology, while Meyerhold embraced rhythmic, acrobatic movement in a training system he called biomechanics. Where Stanislavsky sought representational staging and scenography, Meyerhold embraced constructivism, forgoing realistic interiors for kinetic apparatus featuring gears, platforms, pulleys, and staircases. Yet Meyerhold, like Stanislavsky, was deeply committed to truth-telling. He used theatricality, in Robert Leach's words, to "shadow reality" and to convey "poetic truths."[65] In their staging and design, Blue Blouse, Piscator, and Brecht would follow Meyerhold—and other avant-garde artists like Yevgeny Vakhtangov and Nikolay Okhlopkov—in disaggregating truthfulness from realism, and in embracing a muscular aesthetic that represented the working classes. These strategies informed three distinctive approaches to describing the present, three distinctive modes of theatrical reporting.

### "AGITATION, PROPAGANDA, AND SOCIAL WORK": BLUE BLOUSE'S LIVING NEWSPAPERS

In Russia, *zhivaya ghazeta* ("living" or "alive" newspapers) developed from a tradition of the "spoken newspaper," whereby performers recited news to gatherings of citizens who had not learned to read. After the Russian Revolution of 1917, these recitations of news became more elaborate. František Deák writes: "The reading of the newspaper developed into the presentation of news by visualization (using posters on stage, staging diagrams and statistics), dramatization (monologue, dialogue, mass declamation, and short sketches), and 'musicalization' (news transformed into songs). The structure of the newspaper was followed: There were brief international and domestic news items, slogans of the day, decrees, caricatures, editorials, etc."[66] Starting in 1923, the Blue Blouse movement (Sinaia Bluza) would usher the living newspaper to new heights of popularity by organizing workers across the country into amateur and professional troupes.

Blue Blouse modeled an approach to theatrical reporting that was nimble, local, and massive in its reach. In his extensive study "From Kamchatka to Georgia," the theater scholar Robert Crane traces Blue Blouse's decade-long spread across the Soviet Union. At its peak, Crane notes, Blue Blouse claimed seven thousand troupes and 100,000 members, devising (typically) hour-long performances of song, dance, and topical sketches for beer halls, cafeterias, workers' halls, and factories. Taking their name from workers' signature garments, Blue Blouse troupes nimbly dramatized a range of pressing issues. A sketch on foreign affairs featured actors sticking their heads through a map to represent different countries; a sketch on electrification featured a singing light bulb; a memorial to Lenin featured a history of his life, punctuated by placards and culminating in "The Internationale."[67]

Blue Blouse was undeniably propagandistic, but it saw no conflict between news and propaganda. Indeed, as Crane notes, Blue Blouse was founded by three students at the State Institute of Journalism, and at least one of them, Boris Iuzhanin, would return to journalism later in his career. A publication by the Moscow Proletkult notes: "Thanks to its flexible form, the living newspaper is an excellent instrument of agitation, propaganda, and social work. The two components of the term—'newspaper' and 'living' are equally important. It means that even an illiterate person can 'read' such a newspaper." The living newspaper sought to agitate and to propagate, but it was nonetheless considered a newspaper, albeit a distinctive one. "Its general material," the Proletkult added, "is typical of newspapers, but it needs a different kind of elaboration." Unlike simple recitations of news, the Proletkult asserted, Living Newspapers should "dramatize" and "demonstrate."[68] For this, recommended *Blue Blouse* magazine in Crane's translation, troupes should enlist a director who could adopt the "all-seeing eyes of a reporter."[69] Clear-eyed reporting here was a complement to living newspapers' agitprop mission. An entry march published by *Blue Blouse* magazine, in a translation by Crane, proclaimed:

> We came to tell you, tell you, tell you,
> What you all should learn, should learn, should learn. Yes!
> From our newspaper, living newspaper, living newspaper,
> Everything that happens under the sun,
> You should learn about it all:
> About the international situation,
> And about the union movement,
> About the new way of life.[70]

Emphatic repetition—"our newspaper, living newspaper, living newspaper" ensured that audiences did not forget what they were consuming. So too did instructions for use: an imperative to learn as much as possible, and to cover a wide variety of topics and regions.

Although Blue Blouse conceived of news as a body of knowledge that citizens "should" learn, it also strove to reflect local interests and needs. Indeed, one reason behind its eponymous magazine was to encourage locally specific performances by providing sample scripts and instructions. It was also a reason why Blue Blouse celebrated amateur troupes. An article in *Blue Blouse* argues that while professional troupes had to "bring problems to attention and interest the audience in them," amateur troupes could play directly to the interests of their communities.[71]

TECHNOLOGICAL "ARABESQUE": PISCATOR'S DOCUMENTARY THEATER
The flexibility that allowed living newspapers to adapt to different communities across the Soviet Union also allowed the diffusion of its techniques in other countries. German artists were especially receptive to Blue Blouse. The company toured Germany in 1927, stopping at the theater of Erwin Piscator. There it would inspire both Piscator and Brecht, who were developing epic theater techniques

aligned with *Zeittheater,* which literally translates as "time theater" but might better be interpreted, as C. D. Innes suggests, as "topical theater."[72] Though epic theater is often associated with an episodic, dialectical structure, a cool, didactic tone, and Brecht's now canonized "alienation effect," epic theater is not easy to define. As Brecht's student Fredric Jameson would comment, epic theater is better understood as an ever-changing tool kit than a singular doctrine.[73]

As a tool kit, however, it was most often deployed by Brecht and Piscator toward the same overarching purpose—to cultivate critical reflection on the material conditions that led to class inequality. The Russian Revolution had been a source of hope for both Piscator and Brecht, and they shared Blue Blouse's political commitments to timely depictions of working-class struggles. Early in his career, Piscator's Proletarian Theatre had performed agitprop theater in workers' halls, and even when Piscator moved to more conventional theater spaces, he would strive to dramatize social conditions in vivid and economical ways.

It was a journalist, Alfons Paquet, whose play *Flags* would provide Piscator's first foray into epic dramaturgy. In the admiring words of Piscator, "Paquet aimed consistently at baring the roots of the case." Although the Haymarket riots in Chicago had happened over thirty years before *Flags* debuted in 1924, it nonetheless revealed a prescient class struggle. "Flags was in a sense the first Marxist drama," Piscator claimed, "and this production was the first attempt to make the forces of materialism tangible and comprehensible."[74]

Piscator's reporting techniques were technologically elaborate. Whereas Blue Blouse troupes eschewed professional institutions and popped up in public places, Piscator worked in a professional theater, Berlin's 1,800-seat Volksbühne. There, he projected subtitles, photos, and illustrations, not only to inform but also as "a mode of expanding the subject onstage and illuminating the background of the action." By his own account, he was the first to use projections in the theater, and he characterized them, rather poetically, as an "arabesque." Yet he was careful to qualify that his staging was otherwise simple; he aimed to tell the story "as clearly and objectively as possible."[75] Objectivity for Piscator was not about disinterest or political neutrality; rather, it was a commitment to a full but economical account of present conditions.

The use of source materials would become increasingly important to Piscator's work. Piscator, unlike Blue Blouse, believed that professional theater-makers could serve proletarian causes, and his collaboration with other artists fostered technical innovation. In 1925, one year after *Flags* debuted at the Volksbühne, Piscator would stage a play entirely based on historical documents. The title, *In Spite of Everything,* cited Communist Party co-founder Karl Leibknecht, shortly after the end of the general strike in Berlin known as the Spartacist uprising. The show aimed, in Piscator's words, "to show that the social revolution continued to take place even after the terrible disaster of 1919." It integrated film and photos, pamphlets, political speeches, and historical artifacts, necessitating "a collective effort" that brought together "the separate tasks of writer, director, musical director, designer and actor." Piscator's label for his work, "documentary theater," conveyed the deep significance of relying on source materials and especially film. The point, he asserted, was "not the propagation of a view of life through formal clichés and billboards, but the presentation of solid proof that our philosophy and all that can be deduced from it is the one and only valid approach for our time." He went on, "It is only from the facts themselves that the constraints and the constant mechanisms of life emerge, giving a deeper meaning to our private fates." Film and photography could counter the psychological tendencies of bourgeois theater by capturing sweeping views of social formations, whether at a rally or on the battlefield. Their novelty could impress upon viewers the horrific realities of war. And they asserted, on a metatheatrical level, that the truth about human life could only be conveyed materially.[76] In Piscator's theatrical reporting, source materials were potent technologies of persuasion.

"COMPLEX SEEING": BRECHT'S EPIC THEATER

Brecht spent part of his career writing in Piscator's theater, and it was there that he witnessed Blue Blouse in performance. His papers, as Katherine Bliss Eaton observes, include notes on their technique. Brecht did not aspire to reinvent the newspaper for performance, nor even—following Piscator—to stage the work of journalists. He was deeply engaged, however, in reporting on social conditions, and in the question of how to position spectators so they could understand and intervene. In one relatively rare reference, he used the newspaper to capture the complexity of this endeavor. Calling for new theatrical forms, he asserted: "Even to dramatize a simple newspaper report, one needs something much more than the dramatic technique of a Hebbel or an Ibsen. This is no boast but a sad statement of fact."[77]

"The essential point of epic theatre," he wrote in 1927, "is perhaps that it appeals less to the feelings than to the spectator's reason. Instead of sharing an experience the spectator must come to grips with things. At the same time, it would be quite wrong to try and deny emotion to this kind of theatre. It would be much the same thing as trying to deny emotion to modern science." Indeed, as he would later explain in an interview, his appeals to reason did not entail an absence of emotion. Epic theater, he clarified, "by no means renounces emotion, least of all the sense of justice, the urge to freedom, and righteous anger; it is so far from renouncing these that it does not even assume their presence, but tries to arouse or reinforce them. The 'critical attitude' which it tries to awaken in its audience cannot be passionate enough for it." Brecht's central preoccupation as a playwright and director was with how to position the audience so that it could adopt the "attitude of criticism" he envisioned. Factual and historical but impassioned, this attitude, he would contend, was not objective. Objectivity, which he defined as "dispassionately balancing pros and cons," was neither politically expedient, dramatically compelling, nor even, perhaps, attainable. "Facts," he noted, "can very seldom be caught without their clothes on, and, as you [playwright Friedrich Wolf] rightly say, they are hardly seductive."[78]

One of Brecht's most prominent techniques for eliciting an "attitude of criticism" among his audiences was to separate theatrical elements. Rather than integrating text, music, and setting to absorb the audience in an aesthetic experience, he sought to create friction. In his 1928 *Three-Penny Opera,* this friction would enlist the audience in a critique of bourgeois life. Actors would not casually slip into song but self-consciously "speak against the music"; subtitles would comment on dramatic action, drawing attention back and forth between stage and screen. The effect, Brecht reflected in 1931, was "an exercise in complex seeing." Rather than being taken in by a sensory experience, the spectator adopted a more critical stance—like a discerning viewer smoking a cigarette at a boxing match. Brecht later associated similar goals with his oft-cited "alienation effect" in his article "Alienation Effects in Chinese Acting." Whether achieved through the "lightness and naturalness" of an actor's performance—as inspired by Brecht's Eurocentric take on Chinese acting—or by unexpected uses of music or text, the alienation effect asked, at every moment of a dramatic narrative, "Is this the way of the world, something that can't be affected?"[79] The alienation effect was a tool, one that Brecht was continually refining and revising, to elicit critical engagement with the present. Brecht was not a journalist, but his aesthetic concerns were profoundly journalistic.

NEWS ON THE MOVE:

AMERICAN LIVING NEWSPAPERS BEFORE THE FTP

Brecht's complex seeing; Piscator's technological arabesques; Blue Blouse's agitation, propaganda, and social work: these forms of theatrical reporting would inspire Living Newspapers at the FTP. At least three key figures in the NYLN's founding, Hallie Flanagan, Elmer Rice, and Joseph Losey, were familiar with German epic theater, and all three had visited the Soviet Union, separately, in the 1920s and 1930s. Reflecting on her trip, Flanagan would write in 1930, "The Blue Blouses, powerful, lithe, vibrant, acting with the precision of machines and the zeal of those who spread a faith, are ready for a new art form as well as for a new form."[80] The following year, at Vassar College, she would coauthor a play called *Can You Hear Their Voices?* that adapted living newspaper conventions. Joseph Losey would visit Moscow in 1935, where he sat in on rehearsals with Meyerhold. Losey admired his non-realistic approaches to acting and mise-en-scène, and eventually integrate them into his work for the NYLN, the 1936 Living Newspapers *Triple-A Plowed Under* and *Injunction Granted!* Two other Russian artists would be formative for Losey: Pavlovich Okhlopkov, whose mise-en-scène would inspire Losey's use of platforms and risers onstage; and Yevgeny Vakhtangov, who would inspire Losey's use of satire and clowning in *Injunction Granted!*[81] Elmer Rice would travel to Russia in 1932, three years before he co-founded the NYLN. There he would reportedly go to the theater "almost every night." He would see plays at the Vakhtangov Theatre, talk with Sergei Eisenstein and Meyerhold, and attend a workers' meeting, which he later compared (conscious, no doubt, of anticommunist sentiment) to a "Sunday night parish house meeting in the Middle West."[82]

US-based artists and other workers who had not had the luxury of travel to Europe were nonetheless likely to encounter living newspaper variations and techniques. The possibilities of episodic historical narratives were evident in US pageants of the early twentieth century. "Americans staged pageants," Soyica Colbert writes, "as an expression of democracy. The scale of the pageants necessitated that communities of people work together to produce them." As a result, the pageant form appealed to Americans seeking justice and democracy. In 1913, W. E. B. Du Bois worked with over one thousand African American participants to dramatize ten thousand years of Black diasporic history. *The People of Peoples and Their Gifts to Men* debuted in New York, and subsequently appeared as *The Star of Ethiopia* in Washington, DC, Philadelphia, and Los Angeles. As Colbert argues, "the grand scale of productions and size of the casts" helped Du Bois present "the black world as composed of modern subjects and historical actors" and thus "to quicken African Americans' investment in exercising their democratic privilege to be free acting agents of history."[83]

The same year that *The People of Peoples and Their Gifts to Men* appeared in New York, the communist journalist John Reed mounted a pageant dramatizing a strike of silk workers in Paterson, New Jersey. The so-called Paterson Strike Pageant featured over one thousand workers and members of the public in a panoramic demonstration at Madison Square Garden. Large-scale participatory episodic spectacles like this were not unprecedented in the early twentieth-century United States, but they often conveyed messages of patriotism and nationalism. The Paterson Strike Pageant was distinctive in adapting the pageant form to champion workers' rights, and it would reach an audience of roughly fifteen thousand spectators.[84] Reed's influence, through his activism and journalism, was such that the Communist Party would sponsor approximately thirty

John Reed clubs across the country from 1929 to 1935. They took up many techniques of Soviet workers' clubs, including staging agitprop performances at rallies and meetings.

Living newspapers rose to prominence in the following decade. The Soviet historian Lynn Mally has traced their circulation in her essay "The Americanization of the Soviet Living Newspaper." Some Americans encountered sample scripts in journals such as the "Four Scenes from Russian Living Newspapers" that *Theatre Arts Monthly* published in January 1926. Readers of *Workers Theatre,* a publication of the Workers Laboratory Theatre, would take in guidelines transmitted by Blue Blouse itself. Living Newspapers, according to Blue Blouse, should "give to the worker-spectator in a convincing, entertaining theatrical performance, a clear-cut political show, picturing the need of the present day, organizing for the struggle, and picturing the structure of our socialist society." US workers' theater groups, some even calling themselves "Blue Blouse troupes," would adopt these imperatives. Though they rarely called their work "living newspapers," they helped familiarize American artists and audiences with agitprop techniques.[85]

In the 1930s, as the Popular Front brought together a radical but eclectic bloc of "industrial unionists, Communists, independent socialists, community activists, and émigré anti-fascists," independent US workers' theaters waned.[86] As Mally notes, Blue Blouse groups were in decline by the time the FTP was founded in 1935, both in Russia and in the United States. But the FTP's Living Newspapers would adapt many of their features: the use of documentary evidence; the cast of representative "types" instead of psychologically nuanced characters; the openness of playscripts to revision and adaptation; and a narrator who guided audiences though sweeping historical narratives.[87]

THEATER HISTORIOGRAPHY AND JOURNALISTIC IMAGINATION

In the field of theater studies there have been rich analyses of the FTP's Living Newspapers, but histories and historiographies have tended to focus on the plays' partisan positions—their espousal of leftist issues and Democratic initiatives, their sponsorship by the Roosevelt government, and their origins in Revolutionary Russia. There is good reason for this: Living Newspapers' leftist affiliations (both actual and alleged) played a central role in the FTP's dismantling in Congress. When the Dies Committee charged the FTP with spreading un-American ideas, it would cite Living Newspapers, and their storylines, as some of the most insidious examples.

This charge would follow Living Newspapers through the historical record; the threat of anticommunist sentiment was palpable in some of the earliest documentation of Living Newspapers, in which artists describing their work forgot, ignored, or downplayed the influence of artists outside the United States. In her memoir *Arena,* for instance, FTP national director Hallie Flanagan wrote, "Although [the FTP] has occasional reference to the Volksbühne and the Blue Blouses, to Bragaglia and Meierhold and Eisenstein, it is as American as Walt Disney, the March of Time and the *Congressional Record.*"[88] In 1940, only a year after the FTP was shut down by Congress, Flanagan's selective memory was her first line of defense against hostile critics, and a reminder of the FTP's commitment to US-based artists. Other administrators followed suit. Rather than discussing genealogy, administrators emphasized the craft and technical sophistication of FTP productions to legitimate their state funding and perhaps also to draw focus away from the plays' leftist editorial positions. In this first wave of Living Newspaper writing, Flanagan, Watson, Arthur Arent, and others shared their excitement about what they insisted was a quintessentially American innovation. Their dispatches downplayed leftist messages and influence, emphasizing instead modern technical innovations like the use of projections and loudspeakers.[89]

If the first wave of writing on Living Newspapers emphasized formal novelty over partisan politics, the next wave took the opposite approach. For two decades after the FTP ended, Gerry Cobb notes, the "spectre of communism as subversion and infiltration" discouraged US scholarship on 1930s theater.[90] But between the 1960s and the 1990s, when the intellectual climate in US universities was comparatively progressive, scholars began to recuperate Living Newspapers' partisan positions and leftist lineages. This second wave, much of which grew from the New Left, foregrounded the radical, the oppositional, and the subversive in its descriptions of Living Newspapers' political significance.[91] Arnold Goldman's 1973 article for *Theatre Quarterly* set the tone by indicting the House Un-American Activities Committee's "political suppression" of Living Newspapers. Tracing Russian influences through director Joseph Losey's 1935 visit to Russia, Goldman aligned Living Newspapers with a radical workers' movement that transcended national boundaries.[92] Several works written between the 1970s and the 1990s would parallel or follow Goldman in placing Living Newspapers in a body of early twentieth-century radical leftist theater that adopted Russian and Soviet techniques. These works were crucial in turning attention to transnational political content that the "first wave"—by choice, convention, or political necessity—had largely ignored: they showed how episodic dramaturgy critiqued laissez-faire capitalism, how working-class protagonists mobilized working-class activists, and how agitprop techniques effected calls to action.

In 1974 the theater historians Lorraine Brown and John O'Connor, along with the Library of Congress reference librarian John Cole, uncovered an extensive archive of FTP documents in an airport hangar. Brown and her colleagues won a grant from the National Endowment for the Humanities to organize, catalogue, and preserve the collection.[93] The procurement of these materials allowed for new and detailed studies of Living Newspaper productions and receptions and their relationships to New Deal administration. This is evident in a third wave of scholarship, starting in the 1990s, which has focused, by and large, on identity and representation within and across FTP institutions. This scholarship has illuminated institutional conditions under which FTP plays, including Living Newspapers, were produced and received, not just in New York but across the nation.[94] It has also drawn attention to the politics of representation, including New Deal constructions of gender and race.[95] Rena Fraden, Evelyn Quita Craig, Paul Nadler, and Kate Dossett have assessed the challenges and possibilities facing Black artists in the Federal Theatre, helping to show how the FTP failed to produce a single Living Newspaper by, for, or about African Americans.[96]

Some of these third-wave works complicate Living Newspapers' relationship to a radical left emphasized by the second wave. Loren Kruger, for instance, finds *One-Third of a Nation* to be fundamentally conservative, affirming structural inequality even as it appears to agitate for change. Ilka Saal's *New Deal Theater* emphasizes the form's departures from Brechtian alienation in favor of a politicization through an American liberal tradition of empathy and identification.[97] Third-wave works draw attention to aesthetic techniques that epic and agitprop theater do not fully explain, including radical deployments of modernism as delineated by Laura Browder and "vernacular political theater" as characterized by Saal.[98] They invite reassessments of Living Newspapers' politics beyond their espousal of social welfare (whether defined as leftist or centrist) and in conjunction with aesthetic techniques. Whereas the second wave of scholars depicted a form coalescing around leftist tactics and ideals, the third wave suggests something more complicated—a messy, multifaceted, and at times deeply conservative attempt to represent America and Americans.

This third wave has made space for an exploration of how Living Newspapers negotiated the politics of representation in relation to journalistic institutions. A news-centric understanding of the Living Newspaper reframes the form's precedents and variations, both in Europe and in the United States. It takes seriously the possibility that many agitprop theater-makers, like many modern journalists, understood themselves as accurately representing current issues while espousing partisan (and specifically leftist) commitments. The influence of Blue Blouse and Russian avant-garde, along with the more indirect influence of Piscator and Brecht, points to the NYLN's complicated journalistic inheritance: one in which describing the present was important cultural work, though there was no clear-cut way to do it; one in which facts were important but never, to borrow Brecht's expression, completely "undressed." This book maintains that "dressing up" facts is a crucial component of news-making and not a deviation from it.

In *Staged News* I define living newspapers as a theatrical form that played with news conventions to report on social issues and cultivate journalistic imagination. My understanding of news owes much to three canonical theories—each distinctive and extensive in its own right—of how news co-constitutes social formations. The first of these theories is Carey's "ritual model of communication," which compares reading news to "attending a mass, a situation in which nothing new is learned, but in which a particular view of the world is portrayed and confirmed." The second is Benedict Anderson's proposition, in his intellectual history of the modern nation-state, that newspapers cultivate "imagined communities." The third is Michael Schudson's assertion in a 1995 essay: "news is a form of culture that I will call here 'public knowledge.'"[99] In each of these characterizations, news shapes and reflects communities' knowledge of themselves. In each, to borrow from Schechner's lexicon of performance studies, news is a prompt for "restored behavior." News cues consumers to enact rites of exclusion and belonging—Who do we mourn? What do we fear? What do we celebrate?—that make political communities.[100]

I define "news" as *the cultural production of the present*. By "present" I mean an ascription of temporality (what is happening "now") and of constituency (who "the now" involves and implicates). I see both of these ascriptions, with Africana scholar Michael Hanchard, as profoundly political. As Hanchard shows, European colonizers laid claim to terms like "progress," "history," and "modernity" as an extension of the colonial project and their legacy persists in depictions of African-descended peoples as behind- or outside-of-time. News-makers can be instrumental to the maintenance of this regime, which Hanchard calls "racial time," by presenting a single, white, and colonial account of the present. Yet news can also offer a site of intervention and resistance.[101] As a theater and performance scholar, I see "cultural production" as reflexive and revisable because it is a social and material process that works through the bodies of individuals. In the case of news, the process is that of embodying information, of taking in and responding to information at the moment it arrives at the body. (A person preparing to share news might even offer choreography, prompting her listener, "Are you sitting down?") In "staging news," journalists both convey information and create the scenario in which consumers receive it. When it is staged in a literal theater, the scenario is readily available for analysis: the scholar can consider how text, image, time, and space work together to create conditions for witness. The workings of imagination become perceptible.

Scholars, critics, and journalists themselves have inferred, at times, that a commitment to factual accuracy leaves little room for imagination. Yet as Barbie Zelizer has argued: "The very essence of journalism is creating an imagined engagement with events beyond the public's reach. How that is accomplished is also imagined because journalism operates largely out of the public eye."[102] If facts and observations are important to news-making, so too is the imaginative work that the journalist undertakes to make meaning out of observations, and the imaginative work that the news reader undertakes to involve herself in what she reads, hears, or sees.

In this book I theorize journalistic imagination as *a capacity to reflect on how news produces newsworthy subjects, and how it might do so more critically and expansively*. Other journalism scholars agree on the importance of imagination but differ on what it means: for Schudson, it is "the play and imagination" required to make stories; for G. Stuart Adam, it is "a distinctive approach to understanding and representing the affairs of the world"; for Richard Keeble and Sharon Wheeler, it encompasses literary journalism by authors, poets, and playwrights.[103] My theorization of journalistic imagination builds on but diverges from this small body of scholarship. I argue that if news is the cultural production of the present, journalistic imagination attends to what—and who—is present, and how "the present" might be constructed otherwise. I understand journalistic imagination as a capacity to reflect on *how* the present is culturally produced. It requires self-conscious attention to how journalism works.

Who and what constitutes "the present" is significant because it directly affects what is deemed newsworthy—by journalists, publics, and counterpublics. A call to expand journalistic imagination is also a prompt to revise conceptions of newsworthiness. I see journalistic imagination, like the "sociological imagination" theorized by C. Wright Mills, as a capacity to think carefully and creatively about the relationship between personal experience and societal structures.[104] Imagining journalistically, like imagining sociologically, makes possible an understanding of the world that is sharper, fuller, and perhaps more just. It entails a capacity to identify—and, more importantly, to revise—who and what deserve attention and care. Journalistic imagination need not diminish the importance of factual reporting nor displace the capacity, often called "news literacy," to disentangle fact from fiction. Rather, it offers a complementary concept that centers the politics of interpretation and representation so that revision can occur. In drawing attention to who and what are deemed newsworthy, journalistic imagination renders both categories available to change.

## THE FTP'S LIVING NEWSPAPERS IN NEW YORK

One could analyze the possibilities of journalistic imagination in and around any news story or newsroom, but the FTP's Living Newspapers in New York are an ideal site of analysis. First, as I explain in chapter 1, they were designed from the outset to comment on news items that were already in circulation. As a result, they directed attention to what was reported and how. Second, as an experimental artistic medium, they drew attention to news form and how it could be reimagined. Third, as the output of a single unit, or in the case of *Liberty Deferred,* artists who worked alongside it, they reveal a relationship between journalistic imagination and its material conditions in a single institution.

Though I do not offer a comprehensive study of the NYLN's repertoire or a metanarrative of its history, I follow the lead of Kim Gallon, a historian of the Black press, in offering a "critical curation."[105] I present case studies (chapters 2, 3, and 4) in chronological order, allowing the reader to gain a sense of how the NYLN's approach developed over time. I use images, play texts, production notes, reviews, and other archival materials to suggest what each production might have looked, sounded, and felt like. And finally, I draw connections between the propositions made by Living Newspaper productions and contemporaneous public discourse about journalism and the possibilities of democratic communication. My focus on staged news draws attention to journalistic archives that FTP historians have tended not to consider. In addition to the Federal Theatre Project archives located at the Library of Congress, National Archives and Records Administration, and George Mason University, my sources include the Morris Watson papers at the University of Oregon, the Newspaper Guild of New York papers at the Tamiment Library and Robert F. Wagner Labor Archive, and the historic style guides digitized by the Associated Press.

My point of departure in chapter 1 is that journalistic imagination emerges from the social, cultural, and material conditions in which news is made. Here I examine the development and production of journalistic imagination in the NYLN newsroom by way of an institutional analysis. Rather than analyzing specific productions and conventions, as I do in subsequent chapters, I analyze the resources, people, processes, and practices that guided the NYLN's mission, and subsequently its decisions about what needed to be made present for audiences. I spend some time discussing *Ethiopia,* the NYLN's ill-fated first attempt. Though *Ethiopia* would not see public production, I argue that it was nonetheless formative in two ways: first, in revealing constraints around who and what could be staged under the auspices of government theater; and second, in systematically sidelining the work of Black journalists, an issue I return to in chapter 4. With *Ethiopia* as a springboard, I show how the NYLN drew attention to its journalistic process, or at least an idealized version of it. I reveal a vision of journalism as collaborative interpretation: a form of labor that aligned journalism with other creative professions in a bourgeoning coalition of white-collar labor.

Turning from process to production, chapter 2 examines the NYLN's least popular play, *The Events of 1935*. Although critics—and even NYLN artists—dismissed the play as a superficial review of a year's worth of news, I propose that *1935* was a piece of press criticism, one that used theatrical conventions to engage with the possibilities and limitations of the American public. To make the case, I reconstruct a now canonical debate between the columnist Walter Lippmann and the philosopher John Dewey. Closely reading the playscript, production notes, and reviews, I show how *The Events of 1935* depicted a passive public onstage (much like the "phantom public" theorized by Lippmann), but juxtaposed it with an active, Deweyan public in the audience. I analyze reviews to show how spectators bristled and even spoke out when they encountered their underachieving double onstage. I argue that *1935* cultivated journalistic imagination by drawing attention to the challenges of representing a singular American public and editorially catering to its presumed interests.

In chapter 3 I turn to the possibilities of mass media and their dangers and possibilities for engaging citizens. To do this, I analyze *One-Third of a Nation*, focusing on the interplay between a self-deprecating Little Man and an omniscient Loudspeaker. I situate their interactions in an ongoing debate about mass-mediated propaganda and its eventual uses against the FTP. My argument is that *One-Third of a Nation* presented political action as an embodied process of speaking up.

Continuing to grapple with the theme of representation, chapter 4 turns to how Black American artists challenged white constructions of "the present" within the NYLN. My case study is a Living Newspaper developed outside the NYLN in 1938–39 by the Black playwrights Abram Hill and John Silvera. *Liberty Deferred* chronicles an unfinished struggle for civil rights in the United States. Through an examination of the tactics of anachronism and deferral, I characterize *Liberty Deferred* as an argument for racial equity but also (and controversially, given its institutional context) as a contestation of the whiteness of mainstream news. The FTP's Play Bureau commissioned this script and suggested major revisions that Hill and Silvera would resist; ultimately the FTP would not stage the production. Here and throughout the book, I seek to illuminate roads not taken, to show instances where, by ignorance or design, the NYLN omitted Black issues and reporting. These omissions, I suggest, offer variations on a recurring refrain: a pattern of racist exclusion on the American left, named by Richard Iton the "solidarity blues."

The concluding chapter considers the NYLN's legacies and its insights for contemporary public life. I argue that outside the NYLN, Living Newspapers circulated by way of conventions. I explore the implications of this shift in three brief examples. The first involves a parody that rendered Living Newspaper conventions as clichés. The second is a contested Living Newspaper about syphilis, Arnold Sundgaard's *Spirochete.* The third is a contemporary production at London's Royal Court Theatre. Titled *Living Newspaper: A Counter Narrative,* it reveals the possibilities of convention to critique existing institutions, sparking new engagements with journalistic imagination.

When Watson and his colleagues sought to "combine the newspaper and theatre," their efforts were urgent. In many accounts, the press and the very project of news-making were in crisis. Anxieties about propaganda and mass deception were at a fever pitch. Publishing conglomerates were swallowing up local presses. New media like the newsreel, radio, and motion pictures were running newspapers, and trained reporters, out of business. Journalism in the 1930s was a precarious business. The same might be said of news-making today. Not only has the idea of a "news crisis" resurfaced from the 1930s, but so too have its harbingers, which include cries of "fake news," privatization and consolidation, and quickly changing technology. Nearly a century later, the experiment Watson described is worth revisiting. The time is ripe to reimagine the news.

# CHAPTER ONE

# GETTING A FEEL FOR THE OFFICE

## Reimagining the Newsroom

In a playbill for *Power*, the New York Living Newspaper published a photo series titled "Living Newspaper Goes to Press" (figure 1). As the title suggests, the series presents the process of making a Living Newspaper. It shows a replicable sequence, emulating the systematicity of an assembly line, but with workers engaged in acts of analysis and interpretation. Each of the four panels depicts staff hard at work: in the first three tableaux, they hunch over research and writing; in the fourth, they are poised to rehearse. All participants are intently focused, so absorbed in their work that they face away from the viewer, apparently unaware of the photographer's lens. They also appear to be confident, engaged in skillful, familiar activity. Their workplaces seem to hum with purpose and regularity; they fit together in a well-orchestrated procedure. The stages of production, from research to rehearsal, illustrate a systematized process of interpretation. The panel presents journalists and theater-makers (or at the very least, actors and writers) as skilled professionals.

In this assembly line with variations, there is specialization and hierarchy. Each phase belongs to a distinctive group of personnel, interacting with one another and with texts, engaged in collaborative acts of interpretation. In each image there is a leader, with one figure, always presenting as white and masculine, giving direction to others. Yet the exchanges look more like consultation than the issuing of orders. And with each photo there are new collaborators and new interpreters. The NYLN's journalism appears to be the product of multiple specialties and perspectives, not of lone investigation.

Although these images, like all of the FTP's "backstage photos," were undoubtedly staged to bolster New Deal expenditures, they also intervened

FIGURE 1. "Living Newspaper Goes to Press." Photo series from the playbill for *Power,* Ritz Theatre, New York, 1937. Courtesy of Library of Congress.

in contemporary debates about who journalists were and how they worked.[1] "Living Newspaper Goes to Press" depicted the NYLN's unique brand of news-making as a *collaborative process of interpretive white-collar labor.* It pointed to the social, material, and cultural conditions that shaped journalistic imagination: a white and white-collar workplace; sparse offices and large Broadway theater spaces; a large team of specialized workers; a hierarchical structure of collaboration; sponsorship by the New Deal and a burgeoning news union; interpretation relayed between researchers, journalists, and theater-makers. This vision of journalism represented the material conditions and cultural norms that shaped the experiences of NYLN workers: a professional orientation that Morris Watson would call "news sense."

## NEWS SENSE

In a speech for fellow journalists and labor organizers, NYLN managing producer Morris Watson recounted an early work experience at the *Denver Post.* A creamery company had failed to renew its advertising contract with the paper, and Watson was tasked with retaliation. Publisher Frederick Bonfils, in Watson's words "a wealthy real estate operator," instructed him to "tell the readers of the Denver Post how the Such and Such Creamery Company snatches the milk directly from the mouths of babes." By 1937, when Watson likely delivered his speech, Bonfils was infamous. He had bought a failing paper in 1895 and used an arsenal of yellow journalism tactics to drive up circulation. His thirty-seven-year tenure at the *Post* would be mired in scandal, violence, and corruption, culminating in a dramatic libel suit against his competitor the *Rocky Mountain News.* The lawsuit, which Bonfils filed in 1932, was cut short only by his death the following year. Watson, however, was an idealistic young reporter when he worked at the *Post* and not yet aware of the extent of Bonfils's wrongdoings. He had taken the creamery assignment to heart, preparing himself for a "thorough investigation."[2]

The *Post's* city editor, however, soon disabused Watson of his naïve notions. He would need two columns for the next edition. Thus, not only would Watson's reporting be motivated by a vengeful publisher, but also the piece would be written without adequate research. "The business of coloring the news," Watson continued, though not always this extreme, was nonetheless pervasive in American newsrooms. "It begins," he explained, "with the development in the reporter's mind of a so-called news sense." This, he goes on, "means knowing what to report and what not to report, or knowing what the boss wants printed. It is called 'getting the feel of the office.'"[3]

"Getting the feel of the office" is, of course, a euphemism. It means learning not just who sits where, or where supplies are kept, but what those in power expect their subordinates to produce. It requires reporters to anticipate their supervisors' interests, values, and commitments, whether they are explicit, as in Watson's example, or implied. With an eye to the flexibility this might require, the phrase "coloring the news" reserves judgment; "color," after all, can be vivid or lurid, depending on who you ask.

Rank-and-file reporters by and large could not afford to express opinions on if or how the news should be "colored." Especially under bosses like Bonfils, news sense made reporters' success dependent on their assimilation into workplace culture. And when news sense was lacking, the consequences could be dire. "If a reporter doesn't 'get the feel,'" Watson warned, "a day will come when a new reporter will be put in his place."[4]

News sense, in short, is not only a professional skill but also a set of learned behaviors understood as a survival instinct, the ticket to keeping your job when, as Watson suggests, you can easily be replaced. For historians, news sense offers a glimpse into institutional conditions: how material factors like organizational structure and pay as well as cultural and professional norms direct which stories journalists pursue. Because news sense affects what kinds of stories journalists can tell, it is a crucial component of journalistic imagination. In the introduction, I defined journalistic imagination as a capacity to reflect on how news is produced and presented, and how it might be otherwise. In this chapter I explore how institutional conditions, by way of news sense, both constrained and enabled journalistic imagination at the NYLN. Rather than taking up specific productions, as I will in subsequent chapters, here I explore the NYLN as a whole. My goal is to reveal the key principles that most determined what would get developed and staged—what journalists would call editorial mandate, and what theater-makers might call repertoire.[5]

In the mainstream newsrooms of urban dailies, multiple parties were involved, to varying degrees, in deciding what got printed. Publishers and editors set the tone but could do so with a heavy hand or a light touch. A reporter might pitch a story, but rewrite staff or copy editors could determine headlines and placement.[6] So too in the case of the NYLN, it is difficult to say with precision who made which decisions when. Archival documents do not offer a comprehensive editorial mandate, and the NYLN's personnel, resources, and priorities shifted over time. Therefore, rather than speculating on the rationale for staging any particular play, this chapter outlines the evolving editorial commitments that shaped the Unit's repertoire, offering in the process a history of the Unit's origins and development. I theorize news sense as the institutional influences on journalistic imagination, and I describe the particular news sense that a reporter might have developed at the NYLN. Following Watson's lead, I pay close attention to the tone set by the boss, in this case Watson himself, along with Elmer Rice, Philip Barber, and Hallie Flanagan. But I consider other factors as well, namely, the external organizations, values, and working conditions that shaped the NYLN as an institution.

My understanding of institutions is indebted to the cultural theorist Raymond Williams. For Williams, institution is a "keyword" with dynamic and contested meanings: it appears to describe something "objective and systematic" but is better understood as a set of practices that have hardened into norms and physical spaces.[7] In this chapter and throughout the book, I follow the lead of Ric Knowles and Shannon Jackson in taking institutions and performance traditions to be co-constitutive; that is, creative processes and professional norms have the power to revise material conditions and labor networks, and vice versa.[8]

I begin by describing and historicizing the NYLN's two key sponsors, the American Newspaper Guild (in tandem with the Newspaper Guild of New York) and the Federal Theatre Project, both of which aimed to improve the lives and livelihoods of their workers. Next I show how the NYLN emerged from these two institutions. Then I consider the commitments it inherited and adapted from them, including its relationship to the Franklin Roosevelt administration, its evolving role in the US labor movement, and ultimately a distinctive vision of journalism as collaborative interpretation, subject to continuous reflection and revision, and culminating in theatrical conventions.

## "ROMANTIC FOOLS IN THE EDITORIAL DEPARTMENT": THE BEGINNINGS OF THE AMERICAN NEWSPAPER GUILD

Living Newspapers emerged in a context of economic precarity, and the NYLN was accountable to two key sponsors: the Federal Theatre Project, in conjunction with its New York branch, and the American Newspaper Guild (ANG), in conjunction with its local branch, the Newspaper Guild of New York (NGNY). The financial crash of 1929 arrived on the heels of a century-long golden age for newspapers. Since the mid-nineteenth century, Americans had looked to the newspaper to relay current events. But by the first few years of the 1930s, as the historian David Welky notes, newspaper circulation had fallen by 12 percent and ad income had dropped by 45 percent;[9] overall, according to one federal report, newspapers' income fell by nearly 40 percent between 1929 and 1933.[10] Newspaper workers, like theater-makers, struggled not only with the Depression but also with competition from new media. If news consumers had less money to spend on news, they also had new news options in the newsreel, motion pictures, and especially radio, used to great effect by President Roosevelt.

Amid competition and financial turmoil, editors and publishers found all kinds of ways to shave costs; many scrimped by recycling material, from stories to typewriter ribbon. In some cases they even shrank down the literal size of the paper they used.[11] And if the newspaper industry as a whole seemed to be struggling, then editorial staff, those who reported, wrote, and edited, were especially vulnerable. Not only did new and established reporters face declining job prospects and fewer opportunities for advancement, but also their working conditions were especially precarious, with little improvement in sight.[12] Whereas news workers in mechanical trades such as typesetting were represented by the International Typographical Union (ITU), editorial staff had no union and thus few protections. White journalists worked long hours, with unpredictable assignments, for little pay, and non-white journalists, rarely considered professionals by their white counterparts, often worked for free.[13]

The ANG and NGNY had formed in response to the precarious conditions of editorial staff and, more specifically, in response to a stalled attempt at labor reform. There had been efforts in the 1890s and then after the First World War to join the ITU, but they were short-lived. Editorial workers, the news historian Will Mari infers, were unable or unwilling to pay dues, particularly as they espoused an increasingly distinctive professional identity. The trend continued in the interwar years, which saw a growing cultural divide between production and editorial work. In the 1920s, *New York World* columnist Heywood Broun petitioned the American Federation of Labor for a small New York–based Organization of News Writers; it was not until the following decade that his organizing efforts would become public and national.[14]

The catalyst for organizing was an attempt to codify labor standards for journalists. In June 1933, as part of Roosevelt's New Deal, Congress passed the National Industrial Recovery Act. To implement the act, Roosevelt formed two new organizations, the Public Works Administration and the National Recovery Administration (NRA). The latter was charged with promoting fair competition within industries by regulating wages, hours, and in some cases, prices. Business leaders from a variety of industries raised objections, including the newspaper industry. The American Newspaper Publishers Association (ANPA) asserted that the NRA's efforts, while laudable in theory, could not apply to their industry without doing serious damage. Regulation of editorial work "completely abridge[d] the freedom of the press."[15] Reporters, the ANPA contended, needed flexible hours to pursue their stories and would not want their pay prospects limited by an "arbitrary wage scale."[16]

The ANPA's arguments made creative use of the ideas of independence, impartiality, and other Canons of Journalism to which editorial staff subscribed. But they also relied on popular conceptions of journalism. According to what the historian Daniel Leab calls "the romance of newspapering," journalism was not so much a job as it was a vocation, a passionate pursuit that could not be streamlined or regulated. The romance of newspapering stipulated that "true" journalists were mavericks who did not care for rules and who preferred to work alone. They were lone wolves who chased stories rather than paychecks, and who had little reason to associate with colleagues, much less (according to the ANPA) to organize around common causes. The romance of newspapering was ubiquitous in popular culture, and especially film. As Welky notes, it was evident in early thirties movies such as *Five Star Final* (1931), *Scandal Sheet* (1931), *Scandal for Sale* (1932), and *The Front Page* (1931, adapted from a 1928 play). The protagonists of these films, though often corrupt, were undeniably committed to their stories, sometimes to the point of obsession. (In *The Front Page,* reporter Hildy Johnson is so desperate for a scoop that he hides an escaped convict in a rolltop desk in the newsroom, jeopardizing his chances at marital bliss and a lucrative new job in advertising.)[17]

It was not only moviegoers who were enamored of the romance of journalism. Real-life journalists too accepted long hours, poor wages, and instability as the price for adventure. The romance of journalism persisted even as news work became increasingly collaborative and systematic. The introduction of new technologies like the telegraph, typewriters, and telephones, starting in the late 1800s, called for increased specialization in the newsroom, which scientific management approaches like Taylorism helped to streamline.[18] By the 1930s, however, the Depression and the US workers' movement were prompting journalists to reconsider their work and their professional identities. Morris Watson was one of them. As a cub reporter, he recalled, he had considered a celebrity encounter or praise from an editor payment enough for his work.[19] But with the arrival of a wife and child, his responsibilities grew and he began to seek stability.

When publishers responded to the Depression with cuts to their newsrooms, Watson observed, the romance of journalism became a liability: "[Unionized printers and typists] stood shoulder to shoulder and were in a position to say, 'Cut us and you get out no paper!' We romantic fools in the editorial department couldn't say that. We were individualists. So, he [the publisher] cut us, once, twice, in many cases three times."[20] Journalists, Watson concluded, needed security and stability. Freedom and regulation were complementary concepts, and reporters, however accustomed to solitude, needed to work together both inside the newsroom and beyond. Thus, in the summer of 1933, when the

NRA ceded to publishers the authority to decide if and when to apply labor standards, Watson was dissatisfied.[21] He was not alone.

On August 7, columnist Heywood Broun called for "A Union of Reporters" in the *New York World-Telegram*. Broun was hardly representative of the average reporter. He was one of the best-paid columnists in the country, and his syndicated column in Scripps-Howard papers like the *World-Telegram* enjoyed a loyal following. According to Watson, Broun truly wanted to improve conditions for his worse-off colleagues but "did not expect his column to be accepted at face value."[22] Nonetheless, Watson and a handful of other reporters met at Broun's apartment to discuss the possibilities of banding together. Over the next few months, as the historian Philip Glende recounts, editorial workers would meet in cities across the country. The Newspaper Guild of New York would form in mid-September, with three hundred journalists electing a committee to represent them at upcoming NRA hearings. Two months later, the nationwide American Newspaper Guild was established at the National Press Club in Washington, DC, with Broun elected as its president.[23]

Not all of the ANG's organizers had a union in mind. Rather, Leab suggests that most of Broun's colleagues envisioned a professional association that would avoid trade union methods like strikes and collective bargaining. Collective action would be especially challenging because the ANG represented at least forty local guilds, some of which were wary that New York and the leftist politics its guild tended to espouse would be overrepresented.[24] It would take three more years and many contentious debates before the ANG would decide to affiliate with the American Federation of Labor (AFL), becoming a trade union formally affiliated with organized labor. One year later, ANG members would vote to join the more radical Congress of Industrial Organizations (CIO), in part because of heavy support from the New York guild. This move meant that editorial workers would join ranks with other newspaper staff, including clerks and advertising staff.[25] Watson was a crucial catalyst in the ANG's trajectory. He recalled, "When Heywood Broun . . . published his famous column about organizing newspapermen 'at 10 a.m. tomorrow,' I was one of six who knocked at his apartment door promptly at 10am. Of course Heywood, who seldom emerged from bed before 2 pm, had to be awakened."[26] As well as attending the germinal first meetings in Broun's apartment, Watson went on to hold a series of leadership positions, including chairman of the press unit of the AP, and secretary, treasurer, and vice president for wire services. While at the NYLN, he would represent the guild in high-level meetings, including one with President Roosevelt.[27] Equally important, however, was his symbolic role. The very circumstances that drove Watson to the FTP made him a symbol of the need for journalism unions.

Watson had been fired in the fall of 1935 from his job at the AP, and the trial that followed his dismissal would garner national attention. The Supreme Court had struck down the National Industrial Recovery Act the previous spring, but a few months later, Congress enacted a new set of labor protections in the National Labor Relations Act (NLRA). Also called the Wagner Act after Senator Robert F. Wagner of New York, the NLRA established a legal right for some workers—it excluded domestic and farm workers, many of whom were people of color—to organize or join unions, and to engage in collective bargaining. So the possibility that Watson had been fired just a few months later for organizing activity raised important questions about if and how the act would be enforced. The AP was the nation's largest wire service and a standard-bearer in the newspaper industry.

The AP claimed that Watson's termination was due to unsatisfactory work performance. But Watson countered that it was punishment for two years of organizing with Broun and his colleagues. When Elinor Herrick, regional director of the National Labor Relations Board (NLRB) in New York, investigated Watson's personnel file, she found confirmation. In the memo recommending Watson's termination, the AP's executive news editor described Watson as "an agitator" who "disturbs the morale of staff at a time when we need especially their loyalty and best performance."[28]

Even prior to his firing, Watson asserted, the AP had punished him for his activism: he had been transferred to the night shift and assigned a new role as editor of the South wire, "a confining desk job completely alien to my temperament." For Watson, penance lay not only in staid desk work but also in relegation to the South. He recalled as an example that the Atlanta bureau had a policy of referring to African American women by their first names only, and when Watson refused to correct his copy accordingly (he used the title "Mrs."), he was briefly suspended.[29]

By the time he was officially fired, there was little love lost between Watson and the AP, but he maintained that the termination was unjust. The ANG supported him, lodging a complaint to the newly formed NLRB. Watson's case was quickly publicized as a test case: Would the outcome of his labor activism be punishment or protection? Two years later, in 1937, the Supreme Court ruled in Watson's favor alongside four other key cases confirming that the Wagner Act was to be the "law of the land."[30] The court instructed the AP to reinstate Watson, with back pay, a difference amounting to roughly $100 per month in Watson's move from the AP to the FTP.[31] Yet just over a month after his reinstatement (as well as a few publicity photos at the AP), Watson would opt to return to the Living Newspaper, where he had spent the past two years.[32] When the FTP had begun, just two years after the ANG was founded,

Watson and his colleagues had seen a unique opportunity to find work for their constituents, and to publicize the cause of American journalists.

**AN "ANIMATED NEWSREEL":**
**THE NYLN'S ORIGINS IN THE FEDERAL THEATRE PROJECT**

In August of 1935, the US government established the Federal Theatre Project as one of five initiatives under the auspices of the Works Progress Administration. Like the ANG and NGNY, it aimed to support workers in a struggling industry. Throughout the 1930s, US theater workers appeared to face existential threats in both the economic downturn and the rise of new media, including the radio, newsreels, and film. In New York, the crisis was acute. Just three years before the FTP began, the historian Lorraine Brown notes, 213 of the 253 theater companies playing in or near New York City had closed; only six legitimate theaters would remain open on Broadway. Indeed, when the FTP opened in New York, writes Brown, "thousands of people swarmed Federal Theatre offices on Eighth Avenue, and by December 28, 1935, 3,350 people were at work, 60 percent of them actors, 10 to 15 percent stagehands and technicians and 5 to 10 percent newspapermen and playwrights."[33]

In New York and across the country, national director Hallie Flanagan aimed not only to reemploy theater-makers but also to reflect a variety of American theatrical traditions. Thus, the FTP's local units represented diverse forms, from the classical to the experimental. On October 23, 1935, FTP records document a project proposal for an "animated newspaper" that would be "sponsored by the New York Chapter of the Newspaper Guild." Material would be "collected and dramatized by unemployed newspaper men, and in its presentation, actors, stage hands, technicians, and other theater workers" would be used.[34]

There are divergent accounts of who initially proposed that the FTP produce Living Newspapers. In her memoir *Arena,* Flanagan takes credit, asserting, "I suggested the plan of dramatizing contemporary events in a series of living newspapers."[35] Meanwhile, Lorraine Brown credits playwright and FTP New York regional director Elmer Rice. Rice, too, noted in an interview: "As I remember it, The Living Newspaper project arose out of discussions between Morris Watson, head of the Newspaper Guild, and myself. He asked me if I couldn't do something for the unemployed newspaper men."[36] Designer Howard Bay points to Watson, recalling: "He'd been fired, you know. . . . And he came to Hallie with the idea of a living newspaper. . . . He set up city desks and reporters[,] . . . morgues [to house reference materials]."[37] Actor Norman Lloyd credits ANG founder Heywood

Broun, who "got the original idea because he wanted a place—you see, there were projects for everybody, for painters, for writers, for actors, but none for newspapermen." Broun was, in Lloyd's account, "stage-struck,"[38] and indeed both Broun and his then-wife, the journalist and activist Ruth Hale, frequently published dramatic criticism.[39] Meanwhile, the playbill for *Triple-A Plowed Under* commented that "the idea of living dramatization of current news events was conceived at a meeting of the Re-employment Committee of the NY Newspaper Guild," and that Watson was a referral from NGNY President Carl Randau.[40]

Regardless of whose account is most accurate, the disparity is telling. Some of the accounts credit representatives of the ANG (Broun and Watson) and others credit representatives of the FTP (Flanagan and Rice). By the spring 1936 premiere of *Triple-A Plowed Under,* the FTP's first public production, the ANG and FTP would share top billing as Unit sponsors. Both institutions would provide material support to the NYLN, and both would guide the direction of the NYLN's work. They shaped the sensibilities—or news sense—of NYLN workers.

First and foremost, the Living Newspaper's origins in the ANG and FTP established employment potential as a priority in what and how the Unit would report. The FTP mandate stipulated that 90 percent of each unit's funding go directly to personnel. This meant a decisive break from early living newspapers in Europe and the United States: while Russia's living newspaper movement had been expansive, performance companies themselves often had to be small and nimble, erupting into action with just a few props, on street corners and in meetings. By contrast, the FTP would have to conceive of Living Newspapers as expansive productions that could accommodate large casts onstage and large teams of reporters, designers, and technicians behind the scenes. An early overview of the Unit proposed a head stage director and four assistants, "a house manager and five box office treasurers; three seamstresses, a dozen cleaners, matrons, partners, watchmen, accounts and clerks, ticket-takers, and ushers, etc." alongside a quota of up to 140 actors. The newsroom would encompass "fifteen dramatists, some sixty research workers and copy readers and editors, several librarians, stenographers, etc."[41]

These ambitious plans required some attention to dramaturgy. What forms of storytelling would support a large complement of staff, with varied skill levels and experience? Over its first two years, the NYLN would experiment with two different structures: one was a compilation of multiple stories, the other was an in-depth exploration of a single problem, presented like a piece of investigative reporting.[42] The first had its roots in the forms of montage, vaudeville, variety theater, and revue. The second also drew on these forms but was more closely aligned with US pageants, which cast large companies of amateurs to stage epic historical narratives.[43]

*Ethiopia,* the NYLN's first Living Newspaper, developed somewhere in between these two possibilities, testing and refining the Unit's news sense. It was initially conceived as a fifteen-minute feature anchoring a series of short bulletins, but developed into a full-length production. It would never reach a public audience because of prohibitive last-minute instructions from the State Department. Nonetheless, it was formative in the NYLN's development. It modeled the possibilities of a single-issue focus, and it confirmed the Unit's growing commitment to items of "social significance." Perhaps most crucially, its cancellation would establish parameters for future reporting, reminding staff of their accountability to Roosevelt and New Deal objectives.

## *ETHIOPIA* AND THE CONSTRAINTS OF "GOVERNMENT ENTERPRISE": FROM WAR ABROAD TO NEW DEAL INITIATIVES

Sponsorship from the FTP and ANG released NYLN staff from the possibilities and exigencies of the commercial newsroom. In Watson's account, this meant freedom to pursue stories of demonstrable public interest—a mission that aligned with the FTP's stated goal to represent the American people. When the FTP approved the Living Newspaper as a sub-project in 1935, its mission was simply "to present news events on stage in living dramatized form." As Watson acknowledged, however, this left the field wide open. A "news event," after all, could be "anything from the marriage of two circus freaks to the outbreak of a world war."[44]

Initially, Watson recalled, writers defaulted toward lighthearted fare, playing perhaps to the strengths of its first personnel. Some of the NYLN's actors were former vaudeville performers. Arthur Arent, who would become the NYLN's primary playwright and its managing editor, had spent the previous few years writing musical sketches for resorts in the Catskill Mountains of Upstate New York, colloquially known as the Borscht Belt.

Yet playwright Elmer Rice, whom Flanagan appointed to direct New York's regional division of the FTP, championed items of social significance.[45] He was well known for his sharp critiques of social inequality, materialism, and alienation in *The Adding Machine* (1923) and his Pulitzer Prize–winning *Street Scene* (1923). According to Flanagan, it was the possibilities of the living newspaper that had drawn him to the New York FTP, and he insisted that the form should do more than entertain.[46] With Watson, he envisioned a "sort of animated newsreel" comprising three- to five-minute sketches based on the day's wire reports, and a fifteen-minute "feature" story.[47] The first feature, they decided, would focus on the ongoing Second Italo-Ethiopian War.

Only a few months before, in October 1935, Italian dictator Benito Mussolini had invaded Ethiopia. In 1896 Ethiopia had won the First Italo-Ethiopian War, humiliating Italian colonizers at the town of Adwa. Since then, Ethiopia had been a powerful symbol of African sovereignty and an inspiration to Pan-Africanists. Therefore, as the Ethiopian historian Bahru Zewde writes, with "the advent of the Fascists to power in Italy in 1922 . . . it was only a matter of time before they turned their force against the one country which had stood as a permanent and insulting symbol of the frustration of Italian colonialism."[48]

While the war was far away geographically, many Americans had been following it closely. For many African Americans, as the literary scholar Ivy G. Wilson observes, Ethiopia was a crucial site of transnational Black identity. Nadia Nurhussein elaborates on its significance in her book *Black Land: Imperial Ethiopianism and African America:* "Because most civilizationist arguments assumed the view that black cultures were uncivilized, the antiquity of Ethiopian culture provided African Americans with a well-documented example of originary blackness that exploded the logic of racist accounts of civilization."[49] The Second Italo-Ethiopian War galvanized Pan-Africanist and anticolonial commitments, informed by activist organizations like Marcus Garvey's Universal Negro Improvement Association. As Garvey and others drew attention to the ways that racism and colonialism exceeded national boundaries, Ethiopian resistance became an important focus.[50] Shortly before Italy's invasion, W. E. B. Du Bois and Paul Robeson had drawn ten thousand protesters to Madison Square Garden. Since then, Black activists, intellectuals, and cultural leaders had organized rallies, demonstrations, days of prayer, financial campaigns, and educational events.[51] African American publications with a wide range of mandates and commitments covered Ethiopia's fight extensively and sympathetically.[52] They also offered coverage the white press did not. Indeed, the Black-owned *Pittsburgh Courier,* as the historian Fred Carroll notes, was the only newspaper to send a full-time reporter to the war front. It asserted that correspondent J. A. Rogers, who knew Emperor Haile Selassie and could converse in French, was "the only person, black or white" who was qualified for the job.[53]

Italian Americans too were activated, thanks in part to Italian-language newspapers reflecting a range of ideologies. Some Italian Americans joined antifascist activities and organizations. Others embraced Mussolini's discourse of civilizing colonialism, particularly, as Chiara Grilli writes, at moments when they grappled with the "racial in-betweenness" of Italian identity. In New York alone, Italian American supporters of the war raised over $700,000 to send overseas, and many wrote letters discouraging Roosevelt from pursuing embargos against Italy.[54]

Even Americans without preexisting attachments to Ethiopia or Italy were primed to follow the war. As Nurhussein notes, "There was an inherent theatricality surrounding 'Ethiopia,' and particularly Abyssinian imperial culture in the United States in the 1930s." Haile Selassie was depicted as a flamboyant leader in a range of popular media, from blackface minstrelsy to the cover of *Time* magazine.[55] Indeed, Mussolini had long been a figure of interest in mainstream outlets; Americans had read his monthly columns in Hearst's newspapers or seen him depicted in newsreels or the documentary film *Mussolini Speaks*. Many Americans had been following the development of the League of Nations after the First World War and wondered about its power to prevent another outbreak. On the left, Popular Front discourse was ringing alarm bells about the rise of fascism.[56]

Thus, when Arent was assigned to write about Ethiopia, he likely knew he could count on the interest of many Americans, especially because Ethiopia had recently launched a counterattack on December 15. When he presented an early draft to Rice and Watson, they asked him to develop it into a forty-minute Living Newspaper, rather than the fifteen-minute segment they had planned. They also assigned Arent a more permanent place in the NYLN, or in his words, "kicked me upstairs and made me managing editor of the whole works."[57] With these new affordances of time and space, he could develop his report in greater depth.

Arent's script would dramatize the events of one year, with headlines broadcast on teletype at the beginning of each scene. The play begins at a frontier post, Walwal, on the border between Ethiopia and Somaliland. Ethiopian soldiers are at rest, then suddenly interrupted by machine guns, in a scene capturing the incendiary clash that would become known as the "Walwal Incident." In the following scene, the chairman of the League of Nations reads competing accounts by Ethiopia and Italy, each naming the other as the aggressor. The conflict escalates, with Mussolini and Haile Selassie giving speeches to rouse their troops as representatives from the League of Nations urge peace. The portrayal of Haile Selassie, Nurhussein argues, is fairly sympathetic, depicting him as connected to this people in contrast to Mussolini.[58]

Yet the script's focus, ultimately, is on European leaders. At the play's climax, a stenographer in Paris reads the terms of a peace plan, named for British foreign secretary Sir Samuel Hoare and French prime minister Pierre Laval, and the British public reacts with outrage that the agreement cedes territory to Mussolini and undermines the League of Nations. In the play's final scenes, Hoare resigns and "war drums beat over Europe" as countries declare growing animosities and readiness to fight. The play closes with the kind of compact theatrical metaphor that Arent and the Living Newspaper would become known for. Figures in the uniforms of their respective countries stand in a line, as the sound of marching boots is heard overhead. Stage directions read, "The single word 'war' is passed right down the line, from England to Germany, the music blares out in a mounting climax, the feet tramp louder."[59]

The NYLN's plan for *Ethiopia* was to end each night with a breaking news update. But the vast majority of the play was about events that had come to pass at least a month before the show was set to open. Arent's script established a precedent for other Living Newspapers in that it picked up a story that was already in circulation. Rather than focusing on recent developments, which would put it in competition with print dailies and radio reports, the Living Newspaper would focus on historical context and social significance.

It did so, however, selectively. In *Ethiopia,* this meant espousing a Popular Front focus on the perils of fascism rather than the Pan-Africanist signifi-cance of Ethiopian sovereignty. Other than the opening scene at Walwal, and Haile Selassie's speech from Addis Ababa, the play's setting and perspective are overwhelmingly European and American, and predominantly white. In focusing on European diplomacy, Arent's script neglected the Pan-Africanist and anticolonial solidarities that the Black press had documented and advanced in the lead-up to the war and throughout its duration. Indeed, *Ethiopia's* sole African American character is not aviator-correspondent John Robinson but the flamboyant Colonel Hubert Fauntleroy Julian. Like his rival Robinson, Julian (the "Black Eagle of Harlem") was an aviator who had traveled from the United States to Ethiopia to fight Mussolini's forces. He received a less prestigious assignment, however, having fallen out with Haile Selassie on a previous visit, and he returned to the United States early with harsh criticisms of the Ethiopian army. Watson had sent a reporter to Harlem to interview Julian, but the result was, in Watson's words, "a comic interlude."[60] In Arent's script, Julian talks eagerly to the press about his trip and castigates Ethiopians as "savages." The scene sends up Julian's involvement in the war as naïve and ill-considered, punctuated with the lines "I CAME! I SAW! I QUIT!" *New York Times* critic Brooks Atkinson would describe him, dismissively, as "grandiloquent."[61]

Arent's research drew heavily from the *New York Times,* so it is unsurpris-ing that Arent's sole representative of African American engagement with Ethiopia was one whose views and experiences so opposed those of public sentiment in the Black press.[62] There is no reference to the mobilizations of thousands of African Americans in New York and other cities, nor to the war's Pan-Africanist implications. The latter omission is all the more striking, given that Hallie Flanagan had championed the play, in part, so she could employ a group of Black, non-Anglophone performers as Haile Selassie's courtiers. "One of the first groups of actors sent to us from the relief office (this was, of course, before the prohibition against aliens on WPA) was a large troupe of African Negroes who had come to this country as an operatic company and who, after a brief season, had been stranded," she wrote in her memoir.[63] Although Flanagan asserted that the troupe's performance in *Ethiopia* contained "no caricature," her characterization of a monolithic group of "Africans," unspecialized and hampered by their language skills, suggests that anti-racist and Pan-Africanist politics were far from mind, even in a play ostensibly about Ethiopia.

In mid-January 1936, as *Ethiopia*'s debut approached, Watson wrote to Roosevelt's press secretary, a personal friend, to request a recording of one of Roosevelt's speeches. Shortly after, Jacob Baker, assistant to WPA director Harry Hopkins, issued a directive stating that the State Department would need to approve all representations of foreign heads of state. A few days later, after witnessing a rehearsal, he would issue an amended directive forbidding any impersonations of a ruler or cabinet onstage. The words of state leaders could be quoted by others, but they could not be uttered by actors impersonating them. Flanagan asserted that characters in *Ethiopia* "are characterized with great respect and with no attempt at cartooning. This is particularly true of Mussolini, who is presented sympathetically and with power."[64] But her words seem to have had little effect.

This turn of events must have been striking for Watson, a print journalist, perhaps recognizing for the first time that staging words was different from printing them—and in some cases, more threatening. Mussolini and the other leaders were being not simply transcribed but impersonated, costumed, and lit. It is difficult to know how Mussolini might have appeared in production—but therein was the risk of theatrical staging.

It was Rice who was most publicly critical of the State Department's intervention. Staging the play without heads of state would be, he declared "like putting on Hamlet without Hamlet." It also violated free speech, he asserted, reminding the public of his roles as a board member at the ACLU, as well as vice chairman of the National Council on Freedom from Censorship and chairman of the Authors' League committee on censorship.[65] He resigned from the FTP, and his assistant Philip Barber took up his post as regional director in New York.

*Ethiopia* was postponed and its public performances eventually canceled. Instead, on January 24, a small number of journalists and WPA workers would attend a noon run-through. Brooks Atkinson still reviewed the play in the

*New York Times,* under the headline "'Ethiopia,' the First Issue of the Living Newspaper Which the Federal Theatre Cannot Publish." Atkinson praised his fellow "newspaper men" and artists for a "factual," "objective," and "unbiased" account but asserted that "a free theatre cannot be a government enterprise."[66] Journalist Roi Ottley wrote of chilling implications for the African American press: "I do not think it takes much stretch of the imagination to see that this will eventually affect all newspapers. . . . And in that case, all news that "Washington" considers offensive to its views would be censored to a point where Negroes would not be permitted to raise their voices in protest against existing conditions."[67]

Heywood Broun also had sharp words for the government: "The Living Newspaper must necessarily deal with living events and living men. It seems to me preposterous to attempt to set any sort of censorship upon the Project. That is not life. Censorship is always death."[68] The Newspaper Guild of New York adopted a resolution criticizing the WPA, asserting, "It would be impossible to dramatize news without impersonating important officials who are frequently the very center of the news." It went on, "In sponsoring the Project, the Newspaper Guild relied heavily on the assurances given to Mr. Elmer Rice by the Works Progress Administration that there would be complete freedom from interference and censorship."[69]

Despite the harsh indictment, the Newspaper Guild would not cease its partnership with the FTP. The NYLN would find a way to continue staging news within the considerable constraints *Ethiopia* had revealed. After *Ethiopia,* for instance, Hallie Flanagan herself advocated (unsuccessfully) for a piece on "money," suggesting that it might be less controversial than treatments of war and imperialism. And while Watson countered that any topic could be controversial, depending on its treatment, he seems to have heeded Flanagan's caution. All of the Unit's subsequent productions would focus on domestic issues, circumventing anxieties about portraying foreign leaders. They would also focus on New Deal initiatives, or at least on the values behind them. *Triple-A Plowed Under* narrated the short life of the Agricultural Adjustment Act—recently ruled unconstitutional by the Supreme Court—and heralded its replacement in the Soil Conservation and Domestic Allotment Act. *The Events of 1935,* anomalously, recapitulated a series of stories from the previous year but highlighted the National Labor Relations Act. *Injunction Granted!* traced labor activism in the United States and culminated with the passage of the Norris–La Guardia Act, an anti-injunction bill that preceded Roosevelt's presidency but shared his support for labor. *Power* advocated for the Tennessee Valley Authority, a federally owned electricity initiative, and *One-Third of a*

*Nation* championed the Wagner-Steagall Act, which subsidized housing for low-income families.

Thus, Living Newspapers came to define public interest in reference to Roosevelt's electorate: citizens, mostly white, able-bodied family men. Research into a play on American Indians was quickly shelved, and no Black-authored Living Newspapers saw the stage (see chapter 4), in part, no doubt, because issues of racialized violence so divided Roosevelt's government. Against the entreaties of his wife, Roosevelt would withhold support for anti-lynching legislation throughout his presidency for fear of alienating conservative southern Democrats. Alignment with the Roosevelt agenda, as a component of NYLN news sense, affected what was not produced, nor even considered, as much as it determined what was.

## "OVERHAULING NEWS JUDGMENT":
## SOCIAL SUBJECTS AND PROBLEM-BASED DRAMATURGY

Even though *Ethiopia* established limits and constraints, it also demonstrated some of the Living Newspaper's possibilities. It confirmed the NYLN's commitment to issues of social significance rather than the "sure-fire vaudeville" it initially considered. Reflecting on this shift, Watson asserted that NYLN staff "decided to break with the tradition of newspapers and exercise its own news judgment." He went on:

> We decided that the public was hungry for information about social subjects, and for that reason the Living Newspaper finally evolved as supplement both to the newspaper and to the theatre.
>
> We overhauled our news judgment completely, threw out our ideas for the dramatization of fluff and decided to go whole hog on a dramatization of social statistics which we conceived to be a great deal more vital than most people realized. We went behind the headlines and the news stories which are too often relegated to Page 13 of the newspapers, to find that we could prove that items of seeming academic interest were really items of very vital interest to the people.[70]

It was bold to say that the public was "hungry for information" at a moment when many were hungry in a more literal sense. Yet Watson would insist throughout his career that news was a human necessity, and one that traditional news media did not always serve. *Ethiopia* consolidated the Living Newspaper's unique role in the public sphere: as a "supplement" to mainstream newspapers, it could revisit, reframe, and elaborate on complicated problems. In this light, the slowness of theatrical production—writing, design, rehearsal, and performance—could be an asset rather than a hindrance. Therefore, *Ethiopia* oriented news sense toward stories already in circulation.

This had not always been the plan; at least one undated document proposed that a city night editor would send breaking news stories to the theater during performances so that news bulletins could be projected between sketches. There even appears to have been some infrastructure to support this: the same document notes that "several of our staff went to school with the phone company" to learn how to operate the teletype; and "leg men" (unspecialized reporters on the ground) could be assigned to key sites such as police headquarters.[71] There is little evidence of this practice in production records, however, other than a series of bulletins in the final scene of *Triple-A Plowed Under*. Perhaps routine bulletins were unimportant or logistically unmanageable, or perhaps the problem was aesthetic, with bulletins disrupting the narrative momentum that playwrights worked hard to achieve.

Regardless of the reason, the NYLN's embrace of uninterrupted long-form news instead of quick breaking bulletins would be decisive. From *Ethiopia* onward, Living Newspapers would use an episodic narrative structure, which could weave diverse characters into an overarching narrative about a single problem or concept, even, as I argue in chapter 2, in the anomalous, revue-style *Events of 1935*. In contrast with a series of bulletins, which Watson and Rice had considered, this structure had several advantages. First, as Arent would reflect, it allowed for the "dramatization of a problem": by focusing on a single issue, Living Newspapers could live up to their evolving mandate to "supplement" traditional news media by historicizing current issues and inviting citizens to grapple with solutions. In the context of elaborate problem-based dramaturgy rather than quick vignettes, Living Newspapers, as the rhetorician Sam Smiley notes, could foster more nuanced deliberation about political issues.[72]

A second advantage of this structure is that it echoed the pageant, a form that had become familiar to many Americans over the previous two decades. Indeed, even those who had not seen much theater might recognize the Living Newspapers' sweeping historical timelines from performances they had seen (or taken part in) in churches, workers' demonstrations, and civic commemorations. As these venues suggest, pageants primed communities to look at themselves, their histories, and their futures. Not only were pageants popular, they were also associated with auspicious events, asking communities to see themselves in history as it unfolded. The pageant form drew attention to social collectives, and—like a news broadcast—to their togetherness in specific historical moments.[73] Perhaps most pertinently for the FTP, however, it was an effective vehicle for employment. Long-form, problem-based dramaturgy required a large workforce with varied expertise.

## "WORKING DIFFERENTLY, THINKING DIFFERENTLY": THE NYLN'S WORKFORCE

The NYLN paid close attention to work: who the Living Newspaper could employ and how; how it connected workers to one another; how it represented their experiences onstage. Following FTP directives, it would frequently highlight the sheer number of jobs a Living Newspaper could create and sustain. Playbills, designed to look like newspapers with periodically changing editions, presented audiences with expansive company lists and articles about their work. In a playbill for *Triple-A Plowed Under,* the unit's first public production, an article boasted "two hundred and fifty actors, editors, reporters, rewrite men."[74] Accounts like these reminded Depression-era spectators that their tax dollars were supporting job creation—in the newsroom and in production.

Journalists and theater-makers had closely collaborated since the early twentieth century. A number of journalists, as Marlis Schweitzer explains, launched their careers by working as press agents for actors.[75] But in employing journalists and theater-makers, the NYLN had to accommodate myriad professional practices and ways of working. In the NYLN's newsroom, workers brought a variety of skills and backgrounds. Reporter George Dobson had thirty years of experience at the *Brooklyn Eagle* and the *New York Evening Post;* Frieda Lescher started out as a secretary, and advanced in her time at the NYLN to "senior newspaperman." Internal documents offer a glimpse at how these disparate workers collaborated in the Unit's early days. One of the most comprehensive records is a memo that traces a streamlined chain of command. The managing producer (Watson) and FTP regional director (Rice, followed by Barber) approved a topic, and then the managing editor (Arent) would draft an outline of scenes. The city editor would then create two-to-three-day assignments for research and editing staff, which they would document on worksheets. The managing editor would analyze the research and distribute it to his team of dramatists to work into specific scenes. They would consult with researchers as needed, polish their scenes, and return them to the managing editor and a small team of dramatists for compilation. A team of typists produced and disseminated drafts of the script, including those that would go to the press. Overall, the process described was specialized and hierarchical, emulating the assembly line processes that professional newsrooms were developing. In this respect, long-form problem-based dramaturgy had an advantage: it often enabled

Living Newspaper staff to work together on a single story while allowing for a relatively clear division of labor.

Just as the Living Newspaper's structure accommodated varied skills and schedules in the newsroom, so it did too in the rehearsal hall. Unlike community pageants, Living Newspapers were not designed for amateur performers. They did, however, need to integrate many performers, some of whom were trained in waning styles and genres. NYLN actor Norman Lloyd observed that many of his colleagues were "old American actors who had been in the great stock companies, river boats, gone up and down the Mississippi. Many of them had been in vaudeville acts that went around the country, never being first-rate or second-rate, just sort of traveling."[76]

Some performers used the NYLN to acquire or refine new skills. Add Bates, for instance, a dancer who performed with the Modern Negro Dance Group, would play a speaking role in *One-Third of a Nation,* as one of two tenants who would join the Harlem rent strike. Some of the NYLN's other Black actors, he recalled, had professional backgrounds in minstrelsy, and at least one white director accordingly solicited "teeth showing and them smiling" until Bates intervened and they "started working differently, thinking differently."[77] Meanwhile, Lloyd, among the 10 percent of non-relief workers the FTP could employ, went on to a successful career in film and television. He was one of the few actors to "star" in a Living Newspaper, as the recurring Clown in *Injunction Granted!* and the representative "Consumer" (Angus K. Buttonkooper) in *Power.* News sense at the NYLN sought to reflect a large and eclectic personnel, but it also demanded that workers reflect and adapt to their colleagues.

### "MONTHS OF HYSTERIA": ENGAGING IN REFLECTION AND REVISION

News sense required a commitment to reflection and revision, because NYLN workers had to negotiate different professional backgrounds and approaches. For instance, even though both journalists and theater-makers were accustomed to deadlines, the pace of work was a source of conflict. A heated postmortem of *Injunction Granted!* the NYLN's third production, directed by Joe Losey, offers a glimpse into this tension and others.

*Injunction Granted!,* Losey's second work production for the NYLN, was characteristically radical. *Triple-A Plowed* had culminated in support for the CIO by advocating for the Farmer-Labor Party, and *Injunction Granted!* called on all unions to join the CIO. The latter, as Stuart Cosgrove notes, was the NYLN's "most uncompromising production to date," and it "regenerated the hostilities between the Unit and its administrative superiors."[78] Philip Barber and his assistant Bill Farnsworth raised concerns to Flanagan after attending a rehearsal. Flanagan initially defended the production, asking Losey and Watson to make the script "more objective." In her eyes, they fell short. At 2:30 a.m., after seeing the opening, she wrote a letter lambasting the "one-sided treatment of the CIO rally; the voice reading Hoover; the scene showing judges asleep." It was not news but "biased" and "editorial."[79]

Even as Flanagan's criticism reflected deep disappointment, it revealed her profound investment in the form and her close engagement with NYLN leadership. She reminded Watson and Losey of the project's origins. "As you both know," she wrote, "I am committed to the Living Newspaper. . . . I thought clear and factual presentation of the news done in simple exciting terms, one of the most potent things that the stage can do today."[80] The problem for her was not just *Injunction Granted!* in itself but its reflection of what a Living Newspaper could be.

Both Watson and Losey, it seems, were left reeling by Flanagan's remarks, as well as poor reviews. They too showed a commitment to figuring out what had gone wrong, but from the perspective of process. Though Watson and Losey were friends, they appear to have argued. In a caustic letter penned a few days after the show's 1936 opening, Losey blamed "the inefficiency of your [Watson's] organization." He went on: "Much of this is due to a completely apriori set-up, to a preconceived notion as to the speed at which things should work. Although we have been at work for months, we have been working against a deadline consistently. It was true of the script, rehearsals, score, etc. You had no right either to expect or scream for an opening either on the Tuesday or the Friday set." To Watson, it seems, the theater-makers appeared inefficient and overly flexible. But Losey seemed to feel the same way about the journalists. He argued that his deadlines might have been manageable if the unit's "business, press, and research" divisions had been more efficient. Underlying the issues of time, it seems, were questions of mutual respect. For, adding insult to injury, in Losey's view, Watson was resistant to change: "Both Arthur [Arent] and you are inclined to be unrealistic about production. And I criticize your either nor recognizing this and adjusting your demands or else your not learning about your new field. This is not the old complaint, but I do say that to assume that theatre is a knack merely and everybody's game is to guarantee yourself failure in it. It is an ancient medium and deserves learning." Even with theatrical production as its goal, Losey insinuated, the NYLN's leaders were hindered by anti-theatrical prejudice. He conceded that his colleagues, like him, were exhausted. Arent carried too great a burden in compiling a script out of disorganized research, and even Watson, Losey acknowledged, "must get some rest." A great deal would have to change, it seemed, if the Living Newspaper were to continue. All the same, hope shone through this vitriol. "There is no question," he asserted, "but that the Federal Theatre, with all its handicaps, offered opportunity for experimentation which is not likely to be duplicated." The NYLN had "criminally neglected to utilize its strengths," and "our months of hysteria and our defeat by it [the Living Newspaper] stems directly from lack of clarity and lack of organization within the project."[81] Even as he complained bitterly about its execution, Losey retained high hopes about the Living Newspaper's potential. An ever-changing work in progress, news sense demanded continuous reflection and revision.

### "KNOW HOW TO CARRY THE BANNER": BLUE COLLARS, WHITE COLLARS, AND THE FTP

*Injunction Granted!* closed earlier than planned. Losey, following in Elmer Rice's footsteps, left the NYLN in protest, and Watson's activism, moving forward, would be countered by the more moderate presence of New York regional director Philip Barber.[82] It is not surprising that Elmer Rice and Joseph Losey, two of the Unit's most vocal communists, found the Unit insufficiently radical. The NYLN's company was not the communist hub critics would describe. In fact, a trivia section in the *Triple-A* playbill pointedly noted "that the actor who plays the part of [Communist Party leader] Earl Browder thinks Communists are terrible," though the assertion did little to reassure conservative critics, the House Committee on Un-American Activities, nor a zealous spectator who would disrupt the performance by singing the national anthem.[83] The unceremonious departures of Rice and Losey nudged news sense away from the radical left of the CIO and toward the broader coalitional politics of the New Deal.

Yet the NYLN was not apolitical either. It would promote a culture of labor activism, one that expanded traditional understandings of American workers. More specifically, the NYLN would challenge the US labor movement's traditional focus on so-called blue-collar workers. As the nation's largest and most prominent labor organizations, the American Federation of Labor and the Congress of Industrial Organizations played a significant role in defining the average American worker and his or her interests. Since 1886 the AFL had been at the forefront of labor organizing, representing craft unions. By the 1930s, however, millions of Americans working in "unskilled" mass production jobs, including meatpacking and manufacturing, began to seek representation as well. They started to create a new labor movement in 1935, galvanized by the passage of the Wagner Act two years before. At the helm, John L. Lewis of the United Mine Workers of America demanded that the AFL organize mass production workers. When the AFL refused, the rival CIO formed and soon had 2 million dues-paying members. The CIO quickly established a reputation for being more racially integrated and more ideologically radical, with communists holding significant leadership positions.[84]

Because the AFL and CIO differed ideologically, in some cases they fomented division among workers. At the ANG, for instance, as Philip Glende notes, guild members debated joining the CIO less than a year after they had affiliated with the AFL; in June 1937, they did, seeding discontent among editorial staff who either rejected the CIO's more militant approach or were reluctant to join forces with non-editorial newspaper staff, such as those working in advertising, business, and printing.

The AFL and the CIO would compete for roughly two decades. For all their differences however, they would present a unified front in at least one respect: making "blue-collar workers" the figureheads of the US labor movement and in doing so, conflating labor with white, able-bodied men with families to support. The "blue-collar" referenced a garment favored by craftsmen and manual workers: loose-fitting shirts with soft turned-down collars, dyed indigo to conceal stains.[85] In the 1930s the WPA celebrated blue-collar workers— perhaps most famously in public murals depicting steelworkers, carpenters, and others engaged in physically demanding labor.

The phrase "white-collar," as an antonym to "blue-collar," had been popularized in the 1910s and 1920s. The detachable "Arrow collar" became a symbol of new, refined masculinity, celebrated in the 1934 Cole Porter song "You're the Top" ("You're an Arrow collar"). It indexed work of an "administrative, managerial, or clerical nature."[86] White-collar workers were understood to enjoy higher social status and also material advantages over manual laborers, such as less physical strain and higher earning potential. For some this meant that professional organizations were preferable to unions; they had little in common with—or little need of—a labor movement dominated by blue collars.

FTP employees were a hodgepodge of those who identified as blue-collar, those who identified as white-collar, and those for whom neither identity was possible or desirable. Institutionally, the FTP integrated blue-collar and white-collar identities, espousing blue-collar labor activism while selectively invoking white-collar respectability. Many theater workers were organized through Actors' Equity, the National Alliance of Theatrical Stage Employees, and the Dramatists' Guild. Hallie Flanagan noted in the Dies Committee hearings that FTP administrators were in continuous engagement with approximately twenty-four theatrical unions.[87] These affiliations had trained workers to advocate for their rights, and the FTP, under WPA auspices, encouraged them to do so. Indeed, labor activism was so regular that Flanagan recalled: "I saw a picket line of ten outside our office and I said to the personnel director that every one of the pickets should be fired, not for picketing, which was at that time legal on WPA, but for picketing in such a sloppy and uninteresting manner. Only one, apparently, knows how to walk or carry a banner or anything else indicating theatre training. What are they doing on our project?" (Flanagan's colleague assured her that the sloppy picketers were not trained performers but rather administrators and journalists; the one "carrying the banner" with some competence was, as Flanagan suspected, a dancer.) Of course, not all FTP workers were affiliated with white-led national unions, including administrative and maintenance workers, professional dancers, and those whom white unions excluded on the basis of race and ethnicity.[88] In 1936 Black performers Fredi Washington, W. C. Handy, Paul Robeson, and Ethel Waters would form the Negro Actors Guild of America, but their activism would require them, as Laurie Woodard writes, to "dance gingerly with the [white] Left."[89] The culture of labor activism was alive and well at the FTP, but also selective and exclusionary.

At the same time, some employees and administrators saw the benefits of white-collar status, within their professions specifically and in the FTP writ large. Journalists increasingly identified as white-collar, while printers and typesetters identified as blue-collar. Stage designers had unionized in 1924, but as David Bisaha notes, they resisted a move in the 1930s to reclassify their designs as waged labor. Instead, he observes, "they claimed professional autonomy and intellectual rights, developing a class identity that approached white-collar status within a blue-collar union."[90] Actors, too, as Sean Holmes explains, worked hard in the early twentieth century to claim white-collar professionalism and respectability. While encouraging actors to identify with trade unionism, Actors' Equity "urged their fellow performers to look to the white-collar professions for models of social advancement and to observe the middle-class canon of propriety both on and offstage."[91] Reflecting these white-collar identities in the theater, a bulletin from the FTP's National Play Bureau advised employees, "Remember that this is a 'white collar' Project and that we should look like 'white collar' workers."[92] In what followed, it gave notes about hygiene and promptness. This line of argument—from white-collar work to hygiene and promptness—reveals how notions of professionalism were bound up with race, class, gender, and sexuality. "Promptness," for instance, would be more challenging for those traveling to a Broadway theater from Harlem than from nearby midtown. "Cleanliness" depended, at best, on material access to time, space, and washing supplies; at worst, on racialized, gendered, and sexualized bodily ideals. Even in a relief project with progressive and racially integrated aims, white-collar respectability privileged employees with the time and means to show up early, looking sharp.

The NYLN, like the FTP overall, would negotiate blue- and white-collar allegiances; in fact, it would explicitly cultivate solidarity across these identities, thanks especially to the influence of Morris Watson. In June of 1936, shortly after *Triple-A* closed, Watson had taken on the chairmanship of the Committee of Organizations Representing the Federal Arts Projects of the WPA. In this capacity he represented approximately 45,000 WPA arts workers, from authors to cartoonists to dancers. He met with high-ranking WPA administrators Aubrey Williams and Thad Holt, advocating for a five-point plan that included more funding for federal arts projects, vacation and sick leave, freedom of expression for all artists, and an end to dismissals without cause.

While Watson's ANG work had primed him to advocate for journalists, the WPA role challenged him to consider arts workers as well. At his meeting with Williams and Holt, he spoke passionately about the problems that united journalists and arts workers, how new media, in the hands of opportunistic managers, were diminishing employment prospects: "Canned acting in the form of motion pictures is throttling the legitimate theatre," he observed," and "newspaper staffs still are being cut, and flesh and blood is being replaced by telegraphed photos and syndicated features." In these existential threats Watson saw possibilities for solidarity, for if journalists and arts workers were united in their precarity, they were also alike in their value. "Society and the government, itself," he insisted, "is greatly in need of the talent and experience of all these thousands of workers."[93] Art and journalism provided essential social services, even if—especially during the Depression—they often went unrecognized as such.

At the same time that Watson was creating connections between artists and journalists, he continued the work he had begun with the ANG: to build solidarity between white-collar and blue-collar workers. Thus, in meetings and other public addresses, Watson consistently and emphatically addressed his colleagues as "workers," insisting that to do so did not mean sacrificing professional expertise or integrity. In February of 1937, less than a month before the opening of *Power,* he would embark on a speaking tour with that very message. Addressing journalists across the Midwest, he would challenge his colleagues' reticence to identify with blue-collar activists: "Workers who have heretofore set themselves apart from their fellows in a false class distinction are becoming conscious that their very badge of distinction is a white yoke chained to a vicious economic notion. That notion is that any individualist who plays his cards right is bound to become a millionaire."[94] It was time, he argued, to trade in the "romance" of journalism for material protections. These could be won only when, as his title suggested, "The White-Collar Worker Enters the Labor Movement."

That summer, a few months after he won his case against the AP, Watson would once again broaden his remarks to include artists as well. In a radio interview called "Journalism and the Arts in Everyday Life," he would return to the theme of social value. Watson was convinced, with progressive pragmatists like John Dewey, that people were influenced by form and narrative in their everyday lives. That so many Americans saw the arts as frivolous was a problem that artists and journalists needed to tackle together. His fellow citizens, he would argue, were constricted by a narrow conception of "social utility." It had diminished their "aesthetic appreciation," leading them to devalue the work of artists and journalists. He reflected on his father as an example:

> My father's notion of great art was to lay one brick upon another until a building reared skyward. Anything else was sissified. He saw culture in the terms of tangible social use, and he saw no social use in the sensuous forms of art. . . . I believe my father's instincts were right, and the only trouble with him was that he failed to understand the influence of art on his surroundings and upon himself, even in his everyday life.

It seemed that Watson was still haunted by the gendered, heterosexist threat of work that was trivial, unserious, and effete. (Indeed elsewhere he reiterated that for his father, "the persons who wrote the papers were sissies.") Nonetheless, he sought to expand understandings of work and workers, bridging journalists and artists, blue collars and white collars. Thus he called on the nation to support the "skill and genius" of its artists and to tap "a great untapped reservoir of vigorous talent—the more vigorous now because in the past few years it has known only struggle, because it has been pent up behind that struggle." Only with the support of federal funding and infrastructure might artists meet the needs of "multitudes" that "clamor" for excitement.[95] Far from representing the effete figure of the sissy, artists, in Watson's eyes, contributed to a thriving economy, vigorously supplying that which was in demand.

## NEWS-MAKERS AND BUTTON-MAKERS: EXPANDING CONCEPTIONS OF WORK AND WORKERS

Watson's expansive approach to labor advocacy seems to have resonated with his colleagues at the NYLN. When he won his case against the AP on April 12, 1937, three months into the run of *Power,* they celebrated together in the theater (figure 2). NYLN manager Ethel Aaron (later Ethel Aaron Hauser) recalled: "Of course, the Living Newspaper was so great because Morris Watson was involved.

And after all, he was the man over whom the Wagner Act was decided. So that we celebrated that in the theatre the night that the decision came down from the Supreme Court." Hauser was not alone in her admiration for Watson. A company member identified as "Laura L" penned a poem comparing him to Sir Galahad. But as Hauser went on to explain, she and her colleagues were invested in Watson's case for reasons beyond the outcome for Watson, who by this point did not even want his job at the AP back. She recalled: "There were lots of things like that that were terribly exciting and part of living and part of the time in which we lived. We were all very much involved and very concerned."[96] Those who were engaged in labor activism would know that Watson's victory had implications for others. "The business of the Associated Press," the Supreme Court ruled, "is not immune from regulation because it is an agency of the press."[97] In affirming the Wagner Act, the ruling affirmed the possibilities of organized labor, even for white-collar professionals.

NYLN staff would also show their support for Watson by participating in staging a brief play he created about his legal battle for the Newspaper Guild of

FIGURE 2. "Portrait of Morris Watson." Portrait of Morris Watson, managing producer of the Living Newspaper, reading about the results of his court case in the *New York Post*. Poster of *Power* in the background (bottom left). Morris Watson Papers, Ax 774, University of Oregon Libraries Special Collections and University Archives.

New York. Although it was titled simply *Guild Parade of 1937*, it was a compact Living Newspaper. Actor Charles Dill would play the omniscient "Voice" just as he did in *Power* and, later, *One-Third of the Nation*. Norman Lloyd would play a character named "Publisher." A boxing match between journalist Dean Jennings and publisher William Randolph Hearst was transposed directly from *Injunction Granted!*[98] Another scene would stage Watson's victory in court, with Watson played by actor Jay Williams.

NYLN staff would embody a culture of labor activism throughout their time at the FTP by taking an active role in shaping their working conditions. They argued for sick leave and vacation pay. They asked for more or different office space, for permission to work from home, for more consultation at various points of the creative process. They argued (sometimes successfully) for promotions and raises, though these were somewhat limited by a rigid WPA pay scale. At times they collaborated to make change. For instance, a group of NYLN employees circulated a petition when they felt that administrators like Watson and Arent were too heavy-handed in their management; others wrote a counter-letter to say such claims were unfounded.

Reflecting the unit's culture of labor solidarity, the Living Newspaper repertoire dramatized the experiences of a variety of American workers. Cast lists often identified characters by their jobs or by their relations to capital. Bankers and landowners tended to be unsympathetic. Workers by contrast were sympathetic, and an expansive category.

Living Newspapers dramatized traditional labor tactics and events, such as the Pullman strike (*Injunction Granted!*). But they also depicted workers who were not represented by the AFL or CIO—including farmers, sharecroppers, grocers, and landlords—and explored their political potential. A penny auction in *Triple-A* showed how farmers organized to buy one another's farms when they were threatened with foreclosure.[99]

At the same time as it expanded the representation of American workers, the Living Newspaper repertoire also perpetuated the US labor movement's pattern of racialized exclusion. There were very few racialized characters with speaking roles, and even fewer depicted in significant political action. Native Americans did not appear in any of the Living Newspaper's dramatizations of past or present, with the exception of a brief caricature by Norman Lloyd as a tomahawk-wielding clown in *Injunction Granted!* The 1934 Indian Reorganization Act, which was reshaping governance of and by Native Americans across the United States, did not figure into the NYLN's many treatments of civic engagement.[100] Although African Americans appeared in Living Newspapers, Black leaders were rarely part of the story. For example, *The Events of 1935*, the Unit's second public production, and its least political, favorably spotlighted the Wagner Act and American Federation of Labor organizer John L. Lewis. Paradigmatically however, it neglected the work of Mary McLeod Bethune, who founded the National Council of Negro Women that year. The next Living Newspaper, *Injunction Granted!*, took labor law as its explicit focus, dramatizing a history of strikes and court injunctions. It identified enslaved Africans as early "workers" in the American workers' movement, neglecting the conditions under which they were forced to work, and the ways in which they would resist, revolt, and organize for their liberation.

After *Injunction Granted!* as Loren Kruger has explained, Living Newspapers would drift away from the values of collectivism and organized labor, espousing more centrist politics.[101] Workers were replaced by consumers as the Living Newspaper's protagonists. Whereas *Injunction Granted!* had featured the American labor movement, *Power* and *One-Third of a Nation* featured single individuals defined by their ability and desire to participate in a capitalist economy. In *Power,* the representative "Consumer" wants to be able to afford his skyrocketing electricity bill; in *One-Third of a Nation,* the representative "Little Man" wants to buy "a decent place to live" for his small family. Mirroring the shift from collective protagonists to individuals, the playbills for both plays credit a single author, Arthur Arent.

Indeed, by the premiere of *One-Third of a Nation,* both Watson and the NGNY seem to have ended their formal relationship with the NYLN. Neither is credited on the playbill. Philip Barber is listed as the play's producer, and Irving Mendell is listed as its manager and supervisor. Watson went on to devote his energy to organizing work at the ANG but remained on friendly terms with NYLN personnel: when *One-Third of a Nation* was critiqued on the Senate floor, he put Ethel Aaron in touch with a prominent leftist lawyer for advice.[102]

In Stuart Cosgrove's assessment, "the period between 1937–1939 saw the Living Newspaper shed some of its militancy and become the new dramatic form of state reformism: the drama of the new deal."[103] Yet even as Living Newspapers moved away from overtly supporting organized labor, they still winked at progressive activists. Both Consumer and Little Man identify themselves as "Angus K. Buttonkooper," a name that was not only pointedly generic by white, Euro-American standards but also indexical to blue-collar work and, more recently, to white-collar solidarity. In fact, the name Buttonkooper had acquired special significance in Watson's legal battle with the AP. Watson's lawyer, John W. Davis, had argued: "Watson is like a button maker. A button maker fabricates buttons. Watson fabricated news for the Associated Press!"[104] The claim was that journalism involved a kind of "making," akin to manufacturing. Journalists therefore deserved the same kind of legal protections that their blue-collar counterparts enjoyed under the auspices of industrial unions.

In its operations and theatrical repertoire, the NYLN attuned its news sense to labor. The WPA and FTP brought together blue-collar workers and white-collar workers, allowing the activism associated with organized labor while invoking white-collar respectability. Watson, at the NYLN's helm, called on white-collar workers to enter—and expand—the US labor movement. A preoccupation with work and workers shaped the Living Newspaper repertoire, in its depictions of workers, political actions, and so-called average Americans. These representations perpetuated the racism, sexism, and heterosexism built into white-collar and blue-collar norms while seeking to expand the categories represented by American workers.

The image with which this chapter began, "Living Newspaper Goes to Press," was perhaps the most vivid illustration of this idea. It picked up on a recurring theme, the Living Newspaper's capacity for creating employment, but it also offered a subtle commentary on what the work of news-making could be—one that flew in the face of the ANPA's characterization of journalism as a solitary pursuit of the truth. Synthesizing commitments of the WPA, FTP, and ANG, "Living Newspaper Goes to Press" presented a vision of journalism as collaborative, interpretive labor.

## "THE SCRUTINY AND INVESTIGATION OF A LARGE STAFF": WRESTLING WITH OBJECTIVITY

In its vision of collaborative journalistic labor, "Living Newspaper Goes to Press" also illustrated a dynamic approach to objectivity. On the one hand, it would be difficult for the NYLN to claim anything like independence, especially after the State Department's prohibition on representing foreign leaders and the subsequent cancellation of *Ethiopia*. On the other hand, the NYLN was a journalistic endeavor and committed to the norms endorsed by professional journalists. The American Society of Newspaper Editors' Canons of Journalism distinguished reporting from advocacy and defined impartiality as freedom from "opinion or bias of any kind." FTP administrators like Hallie Flanagan and Philip Barber would champion this standard, demanding, in Barber's words, "factual, unbiased presentation."[105] Yet this was a difficult standard for artists and journalists alike. Moreover, as the form developed, it became clear that the hallmark of Living Newspapers was how they *mediated* facts: by dramatizing agency and implication through fictitious characters; by juxtaposing characters of different classes; by racing forward and backward through history; by rousing audiences with calls to action. These conventions did not neatly align with reigning standards of impartiality. Any pursuit of objectivity at the NYLN would be tenuous.

The NYLN, however, would never disavow objectivity, at least not publicly. Instead, it would redefine objectivity as a commitment to a process that systematically engaged multiple perspectives. Public documents like "Living Newspaper Goes to Press" illustrated this commitment. They showed not only how many people the Living Newspaper employed but also how systematically they tackled the work of interpretation. Processual rigor rather than independence or disinterest became the mechanism for journalistic integrity.

Put differently, the NYLN took an additive approach to pursuing objectivity: rather than stripping a story down to "just the facts," it began with facts and then engaged multiple people and processes to make sense of them. Indeed, according to the FTP leadership, a large, interactive team was the only way to ensure that Living Newspapers retained their factual integrity. The point was not merely that several people happened to contribute to the Living Newspaper, but that it was made in a way that anticipated their disparate backgrounds and expertise. As one manual asserted, "The entire concept of the Living Newspaper technique is that of collective effort. Any subject worthy of this effort is big enough to demand the scrutiny and investigation of a large staff." As a result, it required "the closest co-ordination among the group as a whole" by way of "full and sympathetic discussions between the battery of dramatists and the research workers."[106] Roles were clearly delineated and assigned value in the project's budget, not only to meet the FTP's demands for transparency but also to demonstrate a clear and systematic process of news-making. Starting with *Triple-A Plowed Under,* the NYLN would cite source material in its scripts and archive its research. Playbills invited spectators to verify the team's work by consulting its research at Living Newspaper offices.

The NYLN's critics would not be convinced, but at least some FTP administrators would be: in the years following *Ethiopia* and *Injunction Granted!* both Flanagan and Barber developed more complex understandings of objectivity. In her Dies Committee hearings, Flanagan would concede, "I think we strive for objectivity, but I think the whole history of the theater would indicate that any dramatist holds a passionate brief for the things he is saying."[107] In a 1939 letter, Barber would explain:

> The author may arrange, underline or give unusual theatrical treatment to his material, but he is not, as in the case of a play, simply expressing the workings of his personal imagination and communicating to an audience the direction of his own ego. There must be a vast amount of careful, well-planned research behind a real Living Newspaper. If the research and the morgue (which I consider simply as one aspect of the research) are wiped out, you may be sure that the end of the Living Newspaper will shortly follow.[108]

It is telling that in these comments Barber no longer references the absence of bias; instead he focuses on the volume of research and the multiplicity of perspectives. His account of news-making aligned with the ANG's refutation of the ANPA: rather than lone-wolf reporters engaged in solitary pursuit of the truth, he described a collective engaged in communal interpretation. News sense, at the NYLN, required not impartiality but rather a commitment to extensive research and interpretations that included multiple perspectives.

If processual rigor demanded multiple perspectives, it was also heavily reliant on hierarchy, which reinscribed divisions between white-collar and blue-collar workers. "Unskilled" laborers made roughly $55 per month, whereas "skilled" workers made at least $20 more. Newspapermen, considered not only skilled workers but also "professionals," made $80 to $90 per month. Managers and supervisors, like stage director Brett Warren, manager Ethel Aaron, and morgue supervisor Stephen Madigan, earned in the mid-$100s, whereas the Unit's executive leaders, Watson, Arent, and the business and technical directors, earned between $175 and $200. If the NYLN encouraged collaboration, it was by no means collaboration among equals, at least not materially.

Processual rigor also maintained gendered and racialized hierarchy. Jean Laurent would become chief of research and then city editor, though stage director Joseph Losey would describe her job in condescending and primarily clerical terms: "Research workers must be organized according to a systematic and accepted method which I don't believe Laurent, despite good intention, understands very well—though I think that she could administer such a system under someone else. Nor do I think that she really understands very much about the requirements of the scripts. Research workers must be responsible to script writers—perhaps through Laurent." Although Laurent led the research department—in a project driven, no less, by research—Losey does not credit her with expertise, conceding only that "she could administer a system under someone else." His characterization offers a glimpse into what it might have been like for women to occupy leadership positions at the NYLN. Ethel Aaron, though not employed as a journalist, faced professional barriers too. By her own account, she trained in music at Juilliard, and after several years as a musical director, she joined the FTP to manage the NYLN's "creative promotions." Losey would note that she was "very useful and very responsible, but she talks too much."[109] She went on to become Unit manager during the 1938 run of *One-Third of a Nation.* Her responsibilities included attending the theater every night when there was a show, liaising with Adelphi Theatre staff and the company, sending weekly reports to regional director Barber, and forging community partnerships. She arranged backstage tours and a lobby display with artwork by local youth. In an interview thirty years later, Barber would praise her for initiating group reservations, which were a crucial source of revenue. During her tenure, however, Aaron would struggle for pay and recognition that reflected her management position. Even as Aaron and Laurent acquired relatively high-level positions, male colleagues belittled their work. The NYLN's white male supervisory staff, it seems, either struggled with or dismissed news sense in their female colleagues. This would also be the case with racialized workers.

Systematicity went hand in hand with bureaucracy, a challenge felt disproportionately by workers of color. Limited office space meant that many staff worked at home, including FTP scriptwriters, who nonetheless had to report to the Unit office each morning to sign time sheets. The constant need to track personnel and funds was even more cumbersome in production. Technician Harold Burris-Meyer recalled:

> Superimposing the bureaucracy upon the theatre operation was like trying to make water run uphill. For example, if you wanted to buy something, you had to advertise and get bids. So suppose that at the dress rehearsal you broke the teapot that was used in the second act. So you drew the specifications for the teapot and get it put out for bid and then all the business of receiving the bids and certifying that the stuff proffered filled the specifications and so forth and they figured that if you broke the teapot in January, you might get a new teapot the end of August. Meanwhile the show would be—have to wait for the teapot.[110]

Eventually, Burris-Meyer noted, the FTP established an emergency fund that allowed production teams to fund small discretionary purchases without the bidding procedure. But bureaucracy remained a problem. Indeed, it was the subject of a musical skit called *FTP Plowed Under* penned by Arthur Arent and Marc Blitzstein for the Ladies Garment Workers Union revue. Debuting in November 1937, the sketch seems to have focused on the institutional pitfalls of bureaucratized theater. Bumbling FTP administrators Zealous, Stallalong, and Bureaucrash, together with Mrs. Clubhouse (modeled on Hallie Flanagan) and composer Hippity Bloomberg, manage to mount a play that amounts to nothing but a rising curtain. The sketch was popular until the FTP's 1939 demise, with even President Roosevelt allegedly saying, "I wish the Senate and House could see this one."[111]

Bureaucracy was a powerful source of gatekeeping that seems to have disproportionately slowed development of work by African American artists. Abram Hill and John D. Silvera spent over a year collaborating on a Living Newspaper about Black struggles for freedom and justice, but the Negro Arts Committee observed that it was "lost in red tape." Working under the supervision of National Play Bureau director Emmet Lavery, Hill and Silvera worked through several revisions, but eventually Lavery deemed the play unready for production and turned his attention elsewhere. Impersonal bureaucratic structures meant that there was little accountability for those who enforced the whiteness of objectivity, or white-collar work. As I show in chapter 4, Hill and Silvera would expose this very problem in their playscript. They would also satirize the Living Newspaper form, showing how its conventions were already hardening into something formulaic and predictable. The NYLN was committed to experimentation, but it would take two artists outside the Unit to show the limitations of experimentation, not only in terms of who could engage in it but also in terms of the form itself.

### "THE PROPER GIMMICK": NEWS SENSE AND THEATRICAL CONVENTIONS

I have shown how, under the auspices of two institutions, the FTP and the ANG, the NYLN reimagined the work of news-making. In contrast to the image of pursuit of truth by a single romantic hero, it disseminated a vision of collective interpretation. The workers who joined its ranks acquired a distinctive news sense, one attuned to workers' issues, identification with white-collar labor, and a commitment to collaboration and experimentation.

The various components of news sense help to explain why the NYLN chose to produce what it did: plays that focused on white male workers; subjects that lent themselves to documentary research; issues that were domestic, and current, but not divisive for Roosevelt's supporters. Even so, the NYLN's repertoire is not completely reducible to its process, resources, or approach. Strikingly, NYLN staff discussed this part of their process in quasi-mystical terms, and despite their emphasis on collaboration, did not entirely avoid attributions of virtuosity.

For all of the Unit's emphasis on systematicity, its most popular production came out of an exploratory workshop that took place away from the newsroom, in the summer of 1937. Some NYLN staff were among the participants, and the time and space to create were invaluable. Designer Howard Bay recalled: "I think Arthur [Arent] learned a lot, too, and also being away from the pressures of . . . [the] city room in a newspaper that he had to run in New York. And it gave him sort of leisure and perspective and so forth. I think it was very valuable to Arthur. And you know, looking down your list of Living Newspaper scripts, Arthur was the only one that could write 'em." At the heart of the NYLN's repertoire were vivid stage metaphors, conventions that gave concrete form to complicated social ideas. According to Bay, Arent had a particular talent for creating them: "Arthur had a facility of getting the proper[,] just the proper gimmick for each episode . . . and twisting it. . . . Everybody else [wrote] rather dull stuff. . . . The little man in *Power* and the ventriloquist bit with Wilkie and . . . all those gimmicks were building blocks. You'd think of concrete things that would—or a little burlesque that you'd do. Nobody else had that facility."[112] Philip Barber also credited Arent with a distinctive talent:

> Arthur, I think, was an incredibly brilliant person in his writing. I think that his whole capacity to get essences of things—isn't it in *Triple-A* where there are those scenes about the price of milk the farmers were getting? Well that's typical, Arthur's typical capacity to get a little example, a dynamic scene that suddenly give[s] you a whole picture of a concept of a thought, brilliant effect. Nobody else ever—they fumbled around and messed around. . . . On that type of writing, I think he was an absolute genius.[113]

Arent was not responsible for all of the Living Newspapers' signature conventions: Norman Lloyd, for example, helped develop the Little Man through improvisation; technical consultant Harold Burris-Meyer ensured that the Loudspeaker resounded, god-like, from the entire auditorium.

What is notable, however, is how comments like Barber's and Bay's pointed to theatrical ideas, realized in the bodies of actors, in sound, image, and mise-en-scène. In doing so, they suggested that news sense at the NYLN culminated in theatrical conventions, at once simpler and more complex than a paragraph of editorial prose. These conventions—what Bay called "gimmicks," as I discuss in my conclusion—were fundamental to making news differently. In the chapters that follow, I examine these conventions in production and reception to explore the workings of journalistic imagination in the NYLN repertoire.

# CHAPTER TWO

# THE COURT OF PUBLIC OPINION

## Reimagining News Publics

Amid the debates that animated mainstream journalism in the interwar period, journalists, critics, and scholars grappled with questions about their publics. Who was news for and who should it be about? What did it ask, tacitly or directly, of the people it addressed? What was a public and what could it do?

These questions were bound to preoccupy creators of the Living Newspaper. Within a year of its founding, after all, they had dedicated themselves to public interest. And as news sense coalesced, they had made some presumptions about the public's character: its "hung[er] for information on social subjects,"[1] its preponderance of white American workers concerned with domestic New Deal issues.

In the Living Newspaper repertoire, however, the public would remain a moving target and a site of experimentation. *Ethiopia,* capturing the anxieties of the Popular Front, reminded spectators that they were always on the brink of another war. The public, it proposed, was fundamentally an army in reserve, like the audience overtaken in the play's final moments by the "projection of marching feet and the tramp tramp tramp amplified on the sound system."[2] The NYLN's next play, *Triple-A Plowed Under,* figured the public differently. Shifting its focus to agricultural subsidies, it staged an emerging coalition that included farmers, industrial workers, and housewives. As the Dust Bowl eviscerated American farms, *Triple-A*'s public emerged as rural and urban Americans who recognized their interdependence and shared power. Director Joseph Losey, inspired by experimental Soviet theater, staged a literal coming-together over a series of multilevel risers. A "Chorus of Unemployed" jumped "close together, arms extended." Directly addressing the audience, in agitprop style, the chorus enlisted the audience too, ending the play with the words "We need *you.*"[3] Across its repertoire, Living Newspapers searched for the elusive "American public" between the stage and the audience.

It was the third Living Newspaper, however, *The Events of 1935,* that most explicitly grappled with this challenge. Also called *Highlights of 1935* and simply *1935*, this Living Newspaper was unusual and by most accounts unsuccessful. It was the only Living Newspaper by the Unit to stage multiple stories in a single production. Arriving on the heels of two explicitly single-issue-based plays— *Ethiopia* and *Triple-A Plowed Under*—*1935* with its tabloid structure did not gain much traction among audiences, artists, or historians. Losey, initially hired to direct, found the play so "superficial" that he handed the reins to his assistant H. Gordon Graham.[4] Reviewers by and large praised memorable moments but compared the production unfavorably to its single-issue predecessor. The New York production played for only a few weeks and inspired few variations in other cities.[5] It netted about a sixth of the attendees and revenue of productions that came before and after. Within a couple of years, even FTP staff were writing *1935* out of Living Newspaper history. In "The Technique of the Living Newspaper," managing editor Arthur Arent characterized the form as the dramatization of a single issue and made no mention of *1935*.[6] In "Writing the Living Newspaper," managing producer Morris Watson devoted only a sentence to *1935*, citing its effective use of puppets. Historians have tended to follow their lead, offering minimal analysis of the production or neglecting it entirely.[7]

*1935* is worth revisiting, however, precisely because it is so structurally and thematically different from the majority of Living Newspapers. As one of the FTP's earliest experiments with the form, *1935* reveals how the NYLN critiqued news consumers in its first year of production. It did so by uniquely combining the modalities of public address that the theater and newspaper combined. *1935* dramatized the public onstage, and it also addressed constituents of an "imagined community" in and beyond its audiences. The friction between these two publics—one represented onstage and the other hailed in the audience—was provocative. As critical reviews would reveal, *1935* incited spectators to reflect on their collectivity and to grapple with a "phantom public" that haunted them. In doing so, the NYLN offered a distinctive response to interwar debates about the public and its possibilities.

## "THE PROBLEM OF PRESENTATION":
### JOURNALISM, THE PUBLIC, AND THE LIPPMANN–DEWEY DEBATE

One way to understand the substance of *1935* (*pace* Losey) is in the terms articulated by an unresolved and now-canonical debate. In the aftermath of World War I, Americans had to reckon with the effects of propaganda. The result, as the communication scholar John Nerone observes, "included a broad intellectual crisis of confidence in the ability of democratic publics to operate with real intelligence."[8] Journalists were enmeshed in this crisis. In a liberal democracy, it was their role to inform citizens so that citizens, in turn, could govern themselves through their elected representatives.

Liberal democracy's fallacies were evident to many—those whose families had been colonized, erased, or enslaved in its name; those who were still systematically excluded from voting—but it remained the reigning paradigm in professional journalism. Indeed, the Canons of Journalism, in less than two pages, used the word "public" six times. Considerations of public welfare, public interest, and public attention: these were professional journalism's raison d'être. It is unsurprising therefore that debates about the public also revolved around journalism.

The public intellectuals Walter Lippmann and John Dewey vividly captured this challenge for interwar Americans. Communication scholars have canonized their successive books *The Phantom Public* (1925) and *The Public and Its Problems* (1927) as "the Lippmann–Dewey Debate." Neither book addressed the other directly, nor were the books even widely circulated when they were first published. Yet their arguments crystallized interwar anxieties about the public and the news.

In *The Phantom Public* Lippmann argued that the scale and complexity of American society had rendered predominant ideas of democratic participation all but obsolete. The book opened, it is worth noting, with a theatrical simile. "The private citizen today," Lippmann proclaimed, "has come to feel rather like a deaf spectator in the back row, who ought to keep his mind on the mystery off there, but cannot quite manage to keep awake."[9] The distance between stage and audience, reinforced with an ableist ascription of deafness, captured an experience of being peripheral, out of range; the norms of spectatorship (and by contrast, the embarrassment of drifting off in public) captured the moral imperatives associated with consuming news.

A journalist and political commentator, Lippmann was better informed than most. When *The Phantom Public* came out, he was working as a columnist and editor for Pulitzer's reformist *New York World* and had already published his pathbreaking book *Public Opinion;* in the 1930s he would go on to write a column, "Today and Tomorrow," syndicated in more than 250 newspapers. Yet even he maintained, "I cannot find time to do what is expected of me in the theory of democracy; that is, to know what is going on and to have an opinion worth expressing on every question which confronts a self-governing community."[10] The "private citizen," Lippmann surmised—saying nothing of those who did not "count" as such—lacked the expertise necessary to weigh in on decisions that could orient state politics.[11] Yet political speeches, news media, and the burgeoning field of public opinion research continued to address citizens as if they could, and as if they could do so in concert.

Lippmann believed that his colleagues in politics, in the press, and in political science and theory were working with an ideal that was hopelessly anachronistic. They "remembered" an American public from ancient Greece and Rome, where citizens could routinely gather and deliberate in the agora or forum. Yet for Lippmann, neither gathering nor deliberation was realistic for the sprawling industrialized society of modern America. The "public" invoked by his peers might have lived and breathed in antiquity, but it was long gone. The idea of it lingered like a phantom in democratic imaginaries, as persistent as it was ineffectual.

Two years after Lippmann published his assessment, the philosopher John Dewey offered an alternative in his book *The Public and Its Problems.* As his title suggests, Dewey tacitly rejected Lippmann's premise that an active American public was a dead idea. Rather, Dewey felt the public was incontestably alive. Its existence was guaranteed as long as there were citizens with shared interests and experiences. Turning to analogy, Dewey compared America's social problems to a shoe in need of repair. Lippmann's argument implied that Americans should relinquish their shoes to the cobblers—the policy specialists, social scientists, and political leaders who were figurative experts in shoe repair. Yet Dewey contended that there was crucial expertise to be gained from ordinary citizens who were the *"wearers"* of the shoes. Turning to the adage "the man who wears the shoe knows best that it pinches," Dewey asserted that the American public best knew the pinch of social issues like unemployment and housing shortage. Their experiential expertise was invaluable to government, just as the knowledge of the shoe wearer was crucial to the cobbler.[12] Dewey shared Lippmann's concern that Americans were inactive and, at times, under-informed. If Lippmann's public was a phantom, Dewey's was a living body, albeit perhaps a dormant one.

At issue, Dewey believed, was "a problem of presentation." If the public was simply dormant, as Dewey implied, then what it required were more and richer ways to communicate, and artful reminders of the interests and issues it shared. To facilitate this, journalists needed to turn away from sensational stories of scandal toward significant issues with public impact; in turn, consumers of the news needed to reflect on the significance of what they read and saw. Dewey explained:

> "News" signifies something which has just happened, and which is new just because it deviates from the old and regular. But its *meaning* depends upon relation to what it imports, to what its social consequences are. This import cannot be determined unless the new is placed in relation to the old, to what has happened and has been integrated into the course of events. Without

> coordination and consecutiveness, events are not events, but mere occurrences, intrusions; an event implies that out of which a happening proceeds.

In short, news needed a self-conscious public to give it coherence; the public needed news to help it identify shared narratives of the present and future. In this regard, Dewey thought, journalists had much to learn from artists. "Artists" he wrote, "have always been the real purveyors of the news, for it is not the outward happening in itself which is new, but the kindling by it of emotion, perception and appreciation." For Dewey, artists could assemble new collectivities by helping their audiences perceive together, and in new ways. They could "break through the crust of conventionalized routine," the repetitions and clichés that rendered news consumers numb to violence, oblivious to common ground, and forgetful of their capacities for change.[13]

The challenge that Lippmann and Dewey issued to describe the public more accurately would resonate into the next decade, both in their own elaborations and in the work of press critics like George Seldes. These qualitative discussions would also become inflected by the rise of public opinion research. The 1930s would see "the public" come into focus as an object of quantitative study. In 1935 Elmo Roper Jr.'s Fortune Survey would correctly predict Roosevelt's 1936 victory, helping to establish credibility for opinion research. That same year, the journalism professor George Gallup founded the American Institute of Public Opinion. Its goal was "impartially to measure and report public opinion on political and social issues of the day without regard to the rightness or wisdom of the views expressed."[14] The so-called Gallup Polls would survey Americans and, notably, their findings would constitute news, disseminated as press releases to subscribing newspapers.

As works of art, Living Newspapers implicitly promised to reframe "outward happenings"[15] as Dewey hoped: they could revise and reimagine routines of making news. But Living Newspapers also brought distinctive resources to the Dewey–Lippmann debate, which is to say, to the specific problem of what the public was and how it could relate to news.

In "combining the newspaper and the theatre," to borrow Morris Watson's phrase, Living Newspapers combined multiple modes of public address. The modern newspaper, as Benedict Anderson has famously argued, interpellated "imagined communities" by disseminating news at regular intervals. Geographically dispersed mass populations came to understand themselves as nation-states in part through the newspaper's circulation; and as Michael Hanchard adds, those colonized or enslaved in the name of the nation-state created supranational and countercultural formations. (This dialectic was vividly illustrated in *Ethiopia:* whereas the Black press explored the Pan-Africanist implications of Italy's invasion, Arthur Arent's Living Newspaper grappled with Haile Selassie's modernity, focusing on the threat of war to Europeans and to white Americans.) Living Newspapers could exploit the fact that whereas newspaper publics—national or supranational, countercultural or hegemonic—were characteristically "imagined," theatrical publics were material, at least in the theater. A theatrical public could exceed its audience, as Christopher Balme has argued; reviews, ads, and articles, for instance, could engage witnesses who did not attend the performance.[16] But Living Newspapers also emphasized the distinctive features of togetherness in the theater. In *Arena,* Hallie Flanagan would characterize theater's distinctive asset as "the living body of the actor, emphasized by light, seen from as many angles, massed with other bodies in as many formations as possible."[17] *1935* would illustrate her point, playing with social formations onstage and in the audience.

### THE EVENTS OF 1935 AND "THE GREAT AMERICAN PUBLIC"

*The Events of 1935* was written by the editorial staff of the New York Living Newspaper Unit, under the supervision of managing editor Arthur Arent and managing producer Morris Watson. It was directed by H. Gordon Graham, Joseph Losey's associate director on the previous Living Newspaper, *Triple-A Plowed Under. 1935* boasted a cast of one hundred, sets by Hjalmar Hermanson, and music by Lee Wainer. All other New York Living Newspapers, and the majority of FTP Living Newspapers across the country, would develop a single issue, in depth. *1935,* however, dramatized highlights of the previous year's news; instead of one news item, it staged fourteen. Nonetheless, there was a through-line in the play's dynamic depiction of "The Great American Public."

*1935*'s central image, featured on its playbill, was a crowd of celebrators, mostly made up of well-dressed white men and women.[18] The image comes from the play's opening scene, which takes place on New Year's Eve in Times Square. A voice broadcast by loudspeaker, recurring in Living Newspapers as the "Voice of the Living Newspaper," announces that this is "The Great American Public."[19] The crowd of revelers (figure 3) appears in sharp contrast to their auspicious moniker. There is no trace of Lippmann's "phantom public": no romantic depiction of the agora or the forum; no judicious deliberation or even the casting of votes; instead, the crowd awaits the spectacle of the New Year's ball drop.

In one respect, however, the scene reanimates the ideal that Lippmann thought had passed: physical co-presence. There is nothing abstract or dispersed about this group of assembled strangers. Indeed, much of the play's cast seems to be onstage, with little space between their bodies. Hjalmar Hermanson's expressionistic backdrop exaggerates their proximity, depicting skyscrapers packed together like the people before them. And while the set compresses the crowd visually, sound effects amplify it aurally: stage directions describe a "terrific din" of horns, popping balloons, and whistles (10). The crowd is pointedly together not only in space but also in time. It is New Year's Eve, an event that celebrates and performs the sharing of time. The revelers onstage are partaking in a New Year's ritual, the countdown to midnight; they synchronize themselves in both the "chronic" time of the calendar and the "acute" time of the clock.[20] The Public's bodily presence before the audience, its togetherness in time and space, is undeniable. Like the romanticized Greek *demos* in the agora and the Roman *vox populi* in the forum, this is a collective that is together in ways that modernity seems to preclude—not in its activity but in its embodied immediacy. With many bodies in proximity, sharing time and space in a town square, the New Year's crowd is a public performing itself, year after year.

The Voice tries to make the crowd self-conscious and reflective. Counting down to midnight, it asks the crowd to recollect that past year: "In three minutes it will be 1935. . . . Do you remember the Morro Castle? The $427, 000 truck robbery in Brooklyn? The assassination of King Alexander?" In Deweyan terms,

FIGURE 3. "The Great American Public." The Great American Public celebrates New Year's Eve in the opening of *1935*, Biltmore Theatre, New York, 1936. Courtesy of Library of Congress.

it tries to place the new in relation to the old, to integrate what has happened into a single course of events, in and through which a public's experience might cohere. The crowd cannot ignore the Voice, which overpowers its din and even stops the crowd, according to stage directions, "dead in its tracks" (10). Yet the crowd collectively rejects the Voice's imperative to remember major and ostensibly collective events. According to stage directions, the Great American Public responds to the Loudspeaker's questions by shrugging "its collective shoulders, manifesting complete indifference" before returning to carousal (10).

The collective shrug is emblematic. It is the "gestus," to borrow a word from Brecht, of a public defined by its disengagement. And whereas both Lippmann and Dewey viewed disengagement with some sympathy—an unfortunate spectator, in Lippmann's terms, stuck in the back row—*1935* is less forgiving. Notes to the director call for "automatic gestures, the absence of realistic emotion and color of the crowd" (10). These stage directions hint at the Living Newspaper's debts to Meyerhold, Piscator, and Brecht, rejecting theatrical realism to foster critical spectatorship.

The strains of "Auld Lang Syne" reinforce the crowd's disengagement. As an anthem of collective remembrance among friends, it emphasizes, by contrast, the carelessness of strangers.[21] The unsympathetic crowd soon dissipates—and it gets the trivial news it seems to crave. No sooner has the clock struck midnight than the Voice urges the crowd to "make news." "Well, what are you waiting for?" he asks, "Get going! Make news!" The Voice's urging designates the news as an arbitrary expression of the whims of the crowd. "Bite a dog! Invent a mousetrap. Win the sweepstakes" (11). Invoking the yellow journalism associated with Hearst and Pulitzer, the Voice makes clear that headlines need not be significant, only unexpected.[22]

As the crowd disperses after the first scene, the Voice distinguishes the makers of news from those who consume it. "Only a mere handful" of the revelers onstage, he states, will actually make news. "The others, the millions who make up this nation, will become the Great American Public of 1935. . . . They read the news . . . they react to it . . . we are interested in their opinion, and from this gigantic panel twelve are chosen to represent them all" (11). With these lines, the Voice turns from the inadequacy of news representation—the small handful of news-makers—to the inadequacy of public opinion sampling. The panel the Voice describes is the "Court of Public Opinion," a jury that will observe and weigh in on the events that make news. Like the reveling crowd, the jurors will share time and space, but the emphasis now is on their (in)capacity to represent a whole, a limitation that becomes visible as the Voice quickly assembles a small and motley group of twelve. The Voice calls the jury members by name, creating a comedic contrast between the large body politic and the specific individuals that represent it. The contrast becomes even sharper with the entrance of the final juror, Bixby, who must make his way to the stage from the audience after a spotlight pulls him out of the balcony.[23] Impatient with his slow ascent, the Voice complains, "Why do you have to act like an individualist?" Bixby quips back, "Because I am an *Individualist.*" The Voice however, puts him in his place: "I thought so. . . . That makes you just like everybody else" (12).

The exchange reflects anxieties about recent developments in public opinion research. The Voice wants Bixby to stand in for others; Bixby cannot bring himself to be seen as a mere "sample." He rebels against the metonymy that surveys craft between a group of individuals and a "whole." His rebellion suggests that in reconstituting the Public as representatives of public opinion, the Voice has robbed it of power, recasting it from subject to object. This is the public constructed through samples and surveys—works like Gallup and Roper polls and the Middletown studies—rather than an annual gathering in Times Square. Dispersed and then reassembled through the scrutiny of others rather than its own self-consciousness, the Public of *1935* drifts even further from the heroic democratic protagonist the Voice's moniker ("Great American Public") first suggested. The reassembly of the Public as the Court of Public Opinion satirizes the process of sampling, pointing to the limits of quantitative social science.

The sample that Bixby "The Individualist" joins is, unsurprisingly, ineffectual. As Bixby settles into his place, the Voice announces to the audience: "What you gaze upon, Ladies and Gentlemen, is the court of Public Opinion, and within the jury box the representatives of the Great American Public. . . . As each scene in the panorama of important events of 1935 unfolds before them, they will gaze upon it . . . they will reflect upon it . . . they will render judgment upon it" (12). Bixby and his cohort gaze at a panorama of events (presumably deemed significant, but by whom?) that unfolds before them. Though singled out from the anonymous reveling crowd on New Year's Eve, they are not much more effectual.

At first the jury appears to be a more disciplined social formation than the New Year's crowd of revelers. Conventionally, jurors assemble not for revelry or distraction but for judicious deliberation. They suspend all other obligations for the purpose of thinking together, without bias. The "Court of Public Opinion," in the abstract, encapsulates the model that Lippmann deemed antiquated and elusive: rational, empirical, informed consensus. Surely the audience held this model in mind as it watched the Public in *1935*. The phantom public haunts the jury box even as the very next scene reveals the commodification of justice.

The indictment resonates in *1935*'s first news story—the biggest, in David Welky's assessment, of the 1930s. In 1932 the only child of the aviators Anne and Charles Lindbergh, famous for Charles's nonstop flight from New York to Paris, went missing. Over the next four years, Americans would closely follow the search for Charles Jr. and the recovery of his body from a nearby road, then the arrest and trial of Bruno Richard Hauptmann and his execution by electric chair in April 1936, a month before *1935* opened.

The Lindbergh kidnapping drew more readers than "the Crash, the New Deal, and the onset of the European war."[24] It revealed the underbelly of public interest: an appetite for stories of intimate anguish, fed by mainstream newspapers. The Lindberghs' story, as Welky notes, contained compelling elements from the start: the Lindberghs' fame; the loss of a child from a family that was wealthy and white; the mystery surrounding who was responsible; followed by the scrutiny of the German-born suspect. Yet journalists and publishers had done much to cultivate attention. Reporters swarmed the Lindberghs' hometown, drawing analogies to Times Square; and as Welky points out, when Hauptmann decided to hire a new defense lawyer, Edward J. Reilly, the Hearst Corporation covered his legal fees, anticipating that the addition of the flamboyant attorney, though ailing, would drive up circulation.[25] For anyone seeking to understand "the public" through the news it sought and consumed, the Lindbergh saga was damning. Although *1935* did not go so far as to call the coverage a "disgraceful orgy," as *Forum* magazine did, it was critical nonetheless.

Having introduced the Lindberg story, the Voice of the Living Newspaper gives way to the "soft ingratiating voice of a refined sideshow barker, reeling off the attractions to be found in a tent" (13). A guide leads tourists through the scene of the trial, and the courtroom erupts in a cacophony of gossip before the lawyers issue bombastic excerpts from their final statements. The foreman reports that the jury has found Hauptmann guilty, and the booking agents immediately swarm the jurors, making offers to monetize their experience. The scene concludes with a grim statement from the highest bidder: "There's nothing like justice for a show" (21). Although the figure of the jury initially promised judicious deliberation, the Lindbergh story reveals that it is susceptible to manipulation.

In the scenes that follow, *1935* skims thirteen more stories.[26] Each is short and compact; the Voice announces the headline and climax of each scene before it unfolds, forgoing any attempt at suspense. In this respect, *1935* adopted the "dramaturgy of the tabloid." As theorized by John Osburn, the very features that make tabloid form desirable are what make it suspect. On the one hand, Osburn argues, "condensed forms" convey an enticing "sensibility of advance revelation, technological novelty, and temporal efficiency." On the other hand, they also evoke the "stigma attached to being both a reduction and a copy." Without the "buildup to climax and resolution that one might expect in the theatre," the tabloid's brand of "truncated experience" is easily dismissed as repetitive and fragmented.[27] In *1935* the tabloid form reflected the public's fleeting attention, but despite the play's critical tone, the outcome was a necessarily superficial treatment of the stories at hand. Though "tabloid" had not yet become a pejorative term when *1935* debuted, the play's condensation of familiar events may have ultimately contributed to its negative reception.

Socially and politically, after all, some of the stories *1935* reported were very much in line with other Living Newspapers that received more positive receptions. In the scene after the Lindbergh kidnapping, for instance, the Voice announces the passage of the Wagner-Connery Act and with it the creation of the National Labor Relations Board. It asserts that "unions representing newspaper men, textile workers, bus drivers and other laboring crafts rush cases of discrimination and unfair labor practices before the new board" (22). In one of the Living Newspaper's few depictions of woman-led labor organizing, the scene culminates in a group of garment workers resolving to strike.

Stories like these, however, were interspersed with lighter, less partisan fare. In "China Clipper," FTP technicians seized the challenge of re-creating the world's first commercial transpacific airmail service. Technical consultant Harold Burris-Meyer recalls the staging of the *China Clipper*'s landing: "We used the sound of the aircraft as it approached and circled over the audience and then landed. And the place it landed was upstage left and for those who had heard the clipper and seen it and so forth, it was a very realistic reproduction."[28] The scene offered a triumphant interlude in an otherwise cynical narrative.

The news stories unfold before the viewer as if on a conveyor belt, inevitable both because they have already transpired and because the "Great American Public" is unlikely to intervene and alter their course. The "jurors" onstage snack on hot dogs while the possibly innocent defendant William Deboe is hanged. They are idle in the face of reports of Nazi activity but frenzied by a baseball game. They comprise shallow "types" unresponsive to nuance, whose labels such as "Yes-Man" and "Querulous One" quickly replace the names called in the opening scene, and denote banal squabbles rather than substantive discussion (38–39). In fact, when "Born Leader" finally prompts an issue-based vote regarding the fatal shooting of Louisiana governor Huey Long, nobody bothers to participate. "Born Leader" declares the resolution, "passed by unanimous indifference," and it is punctuated by a blackout (45).

The jury seems most engaged, in fact, in matters that require no deliberation. The image in figure 4 represents a moment from scene 6 during which the jury takes in a baseball game that made headlines when the Brooklyn Dodgers faced the New York Giants. In contrast to the scene title, "Jury Interlude," the jury is at its most rapt, eagerly following the game. The stage directions characterize the group as "delirious" (26–27). In the image, they seem to spill out of the jury box that encloses them. In fact, the jury box here resembles a holding pen, with contours that emphasize the unruliness of its occupants. The frenzied group crammed into a jury box captures the thin line between crowd and public that waves throughout *1935*. Thus, while the jury box references a thinking public, it also forces physical proximity and contagious affect, connoting an unthinking crowd.

The jury is the kind of "gimmick" that, in Philip Barber's words, is the Living Newspaper's signature: it is a theatrical convention that efficiently conveys a social reality, in this case, the conflict between ideals of how a public should act and the reality of its fleeting attention. The jury as gimmick juxtaposes the phantom public, enshrined in liberal-democratic theory, with the disappointing reality of a mass polity. The contrast was especially stark in the play's final scenes: after the grim sentencing of the Black Communist Party (CPUSA) activist Angelo Herndon, the Voice finds the all-white jury "half asleep" (59).

Herndon had been arrested in the summer of 1932, at the age of nineteen, for organizing a peaceful march to the Atlanta courthouse. As the critical legal

FIGURE 4. The Court of Public Opinion spills out of its jury box in *1935*, Biltmore Theatre, New York, 1936. Margaret Blyden, Harry Brooks, Pell Dentler, Robert Donaldson, Jane Hale, Marie Hunt, Robert Mack, Joe Rose, Harry Ruselle, Ellen Spencer, Lulu Thorne, Edward Wright (order not necessarily as pictured). Courtesy of Library of Congress.

scholar Kendall Thomas notes, it was the largest biracial demonstration in the South for several decades, the show of unity serving "both an instrumental and an expressive function."[29] Herndon was charged with inciting insurrection, his prosecution hinging on CPUSA pamphlets police had seized at his apartment. Herndon had been sentenced in 1933 to eighteen to twenty years of hard labor on a chain gang, but when *1935* was produced, his case was under appeal.

*1935*'s portrayal was sympathetic. It showed Herndon persuading prisoners of the need to organize together for workers' rights. It portrayed a chain gang, in silhouette, as a Black prisoner narrated his experience. No doubt the chain gang account drew inspiration from the work of the white leftist journalist John Spivak, who reported on Georgia's chain gangs. It pointed out the irony that Herndon's sentencing to two decades of hard labor, effectively torture, was viewed by many as a "mercy" because it was not the death penalty. At the same time, with graphic detail narrated in a stereotypical dialect, the Herndon scene continued an NYLN pattern of positioning African Americans as objects of white sympathy and condescension even as they enlisted interracial solidarity.

*1935*'s attention to racial violence, however, much like its jury's, is short-lived. Soon the Voice rouses the jurors, urging them to "sit still in silent judgment while we go ahead and finish off the year" (59). He races through a few more headlines before announcing New Year's Eve. A year has passed since the dramatic narrative began, but nothing has changed. The jury loses itself in a crowd of revelers, repeating its gestic shrug when the Voice asks if they remember headlines from the year. In the play's final lines, the Voice cedes the loudspeaker to the "Voice of a Vendor" hawking peanuts and popcorn as "Auld Lang Syne" swells (60).

### THE AUDIENCE'S GAZE

I have shown so far how *1935* depicted the Great American Public through a dramatic convention or "gimmick," presenting a forgetful crowd ghosted by a deliberative jury. Yet *1935* also reimagined its public through interpellation, by addressing its audience as a public in the making. *1935* sought to make its audiences self-conscious of two publics of which they were a part. The first public was, to borrow Michael Warner's phrase, "a crowd witnessing itself in space."[30] *1935* drew explicit connections between the Public it depicted onstage and the group that observed it from the audience; it interpellated a self-conscious audience. The second public was, to engage Benedict Anderson's characterization of newspaper readers in the modern nation-state, "an imagined community." *1935* drew explicit connections between the spectators gathered in the theater and a more expansive, national public, and in doing so, it hailed a self-conscious group of news consumers.

*1935* addressed a self-conscious audience by establishing a relationship between the Public depicted onstage and the crowd assembled to view it in the theater. Just as the revelers in the jury box face the viewer in the photo in figure 4, the Public in *1935* "faced" its Biltmore Theatre audience throughout the play. *1935* used myriad dramaturgical and aesthetic strategies to address its audience directly, as a public connected to the one onstage. The juror Bixby, for instance, self-proclaimed "Individualist," emerged from the audience, a staging choice that visually identified Bixby with the crowd assembled at the Biltmore. And if Bixby was "of" the audience, so too, suggested *1935,* were his concerns. If Bixby was a mere sample of public opinion, despite his protests, then so too, the play insinuated, were the spectators among whom he started the play. The Great American Public, from which the twelve jurors were plucked, was located not only on the stage but in the audience as well. This would be a recurring motif in Living Newspapers: most famously, *One-Third of a Nation,* a 1938 Living Newspaper about housing, would depict a Little Man stumbling from the audience to the stage. The physical transitions that actors made from audience to stage playfully challenged Lippmann's relegation of the average citizen to the "back row" of political life. The spatial separation of audience and spectator, as I discuss in the next chapter, would become an important resource for Living Newspapers' explorations of political life.

Bixby's identification with the audience was not the only way that *1935* connected the Great American Public, represented by the Court of Public Opinion, to the spectators before them. When the Voice first introduces the Public in its jury box, he uses the same word to describe the action of the audience and that of the public. He asserts: "What you *gaze* upon, Ladies and Gentlemen, is the Court of Public Opinion. . . . As each scene in the panorama of important events of 1935 unfolds before them, they will gaze upon it" (12). By using the same verb—"gaze"—to characterize their actions (or lack thereof), the Voice identifies the audience with the Court of Public Opinion in an act of passive looking, one that ultimately renders the Court of Public Opinion ineffectual. No doubt mise-en-scène underscored the point: the strangers seated in a jury box, facing the (mostly) strangers seated in the house at the Biltmore, were positioned to share a single, uninterrupted gaze.

While *1935* was addressing its material public—the theatrical audience—as a reflection of the sample it depicted onstage, it also identified this sample with an imagined community of national news consumers. The most obvious way it did so was through the play's generic framing as a newspaper, evident when spectators opened a newspaper-like playbill. But *1935* did not allow spectators to forget this identity when the play began. Not only did it present them with a series of news stories, but also it did so using familiar conventions of mass news media. As I discuss further in the next chapter, the Voice of the Living Newspaper, wrote NYLN managing editor Arthur Arent, was initially modeled on the moving teletype on the New York Times Building, offering "a non-participating dateline which introduced the various scenes."[31] Yet as a disembodied, authoritative male voice, it also emulated the god-like "Voice of Time" in the popular *March of Time* newsreel.[32] With its references to the *March of Time,* the *New York Times,* and other mass news media, *1935* reminded spectators of an expansive network of readers—of the nation imagined into being by the news. That Living Newspapers were produced across the country, under the auspices of a federal project, could only have underscored their connection to nationwide, imagined communities.[33] *1935,* then, addressed its audience as consumers of the news, members both of an abstract imagined community and a concrete audience embodied in the theater.

## THE SELF-CONSCIOUS AUDIENCE

Arriving on the heels of the single-issue-based play *Triple-A Plowed Under* (produced to wide acclaim), *1935* with its tabloid structure did not gain much traction among artists and critics. The New York production played for only a few weeks, and evidence of similar productions in other cities is limited.

Yet perhaps most striking in *1935*'s reception were the critics who not only doubted the play's merit but also took umbrage at its representations of the public. These strong reactions suggest, despite scant attention from historians and even FTP staff, that *1935* was not categorically unsuccessful. Rather they imply that through representation and interpellation, *1935* provoked at least some spectators to reflect on the nature and possibilities of the American public. If the phantom public had haunted the stage in the obvious shortcomings of the Great American Public, it also seems to have haunted the audience. Fervently asserting that the audience was more active and more judicious than the public depicted onstage, critics would seek to reanimate the phantom public in their reviews.

Reviews demonstrate that some spectators at least recognized that *1935* was about *them,* about the public they constituted—or failed to constitute—and witnessed onstage. *New York Times* drama critic Brooks Atkinson had been suspicious of state-subsidized theater since *Ethiopia,* but his specific critique of *1935* was telling. The play, he wrote, was "a history of our follies," and one that was "harshly accented when the Living Newspaper boys pack it into an hour and a half of tabloid showmanship."[34] Atkinson's "our" is important, suggesting that the disconnected trivia on display were reflective of what constituted news in the public sphere. A *New Yorker* reviewer took a page from Lippmann's book, despairing that important news could never engage the masses: the reviewer conceded that the play's reliance on crime stories was "inevitable, since the events that basically affect the welfare of the nation are apt to be dull, unspectacular and very hard to act out on stage."[35] Less friendly reviewers, too, recognized that the Great American Public was about them, even if they did not appreciate the implications. A reviewer for the *New York Evening Journal* called the Court of Public Opinion not only "very silly and lugged in" but also "vaguely condescending."[36] Whether critical or positive, reviews suggest that spectators recognized themselves represented onstage.

These attestations of self-consciousness were exacerbated, it seems, by another of the play's provocations: its *retrospective* presentation of the news. While all Living Newspapers dramatized news that was already in circulation, it was the critics of *1935* who most disparaged this redundancy. The *New York Evening Journal* critic sardonically commented, "Nothing, they say, is deader than yesterday's newspaper except, perhaps, an obsolete calendar, and for the second production of its journalistic drama the Government Theatre nicely combines the two."[37] A column in the *New York Post* echoed the sentiment, noting, "1935 bumped into the difficulty of presenting highlights from the news headlines of a year which is too close to us and too well remembered."[38] Even in his otherwise positive review in the *Brooklyn Eagle*, Arthur Pollock conceded, "We knew it all before, couldn't help but know it" that "this Living Newspaper cannot keep up to date."[39] Comments like these held *1935* to the standards of mass-mediated news, registering the play's failure to evoke an experience of journalistic simultaneity.

Yet for a *New York Daily News* critic, the presentation of "yesterday's news" prompted reflection—even if it made for bad theater. "These are all recognizable reminders of old news," the reviewer commented, "but that is all . . . it is nothing for the archives."[40] As a form in between the news and "the archives," the Living Newspaper, it seems, prompted this writer to reflect on the *kinds* of stories that he and his public consumed. It is ambiguous, in this review, whether it is *1935* only, or also the news on which it drew, that was truly "nothing for the archives." *1935*'s review may have been too swift and superficial for some, but it generated reflection on what kinds of stories were making the news; the syncopation that defied modern news conventions—a review of "yesterday's news"—was an irritant that promoted reflection in the public sphere.

Whether critical or congratulatory, reviews show that *1935* was a site of contestation. Moreover, they reveal the ghostly encounter the play prompted;

for critics could take offense at this representation of the Great American Public only by invoking a phantom public and its ennobled ideals. And perhaps most striking of all, some of them emphatically defended the liveliness and cohesiveness of their cohort of spectators. The critic for the *New York Sun,* for instance, was careful to tease apart the representation of *1935*'s Public from the actions of its audiences. He complained that "doubt of the brightness of the American public is the view most clearly expressed in the play." Yet he insisted this reflected the play's authors and *not* its audiences. The Great American's Public's failure to "form any idea about 1935. . . was precisely the position the authors of '1935' found themselves [in]." It was only in the rare moments when the authors took a stand, he argued, that they "gave the eager audience one of its few opportunities to express emotion."[41] In taking pains to contrast the authors' apathy with the audience's engagement, the *Sun* reviewer resisted *1935*'s depiction of the apathetic public.

A reviewer in the *New York Herald Tribune* took a similar tack, drawing even more concrete evidence from his fellow spectators' behavior: "Although the American Public, represented by twelve men and women who made inane comments on the significance of each news event, remained indifferent to the end, the audience did not. It applauded vigorously after each blackout and let its feelings be known regarding every headline figure who walked upon the stage." The reviewer later elaborated: "The audience, which apparently read the newspapers more closely than the public's twelve representatives, showed its obvious disapproval of Nazi storm troopers."[42] Arthur Pollock of the *Brooklyn Eagle* corroborated the assessment: "No one [in the jury] votes either for or against and the motion is described as 'passes by unanimous indifference.' Last night's audience was rather less indifferent than its fictitious representative on the stage, however, and a hiss could be heard here and there and enthusiastic applause."[43] It is worth noting that both Pollock and the *Herald Tribune* writer described emotional outbursts from the audience as disproof of their apathy. They sat among audiences that acted out, and in doing so made themselves into coherent collectives—at least in the eyes of critics. The audiences' reactions in both critics' depictions were empowered; far from exhibiting the trivial and contagious affect of a New Year's Eve crowd, these audiences acted up and, in doing so, reanimated the ideals of the phantom public. With its apathetic and ineffectual Public, *1935* goaded some spectators into reflecting upon their own responses to the news, and perhaps even to enact them more loudly than usual. In the theatrical public sphere, these critics contested *1935*'s depictions of the audience, describing an audience that resisted accusations of indifference.

## JOHN Q. CITIZEN GOES TO THE THEATER

It is tempting to read these accounts as testament of a theatrical public triumphing over its casting. There is no evidence, however, that the hissing and applause, albeit powerful interjections in the theater, had any corollary outside of it. Indeed, whatever activity *1935* made possible was clearly not very satisfying; the play ran for only a few short weeks. *1935*'s theatrical audience was more active, more responsive than the spectators it lambasted onstage; yet it was more bounded, and perhaps more temporary, than the imagined community that it addressed. The comments in the reviews just quoted offer something more like a modest rebuttal against the play's charges than a testament to its political effects.

Yet the NYLN would continue to seek to animate the public. In fact, it would revisit the jury gimmick in promotions for its next production. *Injunction Granted!* played from July through October 1936 at New York's Biltmore Theatre. It was advertised in a pamphlet loosely inspired by a subpoena. The front of the pamphlet announced that the Living Newspaper (plaintiff) was pressing charges against "John Q. Citizen" (defendant) and nightly hearings would proceed at the Court of Public Opinion. Inside the pamphlet were the details of John Q's summons:

> We command you, That all business and excuses being laid aside, you appear and attend before The Court of Public Opinion, at the Biltmore Theatre, 261 West 47th Street, in the Borough of Manhattan, City of New York, on any evening excepting Sunday, at 8:45 PM, to hear evidence in the case of Labor at a performance of
>
> Injunction Granted!
>
> And we command you, further, that having heard said evidence you forthwith testify to other persons, each and every one you meet, in the case of Labor therein presented.
>
> *The Living Newspaper*
> *of the*
> *Federal Theatre*
> *Works Progress Administration*[44]

Here, the jury metaphor worked once again to invoke a sense of duty. In the trappings of a subpoena, theater attendance was recast as an urgent obligation. Or rather, three obligations, for spectators were summoned as defendants ("vs. The Living Newspaper"), witnesses ("to other persons") and jurors (in "The Court of Public Opinion"). All three roles demanded their physical presence. The Court of Public Opinion was once again reimagined as a concrete place, complete with an address and seating capacity. At it did in *1935*, the jury in *Injunction*'s subpoena would draw attention to the act of assembly.

*The Events of 1935* was in many ways an anomaly among Living Newspapers that came after it. Its tabloid-style presentation of a year's worth of stories would give way to dramatizations of a single issue; its unwieldy "Court of Public Opinion" would give way to other, subtler representations of the public; and its satirical tone would give way to more earnest calls to arms. But the gimmick of the court would not entirely recede.

*1935* challenged audiences to look backwards and inwards. By presenting "yesterday's news," it prompted audiences to consider whether the stories that made the previous year's headlines were, to borrow Dewey's distinction, meaningful and significant or merely sensational. By staging the Great American Public before its audiences, *1935* invited those audiences to confront its possibilities and shortcomings as representatives of the public. The propulsive possibilities of bodies sharing time and space; the jury box that symbolized its deliberative capacities; the newspaper rhetoric that invoked its embodiment of the nation: these features of *1935* invited the phantom public into the theater to consider the news alongside its audience. The NYLN attempted to represent the public—a preoccupation among news-makers, critics, and consumers—when it seemed to defy representation. In doing so, it cultivated journalistic imagination, asking spectators to consider how political subjects could be together in meaningful ways, and how individuals could enter public life. In the next chapter I explore the latter in the recurring characters of the Little Man and the Loudspeaker.

# CHAPTER THREE

# THE LITTLE MAN AND THE LOUDSPEAKER

## Reimagining News Media

Just two years after *The Events of 1935* closed at the Biltmore, Federal Theatre Project staff were under official investigation. On December 6, 1938, FTP national director Hallie Flanagan was called to testify before a committee of Republicans and conservative Democrats. The so-called Dies Committee was named for its chairman, Congressman Martin Dies Jr. of Texas, before it was renamed the House Committee on Un-American Activities (HUAC). It had charged Flanagan and her colleagues with spreading "communistic" and "un-American" propaganda among artists and audiences.[1]

The work of the New York Living Newspaper was a flashpoint throughout the hearings. Whereas *1935* had presented an ambivalent recap of the previous year's highlights, the NYLN's subsequent productions had dramatized unambiguous arguments for specific New Deal commitments. *Triple-A Plowed Under* (Biltmore Theatre, 1936) had called for government support for farmers and other workers; *Injunction Granted!* (Biltmore Theatre, 1936) had championed labor rights; *Power* (Ritz Theatre, 1937) advocated for public utilities; *One-Third of a Nation* (Adelphi Theatre, 1938) argued for subsidized housing. In no small part because of the NYLN, the FTP's editorial positions were under scrutiny.

So too, however, was theater's vexed status as a news medium. Early in Flanagan's hearing, Congressman Joe Starnes, a Democrat from Alabama, asked her if it was true that Federal Theatre plays were "propagandistic." It was a predictable question, given the committee's mandate, but it was incriminating all the same. In the decades since the First World War, propaganda had taken on insidious connotations, threatening to infiltrate and even displace news media. Americans had witnessed the nation's first coordinated propaganda campaign, and many were still reeling from its devastating outcome. The threat of propaganda, moreover, did not seem to be going away. Radio, newsreels, motion pictures—new forms of mass media that could reach citizens quickly and systematically—were becoming ubiquitous. And there was no shortage of leaders, at home and abroad, who sought to control public opinion. Within a few short decades, popular conceptions of propaganda had shifted from self-interested publicity to something much more sinister: systematic deception by institutions with power.[2]

Flanagan was no doubt aware of these implications. The path of least resistance might have been for her to reject the word entirely. She might have argued, for instance, that whereas propagandists tightly controlled their messages, she coordinated units with greatly varied repertoires, from Shakespeare to puppetry to Yiddish theater.

Yet Flanagan chose to embrace "propaganda." Rather than refusing the term, she drew upon a more flexible usage. Some of the FTP's plays, she asserted, *were* propaganda, but that did not implicate them in communism or political coercion. "Propaganda, after all," she asserted, "is education. It is education focused on certain things."[3] Before New Jersey Republican J. Parnell Thomas cut her off, she added, "I should like to say very truthfully that to the best of my knowledge we have never done a play which was propaganda for communism, but we have done plays which were propaganda for democracy."[4] For Flanagan, propaganda could empower Americans by advancing the project of self-government.

The notion of "propaganda for democracy" did not fly, however, with Flanagan's questioners. "I think you ought to develop that point right there," challenged Thomas. "You said that some plays were propaganda for democracy," he went on, "what do you mean by that?" Motives aside, it was a good question. Flanagan offered to explain, asking, "Shall we go into a discussion of democracy?"[5] Thomas declined and changed his line of questioning. In this forum at least, the relationship between propaganda and democracy would remain unresolved.

But "propaganda for democracy" was—and remains—a provocative idea because it seems to present a contradiction. When propaganda is conceived as sinister machinations by the powerful, it seems antithetical to self-governance—and certainly to journalistic imagination. Propaganda seeks to naturalize a particular view of the present, so that citizens cannot identify alternatives, much less demand them. Journalistic imagination, by contrast, *de*naturalizes the present by cultivating citizens' capacity to see how a current moment is produced, who is represented among its constituents, and how both could be otherwise. In a paradigmatic World War I propaganda poster, for instance, Uncle Sam points directly at the viewer, exclaiming, "I want YOU for U.S. Army." As propaganda, the poster situated its viewers in an urgent and irrefutable present: one in which war was a necessity, and so too was the viewer's obligation to enlist. There was no invitation for the viewer to question whether war was necessary, nor in whose interest it proceeded. Wartime propaganda made little room, in short, for active questioning and, subsequently, for journalistic imagination.

Flanagan, of course, had a different form of propaganda in mind. Before World War I, as the media scholar Mark Crispin Miller observes, propaganda had far less sinister connotations: it simply described the dissemination of ideas, whether truthful or false.[6] It was this conception that Flanagan seemed to invoke at her hearing when she suggested that propaganda could be oriented toward a democratic purpose.

Even so, however, Flanagan's neologism raises some questions. Flanagan, like many other progressives, saw democracy "as discussion,"[7] best achieved through continuous face-to-face conversations between citizens. But propaganda, even in Flanagan's conception, involved the dissemination of ideas on a broad scale. In short, the very phrase "propaganda for democracy" foregrounded a long-standing tension, as proposed by communication scholar John Durham Peters, between two seemingly opposed models of political communication: on the one hand, the frank face-to-face dialogue represented by the town hall; on the other hand, the one-way, mass-mediated dissemination represented by the loudspeaker and newsreel.[8] Flanagan did not reconcile this tension at her hearing, but she did seem to imply that propaganda and democracy, dialogue and dissemination, could coexist. So too did the NYLN. Indeed, the premise of this chapter is that "propaganda for democracy" was more than an improvised retort to the FTP's critics. Rather it was a way of understanding the Living Newspaper's ongoing exploration into the relationship between mass media, news consumers, and political engagement. And it was in *One-Third of a Nation,* the Living Newspaper that debuted in the year before Flanagan's hearings, that this exploration was at its most vivid.

## *ONE-THIRD OF A NATION* AND MASS MEDIA

*One-Third of a Nation* premiered on January 17, 1938, at the Adelphi Theatre, almost one year before Flanagan's hearing. The script is credited solely to NYLN managing editor Arthur Arent, a move that the theatre scholar Loren Kruger attributes to the Unit's shift away from radical collectivist aesthetics and politics.[9] *One-Third of a Nation* was, however, a collaboration—perhaps more so than any other NYLN work, given that it had originated in an experimental workshop nearly six months before it was completed by the NYLN's newsmakers. In the summer of 1937, the Rockefeller Foundation funded a summer theater workshop at Vassar College. The workshop's forty-eight participants from across the United States included NYLN members Arent and Howard Bay. They participated in a series of multidisciplinary seminars, then created a Living Newspaper called *Housing*. A small audience, made up of artists and supporters, included first lady Eleanor Roosevelt and composer Kurt Weill.

Many elements would change before *Housing* premiered as *One-Third of a Nation* at the Adelphi nearly six months later. What began as a ninety-minute one-act would become a two-hour, three-act production. Moreover, the dramatic conventions would become more realistic, reflecting the Living Newspaper's broader shift after *Injunction Granted!* "away from non-realism and closer to New Deal liberalism."[10] One of the few non-realistic elements to remain from the original workshop production was a movement sequence that came out of a seminar with the modern dancer–choreographer Helen Tamiris: a metaphor for urban displacement enacted by city dwellers on an ever-shrinking grass carpet.

*One-Third* would, however, retain the theme of *Housing*, drawing attention to the lack of affordable, sanitary housing in New York, and across the country's major cities. Like the majority of the FTP's Living Newspapers, it would present a single news story (in this case, a tenement fire in a New York slum) as a symptom of a widespread and unresolved social ill. It presented, episodically, the historical development of New York's housing crisis, dramatizing the impact of greedy realtors and grabby landlords, failed legislation and its human costs on fictional families. Culminating in a call to support publicly subsidized housing, *One-Third of a Nation* was most explicitly about the shortage of affordable housing in American cities. It was also, however, about how to respond to new technologies that were changing mass media.

Back in 1936, in his advocacy for the organizations representing WPA arts workers, Morris Watson had remarked that "canned" film acting was "throttling legitimate theatre" and that "telegraphed photos and syndicated features" were causing newspapers to cut "flesh and blood" staff.[11] Watson does not appear to have played a significant role in *One-Third of a Nation*. By 1938, as noted in chapter 1, the Newspaper Guild of New York was no longer listed as a sponsor of the NYLN, nor was Watson credited as the Unit's managing producer. Yet his remarks about the need for the NYLN remained prescient. For many FTP workers, new media constituted a threat to journalists and theater-makers, and one that federal funding needed to mitigate. Yet in their own way, Living Newspapers were new media too. Their goal was not to reject technological change but rather to supplement it.

This was evident in the ways that the NYLN promoted its work and the ways that critics responded to it. An ad for *Power* boasted, "Actors take the place of type."[12] A Philadelphia playbill for *One-Third of a Nation* described its source material as "verbal skeletons rattl[ing] over the boards."[13] In a review for the *New York World-Telegram*, Sidney Whipple called *One-Third of a Nation* a "human document."[14] The *Literary Digest* described *Triple-A Plowed Under* as a "flesh and blood newsreel."[15] Arthur Pollock called *1935* "a lively sheet" in the *Brooklyn Eagle,* and Brooks Atkinson used similar language to describe *One-Third of a Nation* in the *New York Times*, writing, "The Living Newspaper is no superficial sheet. . . . Most people will want to see it because it is alive."[16] Type replaced by actors; verbal skeletons; human documents; a sheet come alive: all of these phrases are variations of the juxtaposition between dead and living, material and spiritual that the phrase "Living Newspaper" implies. It was *One-Third of a Nation,* however, that would bring the Living Newspaper's status as medium into the foreground.

*One-Third of a Nation* engaged journalistic imagination by reflecting on the embodied, mass-mediated practices of seeing, hearing, and speaking in public. The play explored these questions through mise-en-scène and theatrical conventions and, more specifically, through the interplay of two recurring characters: a resounding Loudspeaker, and a plucky Little Man who represented the "average" citizen. Their trajectories through the play proposed a vision of "propaganda for democracy," one in which responsive mass media and self-conscious political subjects co-produced the present and future.

In the introduction, I issued a reminder that the consumption of news is embodied. I proposed that "news" describes information in the process of being embodied, at the very moment the consumer is "taking it in." Though the "taking in" is often auditory or textual, New Deal rhetoric emphasized the visual. As the communication scholar Cara Finnegan explains, it was rife with calls to witness, capture, and document. Mary Stuckey notes that Roosevelt's public address often described images and juxtaposed them. It appealed to what was "clear" and "evident," and as Vanessa Beasley and Deborah Smith-Howell observe, enjoined the public to "take a look-see" at the state of the nation. "The rhetoric of vision," Stuckey argues, allowed Roosevelt to claim unique powers of apprehension, while enlisting Americans in a project of shared seeing. By combining visual dispatches from citizens across the country into a single panoramic vision, Roosevelt positioned himself at the helm of a "national synoptic state."[17] When New Deal citizens took in the news, they were being entreated to watch and be watched.

Taking up this theme, *One-Third of a Nation* cited, in its title, Roosevelt's second inaugural address and his synoptic observation "I see one third of a nation ill-housed, ill-clad, ill-nourished."[18] In promotional materials, the title often appeared in quotation marks and in lowercase letters, and followed by ellipses—typographical reminders that it was a quote. Often accompanied by sketches of crumbling tenements, it engaged prospective spectators in a doubled act of witnessing before they even entered the theater. They bore witness to the country with Roosevelt, and they bore witness to Roosevelt's already performed speech.

The witnessing continued when spectators arrived at the Adelphi. In the lobby they perused images of slums drawn by neighborhood children, coordinated by NYLN manager Ethel Aaron. The playbill, designed like a newspaper, in the NYLN's style, boasted exhaustive on-the-ground reporting. An article attested that reporters had visited tenements for "first-hand data on slums." Furthermore, "on some of these slumming trips," it read, "a member of the Federal Theatre Project staff accompanied the research worker. This made possible a pictorial record of tenement conditions which may be shown to skeptics who might doubt the story presented on the stage."[19] The ethnographic language of "slumming trips" anticipated the play's liberal middle-class perspective, one that designated witnessing to those who lived outside the slums and, indeed, might not even believe they existed. This account of the NYLN's reporting attested to the play's veracity, all the while drawing attention to the act of witnessing itself. When the curtain rose and the play began, the practices of speaking and listening remained in the foreground.

### THE LOUDSPEAKER

In its opening scene, *One-Third of a Nation* floods audiences with sight and sound. The curtain rises on a four-story tenement, which fills the stage. Because it is presented as a cross-section, spectators can see into and across the entire

FIGURE 5. "Tenement Fire." *One-Third of a Nation* opens with a tenement fire. Playbill for *One-Third of a Nation*, Adelphi Theatre, New York, 1938. Courtesy of Library of Congress.

building. "It was 40 feet high at least," recalled designer Howard Bay, and constructed from the remnants of local tenements subject to demolition.[20] The building bustles with apartment dwellers: children playing, adults doing chores. There is a lot to look at, and according to the stage directions at least, no particular focal point. Nor is there any much context, no indication of exactly where and when the tenement exists.

Soon, however, a voice intervenes. It is the "Voice of the Living Newspaper," also known as "the Loudspeaker." As the name suggests, the Loudspeaker has no visual presence onstage. He is present only through a voice, that of actor Charles Dill, which resonates through the theater. He reports: "February, 1924—This might be 397 Madison Street, New York. It might be 245 Halsey Street, Brooklyn, or Jackson Avenue and 10th Street, Long Island City."[21] As the Loudspeaker finishes his lines, smoke begins to rise onstage (figure 5).

Apartment dwellers realize they are in danger and begin to evacuate as bells and sirens sound. Someone cries "look!" and a crowd gathers outside the building to see a man "cowering on the fire escape" (14). The crowd freezes as the lights go to blackout. The scene ends with images of helplessness: a man on a rickety fire escape, a group of onlookers who cannot help. The crowd onstage and the audience in the theater engage in the civic practices of looking and listening, but to little effect. Indeed, the next scene begins with a report of thirteen casualties from the Loudspeaker.

Especially in contrast to the onlookers' helplessness, the Loudspeaker is a powerful presence. He seems to be omnipresent and omniscient. He introduces the scene, and he speaks in short, staccato sentences. His voice bears the trappings of confidence, education, and authority. Featured in all of the NYLN's Living Newspapers, the Loudspeaker seems to have impressed even the artists who conceived him. Arent identified the loudspeaker device with the origins of the form. He noted that while the Loudspeaker was initially imagined as completely expository—something like the moving teletype on the *New York Times* building—it soon took on a character, albeit an ever-changing one.[22] Much like US newspaper reporting,[23] the voice of the Loudspeaker increasingly offered explicit interpretation and commentary, as well as factual description. Arent marveled: "It was at various times in the same play ignorant, thirsting for information and a veritable Britannica of esoteric facts and statistics. . . . It was all things to all men, and particularly to the dramatist."[24] The versatility of the Loudspeaker figure became a source of awe, even to a playwright who helped write it into being.

Arent clearly appreciated the Loudspeaker's malleability in the service of dramaturgical function. Yet there was also a Frankenstein-ish tinge to Arent's account that hinted at the Loudspeaker's powerful presence. Like an invention that had taken on a life of its own, the disembodied voice shifted, in Arent's account, from that of a disseminator of facts to that of a controlling (and opinionated) editor. Arent seems awestruck at its capacity for reinvention, as if he had no hand in its dramatic construction. Arent's Loudspeaker succinctly captured the promise and perils of mass media: "all things to all men," it was hugely powerful yet susceptible to endless manipulation.

Arent's mixed feelings were no doubt tied up with the relative novelty of the technological innovations that enabled the convention. For twenty-first-century readers, this might be easy to miss; indeed, in a review of a 2011 revival of *One-Third of a Nation*, *New York Times* critic Ken Jaworowski referred to a "wry, invisible narrator," neglecting entirely its broadcast medium.[25] When *One-Third* premiered, however, the technology was striking. Though loudspeakers had been converting electrical energy into sound since the 1860s, it was only in the mid-1920s that the invention of dynamic loudspeakers allowed listeners to consume recorded sound without headphones and thus communally.[26] Unlike its predecessor the megaphone, the loudspeaker operated from above its listeners rather than among them, and it could carpet swaths of space with fairly uniform sound. In contrast to the radio, too, it was not under the control of its listener, and it commanded public attention.[27] American listeners had heard or seen reports of the loudspeaker's power, whether in the campaigns of Louisiana governor Huey Long, hugely popular and then assassinated in 1935, or in the public address systems used at Nazi rallies in Germany. By 1934, as Ronda Sewald notes, New Yorkers had demanded city officials regulate the activity of sound trucks, arguing they infringed on sonic privacy.[28] In these and other examples, dynamic loudspeakers were creating new possibilities for public space and collective experience.[29]

Given the recent rise of loudspeakers in civic life, and especially in journalism, it is no surprise that the NYLN responded to their power. Harold Burris-Meyer, a technical consultant specializing in sound, described the technical demands of capturing this power in his work with the NYLN: "The voice of the Living Newspaper was the really important element and this voice was reproduced unidirectionally. That is, the voice was there but no place which you could point [to]. And this made it at once intimate and all pervasive." The goal, Burris-Meyer went on, "was to make it [the sound] come from everywhere." In some cases, this meant aiming loudspeakers up at the theater's ceiling so that the audience heard reflected sound that they could not place. While the role of the Loudspeaker was crucial, NYLN technicians aimed to hide the technology that produced it. In Burris-Meyer's words, "We worked with the concept that if you knew there was a sound system involved, then you had to cut it out because it was no good." This commitment required thoughtful

FIGURE 6. "Charles Dill as the Loudspeaker." Promotional photo of Charles Dill, voice of the Loudspeaker, *One-Third of a Nation*, Adelphi Theatre, New York, 1938. Courtesy of Library of Congress.

attention to sound operation as well as design. The NYLN enlisted Vincent Mallory, an engineer who ran sound for Mayor Fiorello La Guardia when he delivered impassioned speeches in New York's public spaces.[30] Perhaps Mallory, with his firsthand experience of the mayor, also advised actor Leopold Badia, who played La Guardia in *One-Third*'s final scene.

The Unit's investment in sound seems to have paid off, because the Loudspeaker's power resonated in *One-Third*'s reception. Many reviews bolstered the Loudspeaker's authority. Although a promotional image featured Charles Dill in action, reviewers tended to refrain from comment on Dill's acting technique and its technological mediations (figure 6). A notable exception came from Brooks Atkinson, who remarked on "the horrid scream of the mechanical voice amplifier, which paralyzes a theatre-goer's eardrums in time."[31] Yet even Atkinson's complaint attributes some power to the Loudspeaker. The metaphor of paralysis suggests the Loudspeaker's spatial dominance; the spectator, or rather the listener, cannot escape it.

Whether a paralyzing scream or background noise, the Loudspeaker possesses an authority, at least at the beginning of the play, that seems to be incontestable. As the next scene begins, however, the Loudspeaker starts to ask questions:

> LOUDSPEAKER: Thirteen persons lost their lives in that fire on Madison Street—four men, two women, and seven children. Another man was killed in an unsuccessful attempt to make his way down a fire escape ladder in the yard. When the fire department arrived the building was in flames. Only a few of those inside could be reached. What started this fire? Why did it spread so quickly? Why was the death toll so high? (15)

Here the Loudspeaker adopts the role of an advocate, asking questions on behalf of the tenement dwellers. In fact, he goes on to challenge a half-hearted inquiry led by the housing commissioner. As the commissioner concludes that "there were no violations" despite flagrant evidence to the contrary, the Loudspeaker breaks in: "Just a moment, Mr. Commissioner. Has *everybody* testified?" (19). He suggests questioning the tenement's landlord, and when the commissioner explains that it would not be legal, it is the Loudspeaker who contacts the Landlord "off the record" to provide new information about the fire (21). He uses his booming presence to seek out a fuller, more inclusive testimony.

The Loudspeaker shifts then from a one-way conveyor of information to a responsive advocate. This is a notable departure from narrators in other media and genres. For moviegoers, for instance, the all-knowing announcer would have been a familiar convention. From about 1908 to the early 1920s, spectators of silent films were often guided by a "film lecturer," an actor who offered "live voiceover narration that would serve to direct audience attention and apprehension of the event." A frequent presence in early silent films, the film lecturer familiarized audiences with not only the combination of voice-over with image but also the supplementing of a relatively new form with a trustworthy expert who could help them to acquire literacy in the new medium.[32] There is some evidence that audiences connected the Loudspeaker with this didactic figure: at least three critics refer to *One-Third of a Nation* as a "lecture," a term that is not used in promotional materials. More recent than silent film was the *March of Time* newsreel. The influential monthly news series featured a guiding "Voice of Time." The film historian Jack C. Ellis notes that actor Westbrook Van Voorhis's narration was a key element of the series: it was "deep and commanding, ominous and reassuring at the same time." Van Voorhis's role was truly god-like, signaling its omniscience in the signature refrain "Time marches on." Ellis points out that *The March of Time* relayed mostly stock footage without dramatization. Therefore Van Voorhis's role was also more dramatically significant than Dill's, carrying the brunt of the narrative in any given episode. His over-the-top presence was inevitably subject to parody as the "Voice of God" and the "Voice of Doom."[33] These nicknames, in their irreverence, suggest discomfort with a voice that claims to know too much.

By contrast, the Loudspeaker is not quite, or not only, a "Voice of God." Whereas Susan Duffy and Bernard K. Duffy have argued that the Loudspeaker "made a statement about the intrusiveness of technology in daily life,"[34] I see the Loudspeaker as a site for experimenting with mass media's possibilities for democratic participation. Though the Loudspeaker has no human form in the play itself, he transmits a kind of responsiveness that is rarely attributed to mass media. The Loudspeaker not only disseminates information but also seeks to amplify the voice of others. Moreover, within a few scenes, the Loudspeaker meets a foil.

## THE LITTLE MAN

About one-third of the way through the play, a man in contemporary dress emerges from the audience. His name is Angus K. Buttonkooper, but reviews and the playscript itself refer to him as the Little Man. Whereas the Loudspeaker models an alternative to propaganda as a responsive mass medium, the Little Man models an alternative to propaganda as a self-conscious public speaker. The Little Man interrupts "the show" and asks questions about what he sees and hears. He speaks frankly from his own experience, using common sense to interpret the social conditions that affect him. And by the end of the play, he raises his voice to advocate on behalf of allocations for public housing. In his trajectory, the Little Man is positioned as a representative of the "average" American—a notion, as discussed in chapter 2, that opinion research was helping to popularize. In the United States, the very idea of averageness was on the rise: the years after World War I surged with social-scientific characterizations of typical Americans.[35]

As with the Loudspeaker, variations of the Little Man appeared in several Living Newspapers. The first of these was the Clown in *Injunction Granted!*, who offered an identifiable point of continuity in and between scenes. The comedic actor Norman Lloyd, who developed the character through improvisation, recalled: "When I did the clown, I kept thinking, 'What was the audience?' Angus [Buttonkooper] was definitely the guy sitting out there."[36] In the next Living Newspaper, *Power,* Buttonkooper made his debut; he appeared as the average American consumer, seeking to understand his electricity bill. In *One-Third of a Nation* Buttonkooper was humbler still, appearing not as "Consumer" but as the "Little Man."

The phrase "little man" had circulated since the eighteenth century. It connoted a typical man of limited means,[37] and in the 1930s, vulnerability, working-class identity, and averageness became closely intertwined in popular imaginaries. In Germany, the author Hans Fallada had published the popular book *Little Man, What Now? (Kleiner Mann—was nun?)*, which addressed workers' struggles in the early years of the Great Depression.[38] In 1933, a year after its publication, it became a film, heavily censored by the Nazis. It is telling that the average man in the 1930s was described as "little": this qualifier, implying a need for protection, reflected populist and fascist discourses that told average citizens they were vulnerable to manipulation and deception.

In *One-Third of a Nation,* the Little Man figure continued the rhetorical work of combining the ideas of vulnerability, working-class identity, and averageness. Reflecting the NYLN's vision of coalition between blue-collar and white-collar workers, Buttonkooper represents both. His name identifies him with blue-collar craftsmen; his dress—a suit—identifies him with white-collar professionals. In the guise of the Little Man, as in so many popular representations, this archetypal worker is a white, comfortably married man. As I further discuss in the next chapter, however, averageness, as humble an attribute as it appeared to be, was only legible on white bodies.

*One-Third of a Nation* depicted an average American who was meek and bumbling but, importantly, permitted to take the stage. The Little Man bursts onto the scene in *One-Third of a Nation* without warning. He himself does not seem to have planned the intervention. The Loudspeaker has already shown the audience a tenement fire, an inquest, and a trip back in time to reveal the origins of New York's housing shortage; a narrative has been unfolding steadily without the Little Man. Then as scene 4 begins, a voice calls out, "Hey! Give me some light!" (39). His entrance is literally an interjection, and there are no arrangements in place for him to be seen. He even needs to ask for his own light. According to production notes, a follow spot guides his path, representing visually his isolation from the crowd and his ascent to the hypervisibility of the stage. There, the Loudspeaker has not been expecting him:

LOUDSPEAKER:  What is it?
LITTLE MAN:  I'd like some information.
LOUDSPEAKER:  What about?
LITTLE MAN:  Housing.
LOUDSPEAKER:  What are you doing up there in those clothes? (39)

The Loudspeaker is perturbed. The Little Man is unexpected, out of place, and as the Loudspeaker's question reveals, out of time as well. The Little Man's entrance appears to have been spontaneous. Neither methodical nor consistent, his extemporaneous brand of publicity opposes the systematic publicity of propaganda.

The Little Man persists with his improvised intervention. Speaking directly to the Loudspeaker, he demands information:

> LOUDSPEAKER: Well, what do you want?
> LITTLE MAN: Information. Every time something happens that I don't understand I'm going to stop the show and ask questions.
> LOUDSPEAKER: And who's going to answer them?
> LITTLE MAN: You are. (39)

The Loudspeaker seems irritated, impatient ("Well?"), but the Little Man continues, with notable pluck. He does not question his confusion, or try to hide it, and he does not apologize for his interruption. In fact, he bluntly explains his intention to hold up the narrative every time something happens that he does not understand. His metatheatrical language is striking. The "show" he threatens to stop is clearly the unfolding narrative about housing, but it might also be the news writ large. "Show" here suggests an absorbing presentation, and perhaps one that should be distrusted because it is artfully and strategically conceived. It can be quick and spectacular, and leave the witness overwhelmed, like the tenement fire in the play's opening scene, or even, perhaps, like Roosevelt's synoptic sound bite about "one-third of a nation."

A "show," however, as the Little Man insists, can be "stopped." In this respect it is different from another form of news, the bulletin or the flash. The "news flash" entered US discourse in the nineteenth century, thanks to the possibilities of the telegraph. It described a brief broadcast, usually "a preliminary to a fuller report."[39] Truncated forms developed in the twentieth-century news too. Tabloids presented information in compact papers, half the size of a broadsheet. Even in full-sized broadsheets, by the 1920s, journalists typically presented information to readers in order of importance rather than chronology: the inverted pyramid style of newswriting.[40] With the news flash, the tabloid, and pyramidal story structures, modern journalism conveyed public issues quickly and concisely. Popular forms of propaganda seized the trend toward concision. Posters with terse messaging conveyed urgency and afforded little room to ask questions. *One-Third,* unfolding over the course of two hours, offered an attenuated alternative to these forms. It moved episodically, with scenes dramatizing events in a steady, quick progression, often demarcated by blackouts. In *One-Third,* the Little Man modeled the possibilities afforded by this structure, with its expansive temporality broken into discrete units of action. He could intervene, pause, resume, and move backward and forward in time.

Indeed, that is exactly how the Little Man proceeds. Having learned that housing is a deeply rooted problem, he asks the Loudspeaker to take him back to 1850. "I'd like to walk around the town and get acquainted," he suggests. "Got a map"? (51). He is compelled to look and listen, but he does not know exactly what he seeks. His only stipulation to the Loudspeaker is this: "And for the love of Mike, let's see some people—not landlords, people!" (51). The Little Man is adamant that he must see others like him, people whose lives are tested by scarce and unsanitary housing. In the scene that follows, the Little Man traverses a century of urban development in New York. He remains in constant conversation with the Loudspeaker.

As he promised when he first came on the scene, the Little Man spends a lot of time asking questions. And these questions are powerful, in that they shape the play's dramatic arc. Soon after the Little Man steps onstage, it is he, and not the Loudspeaker, who is determining the narrative's movement through time and space. Early in the play, some of the Little Man's questions seek guidance from the Loudspeaker on how to proceed in the play, reminding the audience that his participation is improvised and uncertain. After he witnesses two teenagers planning a desperate escape from their dismal home lives, the Loudspeaker offers to show him more. The Little Man reluctantly asks, "Do you think I'd better?" (52). Later, when the Little Man has reappeared after intermission, the Loudspeaker offers to show him the spread of slum housing in 1933. The Little Man hedges, asking, "Do I have to go alone?" (77). These questions emphasize the Little Man's choice to look, and by extension the possibility of choosing not to look. His decision-making process, captured in innocuous questions to the Loudspeaker, underscores the importance of looking but also opposes the enforced looking that propaganda entails. The Little Man seems to offer a reminder: when a news item appears in a news flash or tabloid, the viewer can choose whether or not to bear witness.

Many of the Little Man's other questions motivate exposition, asking for introductions or clarification. For instance, when he sees two women cleaning a cholera-infested tenement, he asks simply, "Say, who are they?" (61). Some questions are more complex, and elicit causal accounts of historical events. When he hears the chairman of the Council of Hygiene and Public Health deliver a report on a decrepit housing complex, he asks, "What happened after he handed in that report?" (44). The Loudspeaker's responses, here and throughout the play, highlight the perils of apathy. Time and again, the Little Man learns that people in power failed to act for the public good.

As the play progresses, the Little Man's questions grow more critical and more confident. He starts to challenge the motives of powerful leaders. He wonders why Congress does not allocate funds to build more housing (106). Soon after, he starts to pose questions about his fellow citizens. "Tell me," he asks as the play nears its conclusion, "isn't there anybody who's taken the time to figure this thing out?" (112). He begins to address the audience directly.

Over the course of the play, then, the tenor of the Little Man's questions shifts from timid requests for clarification to defiant challenge. By the end of the play, questions are interspersed with arguments. In the final scene it is the Loudspeaker who calls on the Little Man. He is pacing and deep in thought:

> LOUDSPEAKER: Hey! *(no answer; he continues pacing)*
> Hey! What are you doing?
> LITTLE MAN *(without stopping )*: Arithmetic. (114)

The Little Man soon reports that he is calculating the funds allocated by the Wagner-Steagall Act. Also known as the Housing Act of 1937, it subsidized housing, via public housing agencies, for low-income families. The Little Man determines that New York City will receive only a small fraction of the $526 million allocated, half of what Senator Robert F. Wagner originally proposed.

It is significant that the Little Man describes his analysis of the House appropriation as "arithmetic," a subject many Americans learn in their early years. The implication is that it takes little more than common sense and an elementary school education to analyze social issues. The possibilities of common sense were central to what the propaganda scholar J. Michael Sproule calls "straight thinking." In the late 1930s, progressives touted this approach as a way for citizens to interpret political messages and defend themselves against insidious propaganda. Straight thinking emphasizes basic reasoning processes rather than deference to experts or polemical opposition, much like the Little Man's "arithmetic."[41] The Little Man models straight thinking, not necessarily for propaganda analysis but rather for political action. His basic calculations lead him to conclude that the funds allocated for public housing are insufficient. His response, cartoonishly inappropriate, is to get ready for a fight:

> LITTLE MAN: Well what are we doing about it? *(Excitedly)* Are we going to take it lying down like mice? Or, are we men? *(Starts taking off coat)*.
> LOUDSPEAKER: What are you going to do now?
> LITTLE MAN: I'm going to find the guy who's responsible for these slum conditions! I'll tell him something, all right, all right! (115 )

Though the Little Man has come a long way since his entrance onto the stage, he still lacks political know-how. The Loudspeaker steps in, reminding the Little

Man that the problem is not a single "guy" but rather "inertia" (118), "the thing that makes people like you and everybody else sit back and say, 'Well, this is the way it always has been and this is the way it's always going to be!'" (117).

The Little Man is still confused, but his wife steps in. She has appeared once, earlier in the play, calling her husband home to apply for housing in a new development (87). When her husband insisted he needed to stay and finish the play, she decided to stay and watch. Now she ascends comfortably from the audience to the stage and agrees with the Loudspeaker that the problem is inertia (118).

Mrs. Buttonkooper is more self-consciously politicized than her husband. She is impatient with his slow, modest inquiry: "You know about these conditions and so do I and so does everybody else that lives in 'em. . . . What good are all those surveys and speeches to us when we've got to live in a place almost as bad as that twenty-four hours a day!" (120). While the exchanges between the Little Man and the Loudspeaker have thus far depicted information as the path to social and self-improvement, Mrs. Buttonkooper suggests that it may equally be the source of mystification, a layer of obscurity that distances individuals from their experiential knowledge. Mrs. Buttonkooper asks no questions; she proclaims the necessity to act. She demands that Americans "holler" for better housing, and she begins immediately:

> LITTLE MAN (*excitedly*): All right, all right, when do we begin?
>
> MRS. BUTTONKOOPER: *Now! (Shouting)* We want a decent place to live in! I want a place that's clean and fit for a man and woman and kids! *Can you hear me—you in Washington or Albany or wherever you are! Give me a decent place to live in! Give me a home! A home!* (120)

Mrs. Buttonkooper calls for what a loudspeaker does best: amplification. Her husband, unconvinced, wonders if it will do any good. She persists with the auditory metaphor, insisting: "Sure it will. If we do it loud enough!" (120). In her final lines, Mrs. Buttonkooper raises the volume of her voice, becoming, like the Loudspeaker, louder than conversation requires and shifting from a mode of dialogue to one of dissemination. She demands to be heard with little regard to the listener, "in Washington or Albany or wherever you are!" Loud, declamatory, unconcerned who her listeners are as long as they are within hearing range, she is a loudspeaker in human form.

It is provocative that the play's most assertive advocate for action is not its protagonist but his wife, who only enters onstage in the play's final scene. Perhaps NYLN staff, who had already taken heat from conservative critics and politicians, felt that it was safer not to attribute the play's most strident words to its hero. Mrs. Buttonkooper's womanhood could serve to soften what was a rousing call to action. After all, even as she calls for a unified "holler" at Washington, Mrs. Buttonkooper, as the Little Man's wife, primarily represents the domestic sphere. Here, the Living Newspaper melds its socialist influences with New Deal individualism. Mrs. Buttonkooper demands that the Little Man act not just for the public good but for the preservation of his own private domestic life, a normative household (figure 7).

At the same time, in her pushiness Mrs. Buttonkooper requires her husband to be not quite so little, nor to ask so little either. In this respect, as Barbara Melosh argues, Mrs. Buttoonkooper is a typical construct of New Deal gender norms. She is strong, but her strength is above all a rebuke of the "failures of middle-class manhood," evident in her meek husband. Mrs. Buttonkooper fulfills what Melosh calls a "comradely ideal of marriage," one that links marriage to good citizenship.[42] Sure enough, Mrs. Buttonkooper is a catalyst that transforms the Little Man's curiosity into action. It is only after her intervention that the Little Man realizes: "By golly that's right. According to what we've seen here tonight people have been going around for a hundred years or more—taking notes, making surveys—but nobody's ever *done* anything" (118). Mrs. Buttonkooper stirs the Little Man to act by reminding him of his duties to his family.

FIGURE 7. "Mr. and Mrs. Buttonkooper." Promotional photo of Clarence R. Chase and Edith Groome, Mr. and Mrs. Buttonkooper, *One-Third of a Nation*, Adelphi Theatre, New York, 1938. Courtesy of Library of Congress.

## THEATRICAL WITNESSING

Most importantly, Mrs. Buttonkooper's political poise accentuates her husband's awkwardness, an awkwardness that is integral to the play's message about speaking in public. The ease with which Mrs. Buttonkooper ascends to the stage and leaps into action suggests that she is further along than the Little Man in a process of acting on what she sees. So too do moments throughout the play when the Little Man stammers and stumbles in the spotlight. *One-Third of a Nation* dramatizes the Little Man's trajectory from passive looking and listening to active questioning. But the play uses theatrical conventions to show that the trajectory is labored.

If the Little Man's initial entrance appears to be disruptive and improvised, his second entrance, at the top of the second act, is even more so. Here again, the Little Man's entrance is clunky and self-conscious. The audience learns that the Little Man was out for a beer during the intermission. He stumbles, perhaps tipsily, on his way to the stage.

> LITTLE MAN *(hurrying down the aisle of the theatre)*: Hey! Hey! *(He stumbles over somebody's foot)* Pardon me! *(He hurries up stairway from pit to stage, left. Crosses to center on apron step)* Here I am. Hey! (75)

No doubt the stumble serves partially as an endearing moment of comic relief, but it also reinforces the awkwardness of the Little Man's ascent. It arises not from an elaborate physical gag but from the simple, supposedly natural act of walking.[43] The Little Man makes it to the stage twice, but his ascent is clumsy. For him, publicity is neither systematic nor automatic but embodied and unpredictable.

And throughout the play, the Little Man does not seem to want to be onstage. Though he quickly insinuates himself into the narrative, he often draws attention to his status as non-actor. He wears a contemporary gray suit that clashes anachronistically with the historical scenes he visits. When the Loudspeaker comments on his costume, he replies: "Say, I'm no actor. I just came from down . . . *(Pointing to seat in orchestra)*" (75). When the play resumes after the intermission, it commences without the Little Man; in fact, a full scene passes, orchestrated by the Loudspeaker, before the Little Man reenters. While directing dramatic action and modeling political action, the Little Man repeatedly states his affiliation with the audience. As the play approaches its conclusion, after unsuccessfully inciting him to action "offstage," the Little Man's wife sits in the audience to watch him complete the play. The Little Man, reluctantly agreeing, urges her: "But don't look at me up here. You'll make me nervous" (88). Even now, more than halfway through the show, the Little Man self-consciously references his status as accidental actor.

The Little Man's self-consciousness distinguished *One-Third of a Nation* from other political plays of its time. When the Little Man stepped out of the audience, he planted his feet firmly in a modern leftist theatrical tradition: throughout the 1920s and 1930s, theater-makers across Europe and the United States manipulated the spatial division between audience and performer to create—or suggest—participatory dialogues in the theater. In stepping out of the audience to engage the Loudspeaker in conversation, the Little Man joined a long line of interlocutors planted in the theater.

The French philosopher Jacques Rancière has glossed this tradition as a continuous and futile attempt to vanquish the ideological distance between actor and spectator. While Rancière is right to observe a historical pattern, he also flattens out its variations and neglects its complex relationship to varied practices of public dialogue. Many agitprop performances, unfolding in streets and public spaces, had no spatial division between audience and actor to begin with; other productions, meanwhile, created the separation only to disrupt it. In 1928, the Russian director Vsevolod Meyerhold and writer Sergei Tretyakov envisioned a production about eugenics called *I Want a Child*. In a bare theater, set up for arena seating, audiences would participate in discussions as if they were at a workers' council meeting. They would be guided by actors—people, insisted Meyerhold, "we can rely on"—to provoke and direct the discussion.[44] Around the same time, Brecht and his collaborators were also folding audience discussion into performance. Their youth-oriented *Lehrstücke,* or "Learning Plays," invited students to participate in partially scripted plays about social issues. For instance, in 1930–31, Brecht, Hauptmann, and Weill adapted a Japanese Noh play in *He Said Yes* and its rarely presented addendum *He Said No* to catalyze discussion about tradition, coercion, and political consent.

American artists were inspired too by workers' councils, and by works they had seen or heard about in Europe. The Group Theatre's 1935 *Waiting for Lefty* planted actors in the audience to rise, mid-play, and advocate for a strike by exploited taxi drivers. (Watson marveled, "Odets planted characters right in the audience's midst.")[45] At the end of the play, actors invited the audience to vote on whether the strike should occur. Two years later, Marc Blitzstein's play *The Cradle Will Rock*, directed by Orson Welles, offered a variation of this device—albeit, arguably, not entirely by artistic design. When federal administrators ousted the production from its Broadway theater, the company moved to another venue, where Blitzstein, alone, would present the play, cabaret-style. Actors bought tickets as audience members, and in a now canonical act of defiance, many of them rose and performed their parts from their seats. According to Blitzstein, the audience "seethed with excitement" as it followed the action "as at a tennis match from one actor to another."[46]

While the Little Man is one of many planted interlocutors in the leftist theatrical tradition, he is unusually awkward, conspicuously *in-between* spectator and actor, listener and speaker. It was this very awkwardness—*One-Third*'s distinctive interjection in the tradition of plants—that elicited journalistic imagination, drawing attention to *how* the Little Man came into relationship with the Loudspeaker, and *how* he moved from witnessing the present to actively shaping it.

Perhaps the Little Man's stumbles evoked a form of Brechtian alienation (*Verfremdungseffekt*), foreclosing absorption in theatrical spectacle and reminding spectators to take action. Or conversely, perhaps his stumbles made the Little Man sympathetic, masking his power as a middle-class white American. After all, while Arthur Arent proudly attributed the success of *One-Third* to its development of the "human element" of an otherwise complex problem, it is striking that the human element takes the form of the Little Man and not Sammy Rosen, a Jewish tenement dweller who loses his home to the fire in the opening scene. In focusing on the Little Man, the play reserves meaningful witnessing, and thus democratic participation, not just to ethnically unmarked middle-class citizens, as Loren Kruger has observed, but also, more broadly, to the bystander in its inciting tragedy rather than its victim.[47] Here again, *One-Third* focuses on how to transform looking and hearing into action, exploring how average citizens can respond to what they see and hear.

Regardless of how exactly the Little Man hails the spectator, his ascent to the stage is, above all, theatrical. In everyday parlance, theatricality connotes behavior that is over the top and out of place, and these connotations certainly apply to the Little Man's performance. Modern Euro-American spectators learn to sit quietly in "legitimate" theaters, but the Little Man jumps out of the audience. He moves and speaks loudly enough to address the entire auditorium. In the second act, he appears to be slightly drunk.

But the Little Man's behavior is theatrical in another, more technical sense as well, in that it elicits a "sympathetic breach" or dis-identification between spectator and performer. This is how the essayist and historian Thomas Carlyle coined the term "theatrical" in the eighteenth century, according to the theater historian Tracy C. Davis, to describe a critical orientation to the public sphere. Like Adam Smith's "sympathy," Carlyle's "theatricality" describes a relationship between and among liberal subjects. But Carlyle's theatricality, as Davis explains, is what occurs when sympathy fails—when the spectator is attentive to a performer's experience but not so absorbed that she loses herself. The result is an experience of "dedoublement," or splitting in two, whereby the spectator is aware of herself even as she engages with the performer. In other words, the experience of theatricality may be *caused* by phony-looking acting, as when a political leader is accused of "theatrics" rather than genuine communication, but theatricality does not reside in the actor. Rather, for Davis, theatricality emerges from the spectator who has been absorbed in a performance, remembers herself, and "acts back."[48] The Little Man's performance was theatrical in Davis's sense because it did not encourage spectators to forget who or where they were. They were, after all, watching an actor, playing a spectator, stumble to the stage and insist he was no actor.

In its insistent self-deprecation, the Little Man's theatrical performance might have conjured the language of populist politicians, those who asserted that they were just ordinary people, and implied that their very claims to ordinariness merited the extraordinary job of representing the body politic. Yet the Little Man's character resisted many demagogic features often associated with New Deal–era figures like Huey Long and Father Charles Coughlin.[49] He seemed to distrust publicity. He hesitated to take the spotlight. He insisted that he did not belong onstage. And insofar as this was a lie—he was, after all, played by an actor—the audience was fully aware. Drawing on the long history of theatrical confederates, "plants" who the audience knows are not one of them, he likely fooled nobody in the Adelphi Theatre.[50]

In short, then, the Little Man's trajectory from audience to stage was theatrical in two senses of the word. First, it was theatrical in the colloquial sense of the word: loud, exaggerated, and unsubtle. Second, it was theatrical in Carlyle's sense, as interpreted by Davis: a layered self-presentation that enlisted self-conscious spectatorship. The Little Man modeled a process of stepping onstage, becoming publicly visible, or participating in democratic life. But his theatricality showed that this process was labored, awkward, and perhaps even unnatural.

In her theorizations of activism, the performance scholar Lindsay Goss notes that theatricality might be an unavoidable liability for people seeking social change, "an inevitable and critical component of activist practice." Activism, after all, involves making "an existing reality register and appear," a process that will always make performer and spectator self-conscious as they negotiate the appearance of something new.[51] In the case of *One-Third of a Nation,* the NYLN used the Little Man to make visible the possibility of taking action, even if imperfectly. For the Little Man's stumbles reflect the challenge of responding to news. Public speech, he shows, is not a natural extension of everyday talk but an awkward process of fumbling into the spotlight. In this regard, the theatricality elicited by the Little Man's move from audience to stage was not an aesthetic failure but one of the play's most interesting provocations. While the Little Man models one vision of democratic participation, in which the average citizen can move from spectating to being heard, he also models its frustration.

## PROPAGANDA AND JOURNALISTIC IMAGINATION

The Little Man's fumbling, stumbling movement from watching to acting offered a vision of who might be the subject of "propaganda for democracy." When conceived as systematic manipulation by the powerful, as it was by the Dies Committee, propaganda sought out passive citizens. When conceived as a tool for interactive, dialogical exchange, as it was by Flanagan, "propaganda for democracy" sought out self-conscious questioners.

The Little Man's ascent to the stage was a significant departure from other models of civic engagement. The Dies Committee was not the only cohort concerned with propaganda, nor were public hearings the only approach to resisting it. In the previous decades, progressive muckrakers like Upton Sinclair and Ida Tarbell had set their sights on those with too much power in public discourse. Historian Charles Beard and critic George Seldes attacked the publisher William Randolph Hearst, calling his newspapers "the cesspool of American journalism."[52] For the muckrakers, the best defense against propaganda was to undermine those with the power to disseminate it. Others, however, took a less polemical approach. Just one year before *One-Third of a Nation* debuted, progressive journalist Clyde Miller, geologist Kirtley Mather, and business philanthropist Edward A. Filene founded the Institute for Propaganda Analysis. The IPA created and distributed educational bulletins that cautioned readers against a range of propaganda tropes, including "glittering generalities" and "bandwagoning."[53] For Miller among others, the best defense against propaganda was the informed citizen. Indeed, what was initially called the "propaganda analysis" school became the "straight thinking" school.[54] It shifted focus from the workings of mass deception to the cultivation of reason and clear thinking in individuals. Rather than revealing the powers behind the media, it aimed to empower consumers.

There are significant connections between the work of the IPA and that of the NYLN. As Elisabeth Fondren notes, the institute's monthly newsletter, *Propaganda Analysis,* encouraged self-reflectiveness combined with humility so that citizens—much like Little Man—would not "feel smug and mentally superior to the people who don't recognize propaganda." In its early years, the IPA asserted that propaganda could "preserve and extend democracy." When a *Harper's* column accused the IPA itself of propagandizing, Miller countered, echoing Flanagan's phrasing, "We are propagandists for democracy." Perhaps most significantly, the IPA would adopt the Living Newspaper form as a way to teach young people about tolerance and news literacy. In an initiative funded by Eleanor Roosevelt and endorsed by Theodore Roosevelt Jr., the IPA trained New York high school students to make Living Newspapers about their neighborhoods.[55]

Even so, *One-Third of a Nation* does not easily align with any single approach to propaganda resistance. The Little Man's "arithmetic" certainly demonstrates "straight thinking," but his wife's impassioned call to arms rings of polemic. The Little Man stumbles to the stage, stops the show, and asks questions. He looks and listen, then forms conclusions, using common sense and some basic arithmetic. He models a form of public speech that is self-conscious and spontaneous, neither automatic nor systematized. The Loudspeaker uses his booming voice to amplify the concerns of citizens.

Rather than comprehensive program or theory, *One-Third* offers a series of provocations by way of gestures. The Little Man stumbles to the stage; perhaps average citizens, too, could find meaningful paths to political action. The Loudspeaker gives information to the Little Man and amplifies his concerns; perhaps mass media, too, could advance civic engagement. These provocations were resonant. For critics, spectators, and artists alike, the conventions of the Little Man and the Loudspeaker became hallmarks of the Living Newspaper form. A review in *Time* singled out the Little Man as the character who "springs out of the audience and wants to know."[56] Reviewing the DC production at the Civic Theatre, Nelson B. Bell points to the Little Man's "colloquies with the 'Voice of the Living Newspaper.'"[57]

From the beginning, however, Living Newspaper conventions were malleable. They looked, sounded, and *meant* differently from one Living Newspaper to the next. This is perhaps nowhere clearer than in *Liberty Deferred*, Abram Hill and John D. Silvera's dramatization of racialized violence and the struggle for civil rights. In this unproduced Living Newspaper, the singular Little Man appears in multiple forms: a white couple, Jimmy and Mary Lou; an African American couple, Ted and Linda; a French visitor named Felix Deveaux. Throughout the play's narrative, all four characters would argue heatedly about what they want to see and hear. The result, as I demonstrate in the next chapter, is a powerful critique of the NYLN's corpus and its representations of race.

# CHAPTER FOUR

# THE KEEPER OF RECORDS

## Reimagining Representation

While Living Newspapers sought to expand the parameters of news, they also obscured and exacerbated racial inequities. In many ways this pattern was in keeping with other progressive initiatives of the time. The problems of racism and white supremacy were neither new nor unique to the New Deal era; as Richard Iton, scholar of African American studies, has shown, racism "unmade" the American left over two centuries of US history. Yet the New Deal, as Iton also shows, made it especially clear how far leftist causes could advance despite structural racism, and in some cases, because of it. White labor activists, feeling threatened by lower-paid Black workers, excluded them from unions or downplayed their contributions; New Deal policies like old age insurance excluded racialized agricultural and domestic workers; and President Roosevelt declined to champion anti-lynching legislation for fear of losing southern white support. In these ways and others, white progressives undercut important gains, including the new incentives for interracial collaboration that came from attention to class, evident in the Congress of Industrial Organizations' adoption of explicitly antiracist policies, and the new voting blocs that Black voters were forming, especially in the North, as the Great Migration gathered momentum. Despite these moves toward antiracism, Iton notes, "The New Deal coalition was never as strong or as progressive as some contemporary analysts might suggest." While seeking to strike a new chord for white-collar workers, the left fell into a familiar refrain, one that Iton calls the "solidarity blues."[1]

The solidarity blues offer a compelling way to understand the dynamics of race and racism in New Deal institutions, and in this chapter I listen for their resonance in the NYLN. The WPA, the FTP, and the NYLN joined the chorus of New Deal institutions that prioritized white representation on the left. Yet Black artists took up the Living Newspaper form and worked to cultivate journalistic imagination. In their unstaged Living Newspaper *Liberty*

*Deferred,* John D. Silvera and Abram Hill would not simply reflect on the cultural production of the present; they would also rewrite its time signature.

## SOLIDARITY BLUES AT THE FTP

Under supervisor Harry Hopkins, the WPA supported roughly 1 million Black families, and it worked to enforce antidiscrimination policy. Yet racial inequities nonetheless pervaded the WPA. Unlike the rival Public Works Administration, for instance, the WPA did not require employers to develop teams that matched Black demographics in a recent census.[2] Like its umbrella organization, the FTP succeeded in some ways and failed in others. Hallie Flanagan's vision of a nationally representative theater focused on geographic coverage and production content rather than the racial and ethnic diversity of the project's workforce and leadership. Perhaps this is why, as Rena Fraden observes, the FTP mandated but never implemented "racial representation in all national planning."[3] And while the FTP boasted Negro units across the country, it rarely, as the historian Kate Dossett has shown, fully entrusted them to Black artists.[4] The New York Negro Unit, for instance, would become best known for a white-authored and white-directed production, Orson Welles's "Voodoo" *Macbeth.* Indeed, the reliance on white-authored plays, even in the Negro units, was one of several key points in a 1939 brief, drafted by a coalition of Black artists and workers.

A similar pattern of white dominance is evident in the records of the NYLN. As I showed in chapter 1, the Unit's leadership, its most visible representatives and its best-compensated employees, were white. This is not to say that people of color did not play significant roles in production, but rather that they were rarely documented or appropriately credited. This precedent was established from the NYLN's first work. *Ethiopia* almost certainly owed a debt to the Black press, whose depth of coverage exceeded that of mainstream white newspapers; yet the play was largely attributed to white artists Arthur Arent and Elmer Rice, especially because of the latter's well-publicized departure from the FTP when the play was censored.

Subsequently, *One-Third of a Nation* quietly benefited from the contributions of Black artists. The composer and playwright Shirley Graham and technical director Byron Webb, both working at the Negro Unit in Harlem, joined the summer workshop that led to the play's first draft. When the production debuted the following year, actors Kermit Augustine and Add Bates (replaced by James Williams when Bates began rehearsals for *Androcles and the Lion*) appeared in a scene about the conditions leading to the Harlem rent strike. The scene was impactful: the *Chicago Defender* noted that the affecting

"Harlem hot-bed" scene, depicting tenants trading shifts in a shared bed, brought its actors "overnight fame."[5] It is telling, however, that this was the only scene in *One-Third of a Nation* to dramatize Black life; characters named "First Negro" and "Second Negro" appeared only in this scene. People of color, more broadly, were scarce and stereotyped across the NYLN repertoire. In *Power,* Milton Williams played an obliging sharecropper, swindled by linemen from a private utilities company. In *Injunction Granted!* Native Americans are a fleeting, comedic threat to American colonizers: Norman Lloyd's "Clown" wields a tomahawk and lets "out a blood-curdling shriek" before turning to the audience with a scalp.[6] The chilling, otherwise silent caricature is the most striking representation of Native Americans in the NYLN repertoire.

The misrepresentation and underrepresentation of non-white Americans—in the NYLN, the FTP, and the WPA—constrained the possibilities of journalistic imagination. Under its predominantly white leadership, Living Newspapers rarely considered the racial and colonial underpinnings of mainstream journalism; nor, when they sought alternatives, could they benefit from the journalistic traditions that grew out of racialized communities. By the mid-1930s, news historian Fred Carroll observes, Black newsrooms were often highly educated places, populated by college graduates.[7] But Black journalists were seldom recognized as such by their white counterparts. Thus, while the umbrella of "white-collar" identity invited new constituents into the workers' movement, as I discussed in chapter 1, it also reinscribed the exclusion of racialized workers by presuming that they were unskilled. The very phrase "white-collar" conflated racial formations with professionalism, and its entrenchment in the NYLN powerfully constrained journalistic imagination by limiting who could publicly criticize journalistic norms.

The play *Liberty Deferred,* however, offered a provocative exception. It was one of three Living Newspapers to focus on racism, and it was the only one credited to Black playwrights, albeit under white "supervision." Playwrights Abram Hill and John D. Silvera wrote the play while working as play readers for the FTP's Play Bureau, and neither the NYLN nor the FTP resourced it with editorial staff. More significantly, the FTP would never follow through on a production.

Yet even without being produced, *Liberty Deferred* issued an important critique. It targeted, as Dossett argues, the "Living Newspaper form"—but also more conventional news media.[8] In this chapter I show how *Liberty Deferred* challenged white norms of newsworthiness and showed how news, defined in the introduction as the cultural production of the present, was deeply imbricated in race and racism. Hill and Silvera's subject matter was at times horrific. Treading a path that Ida B. Wells had broken over forty years earlier, they offered unflinching accounts of lynching and racial violence—a topic that was studiously ignored by much of the white press and by Roosevelt's office. But *Liberty Deferred* not only served to publicize ongoing brutality; it also expanded the frame. Echoing Wells's assertion that lynching was not just a southern problem but a national one, it situated lynching in a white culture that thrived on producing and consuming spectacles of Black suffering and found ways to report on this violence without satisfying white appetites.[9] By adapting the Living Newspaper form, Hill and Silvera devised new possibilities for Black resistance and interracial solidarity.

## *LIBERTY DEFERRED* AND WHITE SUPREMACY

Hill and Silvera developed *Liberty Deferred* under the auspices of the FTP's Play Bureau. It is possible that they already knew each other by the time they collaborated. Both had attended Lincoln University in Pennsylvania but they had very different backgrounds. Silvera, who had been a track star at Lincoln, had little experience in theater when he joined the FTP.[10] Having grown up in a well-to-do New Jersey home, however, he had been taken by his father on frequent trips to New York to see an array of Black professionals at work, and as a student, he lived two doors down from Paul Robeson.[11] At the FTP, Silvera worked for the Negro Unit as well as the Play Bureau. Indeed, for part of the time *Liberty Deferred* was in development, he was also working as an advance man for the touring production of Welles's "Voodoo" *Macbeth*, managing travel and accommodation in the Jim Crow South for over one hundred Black actors.

Whereas Silvera began his work at the FTP with minimal theater background, Hill already had considerable theatrical experience. Born in Atlanta and raised in Harlem, he had enrolled at Lincoln as a pre-med student in 1934. Two years later, however, he had taken a job directing plays for the WPA's Civilian Conservation Corps while also studying, writing, and working in Lincoln University's drama department. During his time with the FTP, he would earn a scholarship in playwriting and analysis at the New School for Social Research. In 1936, he wrote one of his best-known plays, *Hell's Half-Acre*, which he would produce at Lincoln the following year.

Under the supervision of Emmet Lavery and other white playwrights and critics, Hill and Silvera read play submissions and assessed them for production. The Play Bureau aimed, among other goals, to find authentic and non-essentializing depictions of African American life for the FTP's Negro units. It did not enlist many Black readers in the task, however. Silvera recounted in an interview: "Primarily they assigned [me] the scripts that would be involved in the Negro Theatre. And while I wouldn't say that I was the token black, I guess I was the only black."[12] Hill, too, recalled that he mostly evaluated scripts "with Negro characters or Negro themes to see that these were true to honest portrayals of Negro life."[13]

At the Play Bureau, Hill and Silvera were not part of the NYLN, though the two entities were not completely disconnected from each other. For one thing, the Play Bureau used the Living Newspaper form to assess talent: emerging playwrights were given news stories and asked to dramatize them in brief play-scripts. Moreover, in the summer of 1937, the Play Bureau partnered with the NYLN and the Harlem Negro Unit to form a Negro Dramatists Laboratory, with the aim of developing a Living Newspaper on Black youth. Dossett notes that Hill and Silvera might have attended this four-month summer school and taken workshops with Arthur Arent.[14] Beyond that possibility, however, Hill and Silvera's engagement with the NYLN seems to have been limited.

This limited engagement with the NYLN had advantages and disadvantages. On the one hand, developing a Living Newspaper outside of the NYLN allowed Hill and Silvera to work in relative independence, and to critique the Living Newspaper form, as well as the institution that produced it. On the other hand, their work was never given the resources—researchers, editorial staff, and production team—that Living Newspapers enjoyed once their content was approved. Instead, Hill and Silvera seem to have covered the multiple roles of researchers and sources, writers and dramaturgs. They did, however, participate in a long process of multiple revisions, negotiating their own vision with that of Lavery and other white supervisors. Ultimately, Lavery shelved the play. Perhaps if Hill and Silvera had received an equivalent investment of time and personnel afforded to NYLN staff, it would not have been so easy for administrators to slowly withdraw their support.

Kate Dossett has carefully traced the development of the manuscript of *Liberty Deferred* by analyzing five undated drafts, scattered across FTP archives. Before or during the winter of 1937, Lavery came to an agreement with Hill and Silvera about creating an African American Living Newspaper. The writers produced an initial draft, which they discussed with Lavery and revised through the spring of 1938. Lavery appointed Ira Knaster to supervise their work; he is also credited as supervisor in an earlier draft of the script.[15]

Although the play was never produced by the FTP, the FTP did preserve drafts and limited correspondence. It is worth noting that the published version of *Liberty Deferred*, found in Lorraine Brown's 1989 volume *"Liberty Deferred" and Other Living Newspapers of the 1930s Federal Theatre Project*, is most likely based on a 1980s revision by Abram Hill. There is a note referencing this version in the back of one of the unpublished, undated archival drafts. Further supporting this chronology, the final scene in the published script references a march on Washington planned by A. Phillip Randolph in 1941, two years after the FTP shut down. In what follows, I focus on the two drafts created during the FTP. I refer to them as "draft 1" and "draft 2" not to ascribe a chronology but to distinguish them in my analysis as relevant.

By the time Hill and Silvera started their work together, the Living Newspaper was solidifying as a form, with conventions, like the Loudspeaker and the Little Man (chapter 3), that the NYLN had begun to document and disseminate. *Liberty Deferred* reflected close attention to these conventions. Like almost all Living Newspapers, *Liberty Deferred* used an episodic structure to show conflict between the predominantly opposing groups: in this case, those who advanced racial equality versus those who resisted it. With the Living Newspaper's characteristic sweep, the narrative spanned hundreds of years, dramatizing the enslavement of African people in the United States, the Civil War and Reconstruction, and the rise of Jim Crow, before culminating in a call to action for Black emancipation. A Little Man (or rather, a few Little Men and Women) sought to engage in political life, the Loudspeaker provided dates and locations, and a combination of fictitious and historical figure disseminated facts and numbers, quotations, and legislative excerpts. Though the script did not integrate references, it nonetheless reflected extensive research. For any readers familiar with the Living Newspaper, *Liberty Deferred* would have borne obvious resemblances. Connected to these resemblances, however, were significant variations—variations that satirized the Living Newspaper form. These variations may be characterized, through the work of Henry Louis Gates Jr., as "Signifyin(g)," an African American rhetorical strategy that doubles and redoubles signs and playfully alters them, destabilizing their referents and creating a coded Black vernacular. While Gates analyzes Signifyin(g) as a trope in the Black American literary traditions, it might also be understood as a convention in Black American theatrical traditions, one that upends and complicates white mise-en-scène.[16] In *Liberty Deferred,* Hill and Silvera Signified on three key conventions of the Living Newspaper form: the Little Man, the journalistic present, and the call to action. In doing so, they exposed the predominantly white perspectives that limited the NYLN's approach and offered alternatives.

## SIGNIFYIN(G) ON THE LITTLE MAN

If the modern newspaper, as Benedict Anderson argues, calls forth the "imagined communities" of the nation-state, then its constituents may be understood as *newsworthy subjects.*[17] They are "subjects" in the sense of being formed through ideological processes; they are "news*worthy*" in the sense of being worthy of representation in the eyes (and actions) of news outlets and the state. Newsworthy subjects are those people who are rendered as participants in the goings-on of the nation, whose interests, concerns, and commitments constitute a shared horizon. Historically, in the commercial American press, the newsworthy subject has looked something like *One-Third of a Nation*'s Little Man: a white male citizen who, if not middle or upper class, at least has time and money to spend on consuming news; he is the imagined reader of dominant news media, and his interests have shaped their tone, tenor, and content. In *One-Third of a Nation*, the Little Man challenges the news he witnesses and the limited possibilities for engagement that mass media seem to afford; he stumbles and fumbles as he finds ways to "stop the show and ask questions." But "Little" as he is, the Little Man never doubts that he is entitled to consume news that is relevant to him; when he cannot relate to what he sees, his repeated interjection is a clumsy but indignant "Hey!" Thus, while the Little Man's capacity to influence politics is in question, his newsworthiness is not. In *Liberty Deferred*, however, newsworthiness is a central theme, one that Hill and Silvera explore by Signifyin(g) on the very idea of the Little Man. By replicating, fragmenting, and reimagining the Little Man, they satirize the NYLN's efforts to represent a singular average American.

Like the Little Man in *One-Third of a Nation*, the protagonists in *Liberty Deferred* embody the act of witnessing. But in *One-Third*, the witnessing is metatheatrical, with the Little Man spending several scenes in the play's audience before ascending to the stage. *Liberty Deferred*, by contrast, opens with two of its protagonists onstage: the witnesses are also, from the very beginning, being watched. They are "well-dressed white people" taking in the sights and sounds of a New York City cocktail bar. A "rhapsodic arrangement of Negro spirituals, American Revolutionary and Civil War airs" crescendos into the blues, and then into modern dance music. Mary Lou, a southern woman, is in New York for the first time with her companion, Jimmy, and she is impressed: "I do declare Jimmy, this is living! . . . [E]verything is mighty different down home. . . . [I]t's so cosmopolitan." Encoded in the language of cosmopolitanism, difference, and deep feeling, Mary Lou expresses her delight in experiencing what she takes to be urban Black culture. Jimmy, a New Yorker, enthusiastically suggests they venture to Harlem, where "the blues were born" and where Mary Lou can "let [her] hair down."[18] For Jimmy, Harlem is a portal to novel forms of entertainment and exotic ways of being.

Jimmy and Mary Lou are far from the bumbling, stumbling Little Man of *One-Third of a Nation*, but they are "average Americans": their generic names and contrasting dialects (northern and southern) hint that, like the Little

Man, these figures will represent their fellow citizens. Moreover, like the Little Man, they first appear in the act of watching and listening. For the Little Man, however, witnessing is an expression of powerlessness: America's housing crisis would continue until he stepped onto the stage, asked questions, and made demands of his congressional representatives. Watching and listening, *One-Third* suggests, is passive until spectators "stop the show and ask questions." But *Liberty Deferred* reveals that the acts of watching and listening can also be forms of domination, because white consumption of Black culture perpetuates a history of racial violence. "Come on uptown," Jimmy entreats Mary Lou, "and you'll see why Abe Lincoln wrote the Emancipation Proclamation" (3). The comment is glib but illustrative of a racialized politics of witnessing. It insinuates that Black Americans justify their freedom from enslavement by entertaining white Americans. Indeed, as Jimmy escorts Mary Lou to Harlem, a series of "flashes" depict Black stereotypes that circulate in mass media. A porter grins from a railroad ad; Black men pick cotton and play craps; vaudevillians perform in minstrel makeup (4–5). These clichés undercut Jimmy's insistence that he "knows these people," challenging the notion that consuming Black entertainment is a way of "knowing" Black cultures.

The play develops the point further when a stage direction explicitly links these mediated representations to white supremacy: "Note: These are some representative flashes which should all be done in an elaborate satirical manner—the object of which is to portray the Negro as he is too often shown on the screen, stage and over the air; in fact, as he is seen through the eyes of JIMMY and MARY LOU, who represent White Supremacy, as they sit at their 'night club table' at left" (4–5). Jimmy and Mary Lou, as representatives of "average Americans," embody white supremacy in their consumption of Black stereotypes.

Crucially, however, *Liberty Deferred* creates two counterparts in the figures of an African American couple, Ted and Linda. As the "flashes" of Black stereotypes subside, Ted and Linda slowly dance to center stage. When they reach the center, stage directions read: "Every one of the characters, hitherto playing his part as the whites expect him to, suddenly stops in his tracks and stares, almost accusingly, at JIMMY and MARY LOU. It is almost as if each one had dropped his clownish mask in self-disgust" (5). In *One-Third of a Nation,* the Little Man's self-consciousness of being watched suggests a mode of Brechtian alienation, one that emphasizes his ascent from audience to stage. Here, Ted and Linda and the other Black entertainers onstage align with what Daphne Brooks calls "Afro-alienation acts," which transform racial alterity into freeing self-expression.[19] As Kate Dossett notes, Afro-alienation was a recurring technique in Black Living Newspapers.[20] Reinforcing the disconnect between what white spectators are expecting and what Black performers do, Ted and Linda stand still, smoking. They are lit by a single shaft of light, in counterpoint to Jimmy and Mary Lou. In Hill's 1980s revision this counterpoint will be developed even further, with the two couples positioned, throughout the play, as opposing spectators who debate the meaning of what they see. In the 1930s drafts, however, the relationship is less about juxtaposition and more about reversal: whereas Jimmy and Mary Lou have been consuming (and discussing consuming) Black media, Ted and Linda redirect the audience's gaze to Jimmy and Mary Lou. "They have blinders attached to their eyes," Ted comments, "blinders that are made out of stuff which is a combination of news-print, movie film and essence-of microphone, with just a dash of grease-paint. . . . You can buy those blinders any day of the week" (6). As Dossett observes, Ted and Linda reveal and reverse the white gaze that dominates American public culture. Ted's comments demonstrate the urgent need for persuasive and wide-reaching revisions of the Black misrepresentation that white consumers buy and sell via mass media.

*Liberty Deferred,* like *One-Third of a Nation,* explored the democratic possibilities and limitations of media, but with some key differences. Its preoccupation was not propaganda so much as misrepresentation, a problem that was connected to but not reliant on modern mass media. America's status as a democracy was not at stake because, as Ted and Linda showed, America was not yet a democracy; rather, what was at stake was the possibility of democracy, America's democratic potential. It is therefore crucial that whereas *One-Third* dramatizes the act of "talking back" to mass media, *Liberty Deferred* shows that the very consumption of media is rooted in social, and specifically racialized, identities. There is no single average American in *Liberty Deferred* but rather Black Americans and white Americans contesting the culture they see and produce.

In a few ways, then, Ted and Linda, and Jimmy and Mary Lou, constitute among themselves a variation on the Little Man. Like the Little Man, they are the only characters apart from the Loudspeaker who recur throughout the play, and therefore offer points of identification for spectators. They are not public figures but couples who, much like Mr. and Mrs. Buttonkooper, demonstrate how social issues affect their ostensibly private domestic relationships. They witness and comment on what they see, and in Ted and Linda's case, on what they can do about it.

But this quartet of characters also represents some important departures from the Little Man and a critique of the convention he embodies. By doing away with the Little Man as protagonist, Hill and Silvera assert that American experience cannot be reduced to a single representative figure, no matter how humble or unassuming. Whereas *One-Third of a Nation* (and subsequently

*Power*) asked spectators to identify with a single working-class protagonist, *Liberty Deferred* asks them to negotiate their affinities and differences with four characters, differently positioned by race, gender, and geography. Strikingly, when Abram Hill revised the script in the 1980s, he made this point even more explicitly. Jimmy and Mary Lou and Ted and Linda *all* sit onstage as the play begins and argue with one another from the start about the content of what they see. Indeed, it is possible that a sketch on the back of draft 2 reflects this mise-en-scène with couples on either side of a central point of focus (figure 8).

Although Hill's 1980s revision intensifies the counterpoint between Ted and Linda on the one hand and Jimmy and Mary Lou on the other, it also excises a second, distinctive critique of the Little Man convention that appears in early drafts. As the play nears its conclusion after a discussion of anti-lynching legislation (to be discussed shortly), a new character is introduced—this one *explicitly* replicating *One-Third*'s Little Man, but with some key differences. As in *One-Third of a Nation,* he interrupts the play's dramatic action from the audience. "Just one moment—one moment please," his voice calls out from the audience until a spotlight picks him up. "I would like to ask one question," he begins, much like the Little Man in *One-Third.* But his audience is hostile; no sooner has the "Man from the Audience" spoken when a second voice from the gallery demands that the Loudspeaker "throw the bum out" (121). This Little Man is an outsider from the beginning.

FIGURE 8. "Sketch from *Liberty Deferred.*" Mise-en-scène sketch on the back of a 1980 draft script of *Liberty Deferred.* Courtesy of Library of Congress.

It is not only the hostile audience member who reveals the Man's otherness: stage directions describe a well-dressed foreigner with a vaguely French accent. A French visitor to America, studying its customs, he might conjure Alexis de Tocqueville, but he introduces himself as "Felix Deveaux." And unlike Tocqueville, he is shocked to witness the workings of American racism.

Like the Little Man, this "Man from the Audience" is defined by incredulity. But whereas the Little Man could not believe housing was so expensive, Deveaux cannot believe the realities of racial violence. He is stunned that "such things [lynching] happen here in America" (121). Oblivious to the workings of race and racism, Deveaux embodies a stance akin to what the cultural historian Robin Bernstein has called "racial innocence."[21] But whereas Bernstein's "racial innocence" is the domain of white children, a tool for maintaining racial hierarchy, Deveaux's ignorance is depicted as a property of his foreignness. It gently satirizes a recurring motif in the Black press, one that figured African American experiences abroad as fleeting glimpses of life outside Jim Crow. The Associated Negro Press, for instance, engaged African American travelers to report on their experiences abroad, and as the historian Gerald Horne writes, "those African Americans sufficiently lucky to travel abroad seemed to feel that it was their duty to report on world events and provide an alternative to the routine suffocation of Jim Crow." Describing her tour through London to Claude Barnett, publisher of the Associated Negro Press, Fay Jackson marveled "to have not met the first sign of prejudice," even at an upscale café.[22]

*Liberty Deferred* playfully positions Deveaux as a person who has, seemingly, not met any kind of racial prejudice. His shock drives his questions about lynching. Like the Little Man, he embodies common sense and demands to know who is responsible. Having witnessed the failure of anti-lynching legislation in the scene before, he is convinced that Congress has little say in the matter, and the Loudspeaker seems to agree. "The responsibility," asserts the Loudspeaker, "rests with one of our most distinguished citizens" (122). The scene continues:

> FELIX:　One citizen! Incredible.
> LOUDSPEAKER:　Yes, one. He's here, he's there, he's everywhere. In fact, there he is right behind you.
> (Felix turns around[,] is startled at the appearance of the figure of Jim Crow.)

These lines reveal Felix, who first appeared to be the Little Man, to be different from the average American. Rather, it is his foreignness that makes him ignorant of American racism and beckons to a different way of life. In fact, when the Loudspeaker asks him if he is "a negro," to determine if Jim Crow will harm him, Felix is uncertain:

> LOUDSPEAKER: Don't be frightened. He won't hurt you. Er——er——a——that is—-Pardon me, (continued) You're not a negro are you?
>
> FELIX: No I'm not. That is I don't think so.

The Loudspeaker shares Felix's indignation at the persistence of lynching in the United States, yet he hesitates to ask if Felix is Black, insinuating that the question is inherently offensive. Felix is so apparently oblivious to race and racism, despite the racist and colonial history of his home country, France, that he is not even sure how he might be perceived or classified in the United States. Notably, Hill and Silvera do not racialize him in their stage directions, leaving open the possibility that he is white-passing and feigning ignorance for his safety. Either way, his ambivalent answer charges the scene with danger. Jim Crow, a "grotesque looking individual," leads Felix "over into the light so that he can see his color." The outcome of the scene hinges on Jim Crow's assessment; once he is satisfied that Felix is white, he offers a friendly explanation:

> JIM CROW: Just call me Jim. I heard you ask who was responsible for the way we keep our darkies in place. Well, I am. I am the master of the Negroe's destiny. I rule from the cradle to the grave.

The Loudspeaker's characterization of Jim Crow as a "distinguished citizen" resonates here. Jim Crow is at once a folksy guy-next-door—"just call me Jim"—and a formidable power (122).

Between Jim Crow and Felix, Jimmy, Mary Lou, Ted, and Linda, it is—provocatively—difficult to say who is the "average American." Hill and Silvera present a generic middle-class white couple—much like Mr. and Mrs. Buttonkooper (the Little Man and his wife) of *One-Third of a Nation*—but then they redirect the audience's attention to Ted and Linda. Like Arent and the NYLN, Hill and Silvera plant a theatrical confederate in the audience to stop the show and ask questions, but his questions stem from an outside perspective on American culture. Moreover, the answers he seeks come not from the omniscient Loudspeaker but from the volatile character of Jim Crow.

By distributing the role of the Little Man across several characters—male and female, French and American, Black and white, northern and southern—*Liberty Deferred* withholds the kind of identification that white spectators might have come to expect from the NYLN repertoire. Instead, Hill and Silvera enlist spectators to negotiate their affiliations across multiple protagonists and multiple representatives of American experience. If *Liberty Deferred* had reached FTP stages, it might have prompted what the dance and performance historian Susan Manning calls "cross-viewing." Using the term to describe dance spectatorship in integrated Red Decade theaters, Manning defines cross-viewing as the experience "whereby spectators from diverse social locations sharing the same theatrical space catch glimpses of one another's perspectives." Because it allows viewers to "watch each other watching," cross-viewing nuances the experience of identification that mimetic representation tends to seek.[23] It asks viewers to consider what others might be seeing. Signifyin(g) on the Little Man to represent different kinds of spectators, Hill and Silvera dramatized a kind of cross-viewing, one that demanded attention to multiple perspectives.

## LYNCHOTOPIA

By Signifyin(g) on the Little Man, Hill and Silvera challenge the NYLN's attempt to represent newsworthy subjects as, exclusively, white men. By extension, they challenge the cultural production of the present by white journalists. But as I have argued throughout this book, "the present" has a second meaning relevant to news-making, one that refers not to people in attendance but rather to time.

The news, like the blues, plays out across distinctive time signatures. The *Oxford English Dictionary* defines both the content and the form of the news through its proximity to the present: the news pertains to "recent events or occurrences," and it unfolds as a revelation or disclosure in the present. What makes the news "news," whether celebrity gossip or a presidential address, is its immediacy, that is, the proximity it claims to the "now." Accordingly, journalistic standards tend to privilege speed and concision. The professionalization of journalism in the early twentieth century supported this convention. Recent developments like the telegraph and photo wire service helped journalists obtain and circulate information with increasing speed. At the same time, journalistic writing embraced brevity. Reporters adopted a pyramidal approach to structuring news stories so that readers in a hurry would receive the most important information first. With these stylistic and technological developments, the commercial news outlets enhanced their claims to the here and now, inviting readers, listeners, and viewers into the shared time that news purported to describe. Living Newspapers could not disseminate news as quickly as newspapers or radio broadcasts but nonetheless embraced journalistic time. Consider their titles: the exclamation point in *Injunction Granted!* invoking urgency; *One-Third of a Nation* referencing a recent public speech; *1935* recalling events of the previous year. Staging, too, embraced an aesthetic of speed: concise, episodic scenes, punctuated by blackouts; the Loudspeaker's terse announcements of setting; efficient metaphors and infographics.

*Liberty Deferred* challenged this aesthetic of speed, presenting an alternative vision of the present. Deferral, the play's primary motif announced in its title, would anticipate the question that opened Langston Hughes's "Harlem" over a decade later. Hill and Silvera juxtapose a centuries-long fight for Black freedom with a story of strategic, systematic delay by white opponents. Hill and Silvera's most biting dramatization of deferral, however, arrives about two-thirds of the way through the play, when *Liberty Deferred* departs from its mostly realistic style for a surreal scene set in an afterlife for victims of lynching.

The scene opens, like the NYLN's *1935,* with New Year's Eve cacophony. There is "shouting, ringing of bells, blowing of horns, striking of clock, intermingled with the singing of 'Auld Lang Syne.'" As in *1935,* the beginning of a new year prompts introspection, but this is introspection of a very different kind: "Lights go up on the KEEPER OF RECORDS in Lynchotopia (the fabled land where all lynch victims go). He is an official looking Negro dressed in a white robe and wearing the insignia of Lynchotopia (a rope about his neck). On his desk is a microphone over which is coming the noises heard before curtain. He listens attentively then closes his ledger." This opening stage direction introduces a chilling tension between what is at stake—ongoing state-sanctioned murder—and the cool bureaucratic professionalism of the Keeper's approach. The Keeper of Records resides in a world that is "fabled, and surreal," but he has a desk. He is "official looking." He wears a white robe, a garment that calls up simultaneously otherworldliness, white supremacy, and white-collar officiousness. His badge of office is also a vestige of racial violence: a rope around his neck. His first, matter-of-fact lines only reinforce his professional detachment:

> KEEPER: Well—thirteen new members for the year. Thirteen— exactly one half of last year. I wonder what 1937 will bring. The decline is no sign though. Let's see. What's the total number of members now, 5,107 since 1882. Old Judge Lynch is really doing his stuff. Would surprise me if they didn't send Walter White down to join us.—Oh, well, who knows. (110)

It is clear from his casual, speculative language—"I wonder," "Let's see," "Oh, well," "who knows"—that the Keeper is curious about the figures he tracks but emotionally detached from their significance. He is, by white professional standards, an ideal source: impartially tabulating without getting emotionally involved.

Even for proponents of objectivity, however, his detachment might have seemed unnerving. Strategically, it exposed the contradiction between cool, dispassionate accounting and the subject of brutal, reckless killing. Perhaps the Keeper's detachment frustrated the expectations of white liberals. Many of those who opposed lynching nonetheless consumed spectacular images of Black pain and trauma. Although some white newspapers, such as the *New York Times* and the *Chicago Tribune,* had editorialized against lynching since the late nineteenth century, they nonetheless circulated detailed accounts of lynching parties.[24]

Some Black newspapers too, as the historian Kim Gallon notes, reported explicitly on lynching. "The *Defender,*" she observes, "featured graphic, sensational headlines announcing regular occurrences of southern lynchings with language that described violence against African Americans in lurid detail."[25] Yet Black spectators might have been a little less surprised by the Keeper's lack of affect. As the theater historian Koritha Mitchell argues in *Living with Lynching,* by the 1930s, African Americans had spent the past forty years using plays about lynching to survive white violence.[26] To some, the Keeper's detachment might have been a steadfast refusal to satisfy white appetites for Black suffering. Indeed, it might have been a strategic use of deadpan, an aesthetic, as Tina Post shows, that Black performers used to withhold expression from white spectators in the early twentieth century.[27]

The Keeper's cool accounting advances the theme of deferral. Satirizing the hyper-awareness of time typical of the news, the Keeper marks calendrical time not with dates but with lynchings. "Well—" he takes stock, "thirteen new members for the year." For the Keeper, lynchings are what mark the passage of time. When he does need to note the date, he asks the Loudspeaker (111). As a mythical afterlife, Lynchotopia is out of place in a conventional news story, and out of time. Lynchotopia is anachronistic, in the sense of being in the wrong time, and in the sense of being outside of time. As such, it contrasts with Euro-American chronological realism that announces dates and adheres to sequence. Yet this scene is perhaps the least ambiguous in the whole play: it presents deferral, unequivocally, as a product of social interactions; it confronts audiences (particularly white liberal audiences) with the harsh realities of who is waiting and who is withholding, who is stalling and whose rights are being deferred. If the news is characteristically timely and immediate, then Lynchotopia, a component of a Living Newspaper that is rife with calendars and ledgers but fundamentally atemporal, shows how the news fails those it excludes or renders abject. If the news claims to describe the present, it does so by deferring some versions of it at the expense of others. Lynchotopia lampoons the very claims to immediacy and shared time that white journalists had enshrined. It exposes the capacity of the news for routinized deferral.

Indeed, the Keeper's only connection to the outside world is the speaker on his desk, described in the text as a "microphone." It broadcasts the cries of white lynch mobs, which prompt the Keeper to prepare for new arrivals in Lynchotopia by opening his ledger. A man named Wesley Johnson arrives, mauled and in tattered clothes, and recounts his murder by one hundred men in Abbeville, Alabama. The microphone gives supplemental details. The Keeper announces his plan to hold a party since Johnson is the first of the year. Other men who have been lynched arrive as the Keeper works frantically to keep up and to assess which state is winning "the race." A buzzer adds to the scene's game-show-like tone; lynching victims become "contestants." Finally, the year comes to an end and the Keeper prepares for the New Year's Eve review, which culminates in an award for the "most brutal lynching" (114). He warns eager "contestants" that the standard has been set by Claude Neal, a twenty-three-year-old farm worker who was brought across state lines from Alabama to be lynched in 1934 at the courthouse square of Marianna, Florida.

Yet, once again defying white appetites for Black abjection, the device of Lynchotopia means that Neal is able tell his own story, even though he has been murdered. And the instructions for staging are pointedly subdued. Neal's lynching itself occurs in shadow, behind a screen. The words "EQUAL JUSTICE UNDER THE LAW" appear in juxtaposition with the action onstage. Rather than focusing on Neal's mutilation, the scene shifts quickly to a young child:

> VOICE OF CHILD: Oh, Mama—mama—let me see—I want to see.
>
> MOTHER: Oh, alright, I'll have to lift you (to one side is seen silhouette of woman holding child over her shoulders).
>
> LOUDSPEAKER (softly): Her first lynching.
>
> BLACKOUT. (116)

In this way, the scene quickly shifts from Claude's brutalization to white complicity, denying the ideology of racial innocence as the white girl relishes a scene of dehumanization.[28]

Back in Lynchotopia, the other lynching victims quickly admit "defeat" by Neal's horrific murder. This presentation of lynching as competition adds to the scene's surreal detachment, its insistence on measuring, comparing, and evaluating. But it also refuses the appeals for sympathy that white liberal audiences might expect. Indeed, in the next scene the ghosts of Lynchotopia are raucous as they visit the US Senate. Senator Robert Wagner has introduced an anti-lynching bill (the Costigan-Wagner Bill), but the ghosts are far from somber: "Lights go up on [the] Senate scene, where a filibuster [is underway]. Off to one side we see the nine lynch victims in typical holiday mood—chewing gum, eating popcorn, munching an apple, or smoking a cigar, they are ghosts of course, and unobserved." A note reads that Hill and Silvera planned to "write in antics of ghosts in courtroom" (117). The scene bears parallels to *1935*, where the "Court of Public Opinion" snacks on hot dogs while taking in news of the day (chapter 2). *1935*'s "Court of Public Opinion," all appearing to be white in production photos, takes no interest in the trial of an alleged rapist, reports of Nazi activity, or the shooting of Governor Huey Long. In the context of *1935*, this delinquent jury conveys a blunt indictment of public dysfunction; it represents a public that cannot serve its democratic purpose. In *Liberty Deferred*, the ghostly witnesses are certainly defying the seriousness of what they are watching, but the message is more complex. These witnesses have already been affected by what they see: anti-lynching legislation, and more specifically its absence. Their political influence has already been limited by white supremacy, and by their invisibility as ghosts. But as the stage directions imply, their invisibility is also radically permissive; it allows them to act as they please, free from white surveillance. Past and present collide here to challenge the present-tenseness of white journalistic time. In this Afro-modernist news story, current events are witnessed by the restless victims of white terrorism.[29]

## AN UNEASY CALL TO ACTION

After complicating journalistic time and its imagined constituents, *Liberty Deferred* culminates, like all Living Newspapers, in a call to action. Unlike the calls to action that punctuated the NYLN, however, this one draws attention to the precarious coalition that it will require. The play's final scene unfolds at the second annual National Negro Congress (NNC) in Philadelphia. In the preceding scene, the estranged couple Ted and Linda have reunited at a train station after parting ways so Linda could teach in Baltimore. Ted learns that Linda has quit her job because the pay for Black teachers is prohibitively low; Linda learns that Ted is barely making ends meet as a porter. Both agree that something must be done, exposing the urgent stakes behind the NNC, a Communist Party affiliate that fought for Black liberation between 1936 and 1946. As Ted and Linda speak, African Americans stream by with their luggage on their way to Philadelphia.

At the congress, however, Black organizers meet powerful opposition in a disembodied voice that reveals itself to be "the voice of White America." It asserts that legislation cannot rectify inequality because African Americans are "in the unfortunate position of the legal and social nondescript." The NNC's Speaker briefly argues with the disembodied Voice, exposing its antidemocratic principles and its tired rhetoric before asserting: "We came here for action . . . not words. We have heard enough." But the Voice is persistent and loquacious. It seeks desperately to keep the conversation going:

> VOICE:  Wait. . . . Your tragic isolation and helpness [*sic*] in our social order is due to your undying devotion to equality while persistently ignoring the matter of capacity. Equality weakens men, ignores personal element, eliminates the claim to sympathy and weakens the bond of affection."

The NNC's Speaker and delegates refuse the racist appeal to personal "capacity." Instead, the Speaker asks the Voice to "come out and talk in person." Whereas African American characters have been hyper-visible throughout the play—recall that Ted and Linda first appear in a spotlight, even in the intimate act of slow-dancing—the Voice is completely incognito. His alibi is whiteness; its response to the Speaker's invitation is a simple reiteration that he is "the American white public." The NNC delegates resort to force, crying, "Let's riot him out," and rushing around the stage to find him before the Speaker instructs, "Drag him out." At last the white American public is exposed:

> ALL:  Get him . . . get him . . . don't let him get away
> (Several of the group drag a figure out from behind the enclosure at the top of the steps. The light comes up on the figure. It is Jim Crow.)
> It's Jim Crow . . . It's the ever present viper.
> (136–37)

As chapter 3 demonstrated, critiques of the American public were not out of place in the Living Newspaper. But the charge here is especially subversive. For if *1935*'s public was underachieving, it nonetheless had the potential to organize and take positive political action—something like the group that gathers, focused and unified, at the end of *One-Third of a Nation*. The public of *Liberty Deferred* by contrast, at least the white public, is irredeemable. It is the vicious, singular, and obstinate figure of Jim Crow. The Speaker's suggestion to "reason with him" is quickly overruled; delegates counter that he should be killed. Reaching a compromise, the Speaker and delegates agree to tie him up. They hold him at the top of a staircase.

Here the play directly confronts the "solidarity blues," presenting representatives of US unions—historically white—that support integration:

> TELEGRAPHER: "We have no negroes among our two hundred and fifty members. We all work in broker's offices." I haven't seen why you are interested in this union. But now his riddance makes us feel different. (Points to Jim Crow). (138)

Dockworkers, brewers, and waiters chime in. They empower the Speaker to demand the passage of the anti-lynching bill. Jim Crow protests but then "shrieks in terror" as "the crowd surges at him." (139) Threatened with death, he agrees to pass the anti-lynching bill and to allow equal opportunities in education and the workplace. In the play's final moments, Charles Houston, special counsel to the NAACP, leads a crowd of Black workers and leaders. The crowd sings the Negro National Anthem and calls for liberty. But the play's ending is not completely uplifting. Jim Crow "viciously" cracks his whip as the crowd calls for liberty, a gesture that could signify the continued threat of racial violence or Jim Crow's frustration.[30] Either way he makes a sinister claim to space in the play's final moments. The NYLN's calls to action present unified crowds, speaking up against a common, unseen antagonist. This call to action features a group that acts despite the presence of a violent threat.

In many ways, *Liberty Deferred* is the most complex engagement with journalistic imagination across the Living Newspaper repertoire. It presents competing representatives of the average American, common sense, and public opinion: the protagonists, rather than a single Little Man, are a southern white woman and her northern companion, a Black porter and a teacher; the commonsense perspective comes from a French foreigner, unversed in American racism; the Great American Public is Jim Crow. There is no consensus between these characters on what constitutes the present or its most pressing issues; there is no presumption by the playwrights of a single newsworthy subject.

Nor is there a presumption that the news must convey recent or unfolding events, as quickly as possible, and in adherence to Euro-American realism. *Liberty Deferred* lampoons white-collar journalism and its insistence on "immediacy" by situating a central scene in purgatory, where racial terrorism is dispassionately audited by the Keeper of Records. His charges, the victims of lynching, tell their stories and haunt the chambers of an ineffectual Senate. In Hill and Silvera's newspaper, ghosts sit alongside legislators as makers of the news and constituents of the present. If there is anything like a shared present, as white news media tend to suggest, it is inhabited by the invisible, the terrorized, and the absent as much as it is inhabited by politicians and activists.

Yet even as Hill and Silvera deny the white news' utopian promise of a shared present, they join their counterparts at the NYLN in demanding political action. Their story of Black liberation in the United States culminates at the National Negro Congress, where members of unions and leftist organizations speak out against segregation. Even this scene of triumph and progress, however, is nuanced: while voices rise in the Negro National Anthem, Jim Crow, who remains onstage—restrained, for the moment, by a rope—cracks his whip. The production of the present—and the future—is a contested and dangerous endeavor. With each of these elements, Hill and Silvera adapt Living Newspaper conventions, satirically Signifyin(g) on the Little Man and the Loudspeaker, the Great American Public, the epic presentation of American history, and its culmination in an urgent call for action.

## PRODUCTION DEFERRED

On April 16, 1938, the *New York Age* reported that *Liberty Deferred* would soon be playing at a WPA theater in the city. By June, George Kondolf, New York regional director of the Federal Theatre Project, had indicated that the play would be ready for production in the fall.[31] The play's development, however, was slow—unusually so for a Living Newspaper—and eventually it would arrive at a standstill. While it is unclear who made the final decision not to pursue production, nor even if such a decision was made, it is clear that white FTP leadership and staff commissioned the play and were unhappy with the form it took. The play's protracted development suggests a story of bureaucracy, in its slow, indirect way, stifling the FTP's most provocative Living Newspaper. At the same time, Kate Dossett notes, it also reflects Hill and Silvera's creative vision and their refusal to dilute it.

Emmet Lavery was immediately concerned that the play did not adequately reproduce (white) Living Newspaper techniques; that it underplayed Black success stories and the role of social welfare programs like the FTP; that it too stridently critiqued white spectatorship. At many points in the play's development, Lavery offered suggestions to soften its critique of white Americans and focus on a story of Black triumph that would be more palatable to white audiences. Dossett convincingly argues that "the negotiations which took place between black dramatists and white Federal Theatre administrators over *Liberty Deferred* suggest that black dramatists mastered, critiqued, and parodied white conceptions of theatre."[32] Hill and Silvera accommodated some revisions but maintained their subversive focus on white spectators.

Subsequently, FTP play readers bristled at the script's often satirical tone, which was a challenging departure from *One-Third*'s warm pedantry. Morris Surofsky's play reader report, written in August 1938, argued that the white characters were "superfluous" and "stilted," the uses of (satirical) comedy were inappropriate for the subject matter, and the play overall was "too subjective." These ostensibly formal criticisms reveal non-Black resistance to Black critique. It is telling that Surofsky's first substantive paragraph is loaded with the language of overwhelming disorientation: "[It seemed] as though the writers had for a time lost their perspective and *plunged into a maelstrom* of fact and grabbed whatever they could get hold of to *hurl* at an audience. . . . This over-indulgence in sheer fact would result in a panorama that would serve to *bludgeon an audience* rather than convince it."[33] Surofsky's violent verbs—plunge, hurl, bludgeon—may say more about a non-Black reader's discomfort with encountering the realities of slavery and Jim Crow than they do about the authors' technique. Even more telling, perhaps, is how the script was developed to begin with: under the auspices of the playwriting department, in a process of Black creativity and white supervision. At the NYLN, once topics were approved, they were infused with resources: by 1936, the Unit's key figures had agreed that the form was fundamentally collaborative, and they committed to providing lead dramatists with teams of researchers and assistants (chapter 1). By contrast, after FTP administrators approved Hill and Silvera's theme—albeit tacitly—they never followed through with resources. The two-person team appears to have been solely responsible for the play's research and writing. Hill produced ten pages of bibliography and notes; Silvera produced a thirty-page prospectus for "A History of the Negro in the American Theatre." And in a sense, Silvera and Hill were not only reporters but also sources, given that both were initially assigned to the FTP's Play Bureau to "authenticate" representations of American life. All this suggests that if *Liberty Deferred* appeared to be more "subjective" and less "journalistic" than other Living Newspapers, it was in part because its creators were never afforded a journalistic team or the material resources to produced collaborative, multi-perspectival reporting.

It is telling, too, that even though the NYLN championed processual rigor over objectivity (chapter 1), objectivity here became a major focus of critique. "The play," wrote Surofsky, "should have been written wholly from an objective standpoint."[34] Whether or not intentionally, Surofsky reiterated a familiar refrain that white journalists and critics used to maintain their white collars at the expense of Black journalists and Black journalism. Since the development of objectivity as a standard in the early twentieth century, white journalists had continually asserted that Black and otherwise racialized journalists did not—could not—deploy it, particularly when it came to reporting on race relations.[35] Objectivity was integral to white modern imaginaries: it emerged from the technological and colonial conditions of modernity; it constructed a hegemonic view of modern life by insinuating that citizens could perceive a shared reality; and finally, it enabled and denied access to modernity, rendering old news those views that were located and impassioned.

Hill and Silvera were not swayed by Surofsky's review. They remained determined to have the play produced, and in December 1938, Hill contacted Flanagan herself, passing along a positive script review from the *New Amsterdam News* and suggesting a production in Harlem. Flanagan replied the following week with a promise to read the script, but there is no further correspondence documented.[36] Progress after that appears to have stalled.

Black artists took note and spoke up on behalf of their colleagues. That March, the Negro Arts Committee Federal Arts Council, comprising representatives from the NAACP, the National Negro Congress, the Urban League, and the Brotherhood of Sleeping Car Porters, pointed out that although the script had been "acclaimed as worthwhile for production," it was now "lost in red-tape." It was, they asserted, yet another example of discrimination across the FTP's New York offices. Emmet Lavery continued to propose projects related to Black history but seems to have given up on *Liberty Deferred*.[37]

For the theater scholar Paul Nadler, the failure to produce *Liberty Deferred* reflected the political climate that led to the FTP's closing.[38] There is good reason to believe that FTP administrators feared criticism from New Deal opponents: many who opposed the FTP's stance on workers' rights and public resources would no doubt also decry a play about anti-Black racism, lynching, and white supremacy. This content not only opposed conservative values but also could provide fodder for charges of communism, given the CPUSA's anti-racism work, particularly in the so-called Black Belt. Yet as Dossett argues, the fate of *Liberty Deferred* cannot be fully explained by a fear of Martin Dies and his committee. For one thing, *Liberty Deferred* was already in development before the Dies Committee assembled; for another, as Dossett explains, the NYLN did not always shrink from controversy. It continued to promote *One-Third of a Nation,* for instance, long after the play was publicly disparaged in Congress. FTP staff, including the NYLN's Arthur Arent, vehemently defended *One-Third of a Nation* and refused to make concessions on the basis of conservative critiques. Dossett concludes that if *Liberty Deferred* never made it to production, it was not only because it challenged FTP critics but also because it likely offended the sensibilities of white liberals and progressives.[39] To white leftists, as Iton might say, *Liberty Deferred* was an inconvenient refrain of the solidarity blues.

## BEYOND "RELEVANCE"

Iton's analytic aptly applies to the racial politics at the NYLN. The solidarity blues also draws attention to the discordant time signatures of the New Deal and Jim Crow, two concurrent eras of violently different experiences of the present. It is provocative to consider how *Liberty Deferred* might have developed had it been fully resourced and produced by the FTP. Yet as Dossett argues, the significance of Black radical manuscripts has never been limited to the white institutions that constrained them.[40] As she shows, Black manuscripts galvanized Black performance communities, offering crucial forums for discussion and exchange. Dan Burley, for instance, reviewing the script for the Black-owned *New York Amsterdam News,* called the play "a singularly thought-provoking piece of propaganda and a valuable contribution to Negro literature, whether it reaches the stage or not." A pianist, journalist, and chronicler of Harlem nightlife, Burley was attentive to the dynamics of performance. *Liberty Deferred,* he observed, "does something to the reader by unconsciously placing him in the role of a spectator of reincarnated events on imaginative parade." Hill and Silvera had "mastered" the Living Newspaper technique, interrogating the practice of spectatorship while they dramatized historical events.[41]

*Liberty Deferred* would also make an impression on Arthur Pollock, a white journalist who had reviewed NYLN productions for the *Brooklyn Eagle.* In 1944, six years after the FTP had ended, he referenced *Liberty Deferred* in contrast to an unsuccessful play about Harriet Beecher Stowe at the City Center. Calling up the mission of the NYLN, Pollock noted, "A city theatre can be a kind of cultured newspaper for the citizens for whom it exists." The City Center "could do worse," he went on, "than present a play written some years ago by Abe Hill. . . . If I remember correctly the play is called 'Liberty Deferred.'"[42] It is hard to tell from Pollock's comments whether or not he read the play, but it is notable all the same that he remembered it as an example of what a Living Newspaper could be.

Another legacy of *Liberty Deferred* is evident in Hill and Silvera's radical visions for African American theater. Silvera would not pursue playwriting; a critic's assessment that he was "mediocre" would steer him away.[43] But he would continue to grapple with Black representation, theatrical and historical. In 1939 Silvera published an article in *The Crisis,* the official and widely circulated journal of the NAACP, founded by W. E. B. Du Bois. The article, titled "Still in Blackface," drew on Silvera's research, and no doubt his experience at the FTP. In it, Silvera offered powerful reflections on Black representation in American media: "Just as the surest way to misunderstand a person is to refuse to learn anything about him, so it follows that the surest way to misjudge a person is to learn the wrong things about him." For Silvera, new media like film and radio were partly to blame for teaching white people the wrong things, but theater was the original culprit. "More than any other single factor in American life," he wrote, "has the theatre served to keep alive the misunderstanding and consequent prejudices of the white man toward the Negro."[44]

Accordingly, Silvera imagined a Black theater dedicated to addressing prejudice. Like Flanagan (chapter 3), he would not shy away from theater's propagandistic possibilities:

> The purpose of any Negro Theatre worthy of the name should be to devote itself to the correction of false ideas concerning the Negro. Some may say that this would make for a theatre of propaganda and that as such it would not be real theatre. Nothing is further from the truth for with capable writing, themes well chosen, skillfully executed, propaganda can be coupled with entertainment in so subtle a fashion as to increase its driving force and meaning. The job is with the Negro playwright.[45]

Silvera envisioned a new form of propaganda, one dedicated to undoing the accumulation of Black misrepresentations in white media. For Silvera, historiography would become a lifelong commitment. After thirty-two years with the Tuskegee Airmen, he would publish a book about African American service in the Second World War. He would also publish his FTP research on Black theater as *A Treasury of Early Black Plays*. In a 1987 interview with *Florida Today*, he reflected that with the book, "we seek to contribute in some small measure to a realistic and more accurate perception and conception of the importance of Black Americans to the richness of our nation's heritage."[46]

Hill, too, would use his experience at the FTP to reimagine Black theater. In 1940, the year following the FTP's end, Hill went on to found the American Negro Theatre (ANT). By the time Hill moved on to the ANT, he envisioned a theater that explicitly addressed Black people, rather than the FTP's integrated but white-dominated audiences. He also disavowed the Living Newspaper's key value: timeliness. In an interview with Loften Mitchell he commented: "We [ANT founders] were really trying to reach within ourselves and say that if the theatre as it exists now is not to our liking, we're going to try and make it so. We didn't even use the word relevant at that time. We said meaningful and significant to the people who would in turn support us because we were giving them a lift and projecting the Negro as a real human being."[47] What is the difference between relevant and meaningful? In the context of Hill's statement, it seems to be time. Relevance is a relational term, one that predicates significance on a "point at issue" or a "matter in hand."[48] It suggests repetition—a concept that, as Soyica Diggs Colbert, Douglas A. Jones Jr., and Shane Vogel observe, offers a limited and historically white approach for "explaining what makes (some) performance meaningful in and as time."[49] Relevance was a guiding value for the NYLN, just as it has long been for white journalistic practice. But Hill imagined something different: rather than adherence to tacit norms of relevance for an ill-defined, white-dominated public, meaning and significance for Black communities.

# OUTSIDE AND AFTER THE NYLN

## Reimagining Living Newspapers

Throughout this book, I have sought to re-center the newsroom—as a space, an idea, and a set of practices—in the history of Living Newspapers. In doing so, I have argued that the FTP's Living Newspapers must be seen not in parallel with US newspaper history but in conjunction with it, as provocations, elaborations, and responses to journalistic crisis. The American Newspaper Guild sponsored the New York Living Newspaper, and in turn, the NYLN advanced the ANG's cause by propagating a vision of journalism as white-collar labor. The NYLN helped the ANG to secure labor protections for journalists, but its advocacy was selective. A team led by mostly white men drew on gendered and racialized norms of professionalism to maintain credibility. As a result, the NYLN's conception of public interest—of what was newsworthy and why—was limited from the start, and the Unit overlooked crucial angles of the stories they told.

Although the NYLN replicated some practices from mainstream newsrooms, it reimagined several key components of journalistic integrity. Whereas the Canons of Journalism stipulated independence and impartiality, Living Newspapers integrated fictional devices and explicit calls to action that reflected their New Deal funding. Although FTP administrators like Philip Barber and Hallie Flanagan initially insisted that the plays were objective, over time they embraced a new strategy: one that emphasized the rigors of the NYLN's reporting. Living Newspapers claimed truthfulness, not because they set aside values and commitments but because they reflected the "scrutiny and investigation of a large staff."[1] This additive conception of truth-telling—truth-telling as the achievement of multiple interpretations engaged at multiple phases—was integral to the NYLN's reporting. In all these ways the newsroom was formative to the distinctive shape Living Newspapers took under the auspices of the FTP.

It was by leaving the newsroom behind, however, that Living Newspapers were able to circulate—outside of New York, beyond the FTP, and long after the 1930s. *Liberty Deferred,* as discussed in chapter 4, offers one example. The experience of playwrights Hill and Silvera demonstrates some of the constraints and possibilities that came with creating a Living Newspaper outside the NYLN: on the one hand, they missed out on the resources of an editorial team, and they were left to advocate for their work alone; on the other hand, their independence from the NYLN freed them to critique its overwhelmingly white news sense and to develop a compelling alternative. But Hill and Silvera were not the only FTP workers to create Living Newspapers outside the NYLN. In Cleveland and Hartford, FTP workers made topical revues like *1935.* Philadelphia artists rewrote *One-Third of a Nation* to reflect housing conditions in their city. Elsewhere, artists started from scratch, devising original scripts about flax in Portland and flooding in Cincinnati, dirt in Iowa City, sugar in Denver, and timber in Seattle. Starting in 1937, the National Service Bureau began to work with colleges across the country to explore the use of living newspapers as an educational tool. The conditions that produced these Living Newspapers, in some cases as full productions and in others as preliminary outlines, differed from their counterparts in New York. These differences were not only geographic and cultural but also material and creative; away from the ANG's sizable New York contingent, with different budgets, audiences, and personnel, FTP artists elsewhere did not have access to a dedicated Living Newspaper unit.

Untethered from the newsroom, the circulation of practices and conventions prompted questions about what counted as a Living Newspaper and what did not. In 1938, for instance, the Yale-trained playwright Arnold Sundgaard dramatized the spread of syphilis in Chicago. When the FTP published the script that year, it classified the play not as "A Living Newspaper" but rather as "A History." The following year, FTP New York regional director Philip Barber asserted, "I do not consider this a Living Newspaper nor does the author."[2] Their position was understandable. Sundgaard wrote *Spirochete* without the support of a newsroom, and he himself had no journalistic background. Although he conducted research, he relied heavily on a public health campaign and its roster of experts rather than on original reporting. Yet in many ways *Spirochete* looked and sounded as if it could have come out of the NYLN even if it was made very differently. The play was full of Living Newspaper conventions, including projections, a Loudspeaker, and a sweeping, episodic narrative. It staged an urgent and unresolved problem. With these conventions in mind, perhaps, as well as the continued popularity of *One-Third of a Nation,* FTP marketing staff advertised *Spirochete* as a Living Newspaper when it debuted at the Blackstone Theatre in Chicago. Other regional units followed their lead, advertising *Spirochete* as a Living Newspaper in Boston, Cincinnati, Philadelphia, Portland, and Seattle. Hallie Flanagan, in her memoir, would adopt the classification too, as would several historians of the FTP.

The disagreement about how to classify *Spirochete* is doubly revealing. First, it shows that by 1938, the assignation "Living Newspaper" had weight and significance. Second and relatedly, however, it reveals that the criteria for classification were still undefined. Was a Living Newspaper defined primarily by its creative process or by its conventions?

In the remainder of this concluding chapter, I attend to the implications of this question for the Living Newspaper's legacies outside and after the FTP. First, I analyze a parody, titled *One-Third of a Mitten,* which lampooned Living Newspaper conventions at the height of their popularity. Then I consider a series of new works commissioned by London's Royal Court Theatre during the COVID-19 pandemic. Prompted, like the FTP, by social and economic crisis, *Living Newspaper: A Counter Narrative* raised new questions about who and what should be in the news.

### OUTSIDE THE FTP: EISENBERG AND WILLIAMS'S *ONE-THIRD OF A MITTEN*

In the same year that Sundgaard wrote *Spirochete,* while *One-Third of a Nation* continued to draw large audiences, and Hill and Silvera struggled to get *Liberty Deferred* produced, Emmanuel Eisenberg and Jay Williams wrote a "hobble-dehoy take-off" of *One-Third of a Nation.*[3] Like *Liberty Deferred, One-Third of a Mitten* lampooned NYLN conventions, but to very different ends: whereas Hill and Silvera Signified on Living Newspaper conventions to advocate racial justice, *One-Third of a Mitten* was an outright parody, the main substance of which was the Living Newspaper form.

Playfully critiquing Living Newspaper conventions, *One-Third of a Mitten* was written by and for audiences who sympathized with the NYLN's commitments. Writers Eisenberg and Williams were active in US workers' theaters, and their sketch debuted for the Theatre Arts Committee's cabaret before it was added to the Ladies Garment Workers Union's revue *Pins and Needles.* The Theatre Arts Committee, as the historian Michael Denning explains, was a "Popular Front alliance of film, theater, and radio entertainers." It produced magazines, recordings, and radio shows as well as its weekly cabaret. Former NYLN director Joseph Losey noted that "Cabaret TAC" never "came near the

German political cabaret of the late 1920s because we didn't have that kind of sophistication or experience. But it was a tremendously vital thing."[4] Cabaret TAC offered an ideal audience for Living Newspaper parody, an audience familiar with the form and attentive to its possibilities.

*One-Third of a Mitten* achieved its comedic effect by compressing a typical Living Newspaper narrative. In a version of the script from March 1939, Living Newspaper conventions appear without context, in rapid-fire succession. The sketch begins abruptly with the Little Man. "Why can't I get a pair of kid gloves?" he asks. A voice, caricaturing the Loudspeaker, immediately responds with a condescending affirmation: "A very intelligent question. Let's begin at the beginning. The year of 1634." No sooner have the Little Man and the Loudspeaker been hastily established than the next convention follows: a whirlwind history. A man introducing himself as Elbert W. Neemish states that he sold 440 tons of sheep to a buyer at a high price: "Any damn fool can see I made a profit." Further investigation hardly seems necessary, yet the narrative lurches along. "Sign bearers in rotation" present a dizzying array of dates and locations, mimicking the episodic dramaturgy of Living Newspapers' epic roots. "Detroit 1911, Philadelphia 1852! Baton Rouge 1776! Winnepassaukee, 1864!" The sequence is forceful but arbitrary, a point that is reinforced when the Little Man jumps in with a date and location that turn out to be his birthday and hometown. Although the interjection is incongruous, the Little Man turns out to be important. His wife reveals that her husband is in fact "president of the kid-glove monopoly," hardly a representative of the average American.[5]

*One-Third of a Mitten* speeds to its cacophonous finale. When the Little Man's wife insists that her husband return home for dinner, the Voice is bereft. He sputters, "But—my dear lady, do you realize that from 1848 to 1862—"[6] Not knowing how to respond, the Loudspeaker is left speechless. Whereas the mixed promotions for *Spirochete* raised the question of whether, without a newsroom, a Living Newspaper could be made by conventions alone, *One-Third of a Mitten* issues a caution about the limits of genre. It shows how, as conventions harden over time and use, they become *too* replicable, too rigid. As the communication scholar Robert Hariman writes of parody, "When language is placed beside itself, limits are exposed." Parody works, Hariman argues, by critiquing the "inelasticity" of its object. The Voice in *One-Third of a Mitten,* unable to adjust his comments to his interlocutor, is a perfect example.[7] Unfortunately for him, the Little Man's Wife is even more impatient than her counterpart in *One-Third of a Nation.* "Look Mister," she interrupts, "this is 1939, it's 9 P.M., it's raining like hell and his dinner is getting cold—Come on home!" Rejecting the Loudspeaker's attempt to set the scene, the Wife causes chaos onstage. The final stage directions for *One-Third of a Mitten* read: "ALL members of the cast come in a line from both sides and start to repeat their own perticular [*sic*] lines. All sorts of confusion as the LOUDSPEAKER blares out dates. / BLACKOUT."[8] This version of the Living Newspaper is overtaken by a cacophony of talk, confusion, and undifferentiated noise—the very problems of mass-mediated news that the NYLN aimed to address.

Recognizable but ineffectual, the Loudspeaker is demoted from convention to cliché—and also, simultaneously, to gimmick. Whereas "cliché" describes simply a too familiar form, the gimmick invokes ways of working and modes of production. The cultural historian Sianne Ngai defines the gimmick as a "labor-saving device," a characterization that resonates with Living Newspapers' mission to make and reimagine journalistic labor.[9] As the NYLN experimented with new ways to make news, the Loudspeaker, the Little Man, and other features emerged not only as theatrical conventions but also as techniques of reporting and ultimately, as "labor-saving devices." These techniques offered efficient ways to convey information and to elicit engagement. They were thus undeniably useful to both news-makers and spectators. Indeed, FTP designer Howard Bay spoke appreciatively of Arthur Arent's talent for producing "gimmicks." He marveled, as noted in chapter 1: "Arthur [Arent] had a facility of getting . . . just the proper gimmick for each episode . . . and twisting it. . . . Everybody else [wrote] rather dull stuff. . . . The little man in *Power* and the ventriloquist bit with Wilkie [also in *Power*] and . . . all those gimmicks were building blocks. You'd think of concrete things that would—or a little burlesque that you'd do. Nobody else had that facility."[10]

For Bay, Arent's gimmicks were an important contribution to the Unit. They were dramaturgical "building blocks" that held audiences' interest—but they were also expedient. They eased the work of the NYLN's news-makers—saving labor, as Ngai might say—because they were perfectly suited to the scene at hand but flexible enough to be "twisted." Over time, across the NYLN repertoire, they became consolidated as expedient approaches to journalistic problems—as surprising ways to interpellate political communities, to elicit informed participation, to convey complex information while maintaining interest, to produce a communal "present" without making the future appear inevitable.

It is not altogether surprising that Bay invoked the gimmick with reverence. As Ngai notes, the gimmick is historically and etymologically connected to magic, and like magic, it can evoke wonder.[11] It tends, however, to lace wonder with suspicion—and even annoyance. Labor-saving devices irritate spectators because they are always, in some sense, too good to be true. In a capitalist society, where labor, time, and value are entangled, subjects cannot help but distrust anything that promises to save labor while retaining value.[12]

*One-Third of a Mitten* playfully depicts the Living Newspaper as a journalism of gimmicks. It renders the Loudspeaker, with its promise of clear and credible explanations, as babbling and ultimately speechless. The Little Man, with his promise of universal representation, turns out to be a wealthy member of the elite, and the "problem" he wants to solve is trivial. Inevitably, the investigation that follows is not reasoned and deliberative but chaotic and illogical.

By addressing news consumers in novel and surprising ways, Living Newspapers had the potential to evoke awe and wonder. But as their features became increasingly familiar, and thus increasingly efficient, they were also bound to become annoying. As a repository of theatrical conventions and journalistic gimmicks, Living Newspapers enjoyed a popularity that could undermine their capacity to surprise their spectators and elicit novel modes of engagement with news.

### AFTER THE FTP: *LIVING NEWSPAPER: A COUNTER NARRATIVE*

It was not, however, sympathetic critiques from the likes of Eisenberg and Williams that brought down the NYLN. Rather it was conservative critics who called for the FTP's defunding. On June 30, 1939, an act of Congress would dismantle the FTP. Neither Hallie Flanagan nor other FTP leadership could convince the Dies Committee that Living Newspapers were in fact "propaganda for democracy," nor could they quell broader suspicions of the FTP's communist leanings. The committee's mandate to investigate "the extent, character, and object of un-American propaganda activities in the United States" led to the subpoenaing and questioning of FTP staff. The committee, comprising a coalition of Republicans and southern Democrats, succeeded in closing down the FTP. If, as the theater historian Christopher Balme has suggested, censorship is a fairly reliable litmus test for theater's resonance in the public sphere, then the FTP's dismantling by the Dies Committee was a testament to the political significance of the Living Newspaper, which was its primary target.[13] As Arnold Goldman notes, however, the Dies Committee was not the only source of the Living Newspaper Unit's instability in its final years. Arthur Arent had left the Unit in 1938, when he received a Guggenheim Award to travel to Europe and write a Living Newspaper about war.[14] Even Living Newspaper personnel, Arent's move suggests, were turning away from domestic issues and toward perceived threats abroad.

After the FTP closed, the resources needed to staff a newsroom were out of the question for most theater-makers. FTP personnel would continue to explore the Living Newspaper form but worked in relative independence. *The Medicine Show,* which debuted in April 1940 at the New Yorker Theatre, was the work of only two dramatists, Hoffman Hayes and Oscar Saul. $E=MC^2$: *A Living Newspaper about the Atomic Age,* produced in 1948 at the ANT Experimental Series in New York City, was the work of Hallie Flanagan, with help from Sylvia Gassel and Day Tuttle.[15] In a way, then, *Spirochete* and *Mitten,* in their focus on Living Newspaper conventions, predicted a lineage of Living Newspapers after the 1930s. While the newsroom had been crucial in developing the FTP's distinctive brand of the form—sweeping, heavily referenced productions that were very different from their precursors in Europe—it receded in importance, just as it had when it moved outside of New York.

Put another way, although Living Newspapers were profoundly and decisively shaped by their founding institution, it was their formal conventions that allowed them to circulate and survive. It is not surprising that Living Newspapers have often persisted by way of their conventions and not their processes. The funding and infrastructure of the FTP has not been reproduced, though Elizabeth Osborne makes a strong case for a twenty-first-century Federal Theatre Project.[16] The formative collaborations between artists and journalists, catalyzed by white-collar coalition, is also, in many ways, a thing of the past. And of course the conditions of news-making have changed too, economically, technologically, socially, and politically.

Even as Living Newspapers have been dislocated from the newsroom, for better or for worse, they have nonetheless raised important questions about institutions and practices, and who news—and theater—leaves out. For example, in Illinois Humanities' 2014 Living Newspaper *Shelter/Chicago,* a key scene featured actors standing before a projection of the Preamble to the US Constitution—a mise-en-scène that directly cited the NYLN's *Triple-A Plowed Under.*[17] Perhaps more intriguingly, however, *Shelter/Chicago* was written in large part by unhoused Chicagoans, thus following the NYLN in employing unconventional news-makers.

Six years later, amid the UK's COVID-19 lockdowns, London's Royal Court Theatre staged its own series of living newspapers. It employed over three hundred freelancers and the full complement of Royal Court staff. Explicitly billed as a "Counter Narrative," it centered queer, racialized, and emerging artists. Importantly, *Living Newspaper*'s aims were not explicitly journalistic. "We never commission to a brief," commented the Royal Court's artistic director, Vicky Featherstone. [18] Assigning stories in the vein of a managing editor, she worried, would prevent artists from saying what they needed to say. Instead she envisioned a process that freed them to use, adapt, or ignore current events and journalistic norms.

In each of the Royal Court's contemporary living newspapers there was journalistic input, but it was more unidirectional and more syncopated than it was at the NYLN: dramatists pulled source material from the news, but they did not share a newsroom, a managing editor, or a co-evolving news sense predicated on journalistic norms. Despite these factors—or perhaps because of them—*Living Newspaper* deeply engaged journalistic imagination.

Featherstone recalled in an interview the discussions among *Living Newspaper: A Counter Narrative* playwrights: "They said things like, 'Surely, whatever we write is the news. We're writers. Who dictates what the news is? Who owns it?' They talked a lot about—because of the diversity of our writers—who chooses what we see? Who edits? Who's in control of that? How do you enable people to look into the gaps, where things aren't written, to think for themselves?"[19] The Court's writers, like the NYLN, drew attention to who and what mainstream news outlets represent, and how.

These discussions were palpable, if subtle, in production. In a segment called "The Blank Space," playwright Ryan Calais Cameron carved out a quiet space to mourn Oluwatoyin Salau, a Nigeran American Black Lives Matter activist who was murdered earlier that year in Tallahassee, Florida. In doing so, Cameron challenged news outlets to report on anti-Black violence without reiterating the white supremacist culture that enables it. How might such reporting, "The Blank Space" asked, center the people living in fear of racist violence, and the families of victims? How might news create space for retrospection and mourning?[20]

Taking on a different though interrelated issue, in his "weather report" segment, playwright Chris Thorpe challenged viewers to reckon with climate change. Titled "Always Maybe the Last Time," it was set on an abandoned beach. The only human presence was the voice of a woman resounding in an empty room. Instead of a chirpy prediction of afternoon showers, she offered a sobering confrontation with mortality and extinction. "Maybe the best way we've got to prepare for all this going," narrated Jasmine Lee-Jones, "is to act like it's already gone."[21]

"The Blank Space" and "Always Maybe the Last Time" addressed a problem in common: the problem of reporting on issues that are cataclysmic but so pervasive that mainstream news often renders them as routine or even mundane. The familiarity of news can exacerbate this issue; the banality of scrolling through a news feed or tuning in to a podcast can numb us, as news consumers, to what we hear and see. If news literacy is needed, as many communication scholars have argued, to distinguish fact from fiction, then journalistic imagination is needed to assess how values accrue around some facts and not around others. Where proponents of news literacy, grounded in social-scientific approaches, might see imagination as ephemeral and abstract, theater artists and scholars see it as the material of social practices and lived experiences, readily available for analysis.

The news shares with performance the peculiar status of being defined, alternately, by its everydayness and its spectacularity, by continuity and rupture. In this context, experimentation can be deeply generative; the repertoires it produces are worthy of attention. In reimagining conventions and institutions, the NYLN and its legacies have created possibilities for making news otherwise. In cultivating journalistic imagination, Living Newspapers attune us anew to the present we might make together.

# NOTES



1   "The Living Newspapers Festival—The Artistic Home—Chicago," *Theatre in Chicago,*
    accessed September 30, 2020, https://www.theatreinchicago.com/the-living-newspapers
    -festival/3900/; "Injunction Granted," Metropolitan Playhouse, accessed June 4, 2015,
    http://metropolitanplayhouse.org/injunctiongranted; "Living Newspaper: A Counter
    Narrative," Royal Court Theatre, accessed June 7, 2022, https://royalcourttheatre.com
    /home/livingnewspaper.

2   While this issue is not the focus of this book, I have benefited enormously from opportunities
    to witness Living Newspapers over the years: not only in the theater but also in a nightclub, in
    a museum, and of course in classrooms. In 2014, Jackalope Theatre's then–artistic director AJ
    Ware brought the company's annual Living Newspaper Festival to Northwestern University's
    Block Museum. The performances, which featured Northwestern acting students, comple-
    mented John Murphy's exhibition *The Left Front: Radical Art in the Red Decade.* That same year
    I attended *Shelter/Chicago,* a Living Newspaper presented by Chicago's Living News Project, in
    conjunction with the Illinois Humanities Council. Columbia College lecturer Lisa DiFranza
    had collaborated with staff and residents at Cornerstone Community Outreach to create an
    original play about homelessness in Chicago. In 2018 I witnessed *The Paper Machete,* a weekly
    "live magazine" hosted at Chicago's historic Green Mill nightclub.

3   I define mainstream newspapers as commercial, professional, politically conservative, and
    making use of syndicates and wire services. In doing so, I follow the historian David Welky,
    who writes: "Mainstream print culture consists of written material that has a national reach.
    It was distributed across the United States or, in the case of newspapers, assumed a national
    tone through the use of syndicates and wire services. It was a product of profit-driven corpo-
    rations that wanted to appeal to the largest possible audience within a target demographic."
    Mainstream newspapers, he notes, were decidedly apart from the leftist cultural front, though
    they sometimes made use of cultural front advocates and ideas. David Welky, *Everything Was
    Better in America: Print Culture in the Great Depression* (Champaign: University of Illinois
    Press, 2010), 4.

4   Richard Iton, *Solidarity Blues: Race, Culture, and the American Left* (Chapel Hill: University
    of North Carolina Press, 2000).

5   Welky, *Everything Was Better in America,* 67.

6   John Nerone, "Does Journalism History Matter?" *American Journalism* 28, no. 4 (October
    2011): 7–27; "About," *Journalism History,* August 20, 2018.

7   Jonas A. Barish, *The Antitheatrical Prejudice* (Berkeley: University of California Press, 1985).

8   For a history of *New Theatre Review* and an analysis of its editorial positions, see Eleazer Lecky,
    "New Theatre," *Modern Drama,* April 5, 2013.

9   Morris Watson, "The Living Newspaper," *New Theatre* 3 (1936): 6.

10  John Nerone, "Journalism's Crisis of Hegemony," *Javnost—The Public* 22, no. 4 (October 2,
    2015): 321.

11  Raymond Fielding, *The American Newsreel: A Complete History, 1911–1967,* 2nd ed. (Jefferson,
    NC: McFarland & Co., 2011). For histories of mass media in the United States in the 1920s
    and 1930s, see also Joseph Clark, *News Parade: The American Newsreel and the World as Spectacle*
    (Minneapolis: University of Minnesota Press, 2020); Cara A. Finnegan, *Picturing Poverty: Print
    Culture and FSA Photographs* (Washington, DC: Smithsonian Institution Press, 2003); David
    Goodman, *Radio's Civic Ambition: American Broadcasting and Democracy in the 1930s* (New York:
    Oxford University Press, 2011); Jason Loviglio, *Radio's Intimate Public: Network Broadcasting
    and Mass-Mediated Democracy* (Minneapolis: University of Minnesota Press, 2005).

12 William Stott, *Documentary Expression and Thirties America* (Chicago: University of Chicago Press, 1986), 14. Stott includes a brief discussion of the FTP's Living Newspapers as part of the documentary movement.

13 Mary E. Stuckey, "FDR, the Rhetoric of Vision, and the Creation of a National Synoptic State," *Quarterly Journal of Speech* 98, no. 3 (August 1, 2012): 297–319. See also Stott, *Documentary Expression and Thirties America*.

14 Vanessa Beasley and Deborah Smith-Howell, "No Ordinary Rhetorical President: FDR's Speech-Making and Leadership, 1933–1945," in *American Rhetoric in the New Deal Era, 1932–1945: A Rhetorical History of the United States*, ed. Thomas Benson, vol. 7 (Lansing, MI: Michigan State University Press), 8.

15 US Bureau of the Census, *Historical Statistics of the United States: Colonial Times to 1957* (Washington, DC: Government Printing Office, 1960).

16 Following Mark Hampton's gloss of a cultural-history approach to journalism studies, I define journalists as those who self-identify as such. Mark Hampton and Martin Conboy, "Journalism History—A Debate," *Journalism Studies* 15, no. 2 (2014): 154.

17 Will Mari, *The American Newsroom: A History, 1920–1960* (Columbia: University of Missouri Press, 2021), 55.

18 For more on how newspaper publishers met the encroachment of radio and newsreel, see Lynn D. Gordon, "Why Dorothy Thompson Lost Her Job: Political Columnists and the Press Wars of the 1930s and 1940s," *History of Education Quarterly* 34, no. 3 (Autumn 1994): 281–303.

19 Sheila M. Webb, "Creating *Life:* America's Most Potent Editorial Force," *Journalism & Communication Monographs* 18, no. 2 (2016): 60–62.

20 Quoted in Zelizer, "Words against Images," 141; Mari, *The American Newsroom*, 41.

21 Webb, "Creating *Life*," 55.

22 Quoted in Webb, "Creating *Life*," 56.

23 Mari, *The American Newsroom*, 30.

24 Finnegan, *Picturing Poverty*, xi.

25 Michael Schudson, "The Objectivity Norm in American Journalism*," *Journalism* 2, no. 2 (August 1, 2001): 149–70.

26 Harvey Saalberg, "The Canons of Journalism: A 50-Year Perspective," *Journalism Quarterly* 50, no. 4 (1973): 731; Schudson, "The Objectivity Norm in American Journalism*."

27 Associated Press, "A Guide for Filing Editors," 1930, Associated Press Corporate Archives, 1, accessed May 2, 2022, https://www.apstylebook.com/archived_stylebooks.

28 Saalberg, "The Canons of Journalism," 832; Schudson, "The Objectivity Norm in American Journalism*."

29 Jean Folkerts, "History of Journalism Education," *Journalism & Communication Monographs* 16, no. 4 (December 1, 2014): 235, 239.

30 Quoted in Mari, *The American Newsroom*, 8.

31 Fred Carroll, *Race News: Black Journalists and the Fight for Racial Justice in the Twentieth Century* (Champaign: University of Illinois Press, 2017), 8.

32 Mari, *The American Newsroom*, 17.

33 LaShawn Harris, "Marvel Cooke: Investigative Journalist, Communist, and Black Radical Subject," *Journal for the Study of Radicalism* 6, no. 2 (Fall 2012): 91–126.

34 D'Weston Haywood, *Let Us Make Men: The Twentieth-Century Black Press and a Manly Vision for Racial Advancement* (Chapel Hill: University of North Carolina Press, 2018).

35 Kim Gallon, *Pleasure in the News: African American Readership and Sexuality in the Black Press* (Champaign: University of Illinois Press, 2020), 38.

36 Bonnie Brennen, "Newsworkers during the Interwar Era: A Critique of Traditional Media History," *Communication Quarterly* 43, no. 2 (March 1995): 205.

37 Paul Alfred Pratte, *Gods within the Machine: A History of the American Society of Newspaper Editors, 1923–1993* (Westport, CT: Greenwood Publishing Group, 1995), 52, 51, 55.

38 Ishbel Ross, *Ladies of the Press: The Story of Women in Journalism by an Insider* (New York: Harper & Brothers, 1936), 6.

39 Schudson, "The Objectivity Norm in American Journalism*," 165, 159.

40 Schudson, "The Objectivity Norm in American Journalism*," 164.

41 Gordon, "Why Dorothy Thompson Lost Her Job," 296.

42 Mari, *The American Newsroom*, 118.

43  Jean Marie Lutes, *Front Page Girls: Women Journalists in American Culture and Fiction, 1880–1930* (Ithaca: Cornell University Press, 2006); Jean Marie Lutes, "Sob Sisterhood Revisited," *American Literary History* 15, no. 3 (2003): 504–32; Ida B. Wells, *Crusade for Justice: The Autobiography of Ida B. Wells* (Chicago: University of Chicago Press, 2013).

44  Deborah Chambers, Linda Steiner, and Carole Fleming, *Women and Journalism* (New York: Routledge, 2004), 24.

45  Carroll, *Race News*, 8.

46  Gerald Horne, *The Rise and Fall of the Associated Negro Press: Claude Barnett's Pan-African News and the Jim Crow Paradox* (Urbana: University of Illinois Press, 2017), 5, 13.

47  Welky, *Everything Was Better in America*, 11.

48  Welky, *Everything Was Better in America*, 18–19.

49  Welky, *Everything Was Better in America*, 21–22, 26.

50  Helen Fordham, "Subversive Voices: George Seldes and Mid-Twentieth-Century Muckraking," *American Journalism* 33, no. 4 (October 1, 2016): 435.

51  Ida B. Wells-Barnett, *Southern Horrors: Lynch Law In All Its Phases* (New York: The New York Age Print, 1892).

52  Carroll, *Race News*, 26.

53  On the Great Migration's influence on major Black publications, especially *The Crisis* and *The Defender*, see Haywood, *Let Us Make Men*, 28.

54  Upton Sinclair, *The Jungle* (New York: Grosset & Dunlap, 1906), 306; Upton Sinclair, *The Brass Check: A Study of American Journalism* (Pasadena, CA, 1920).

55  Ida M. Tarbell, *All in the Day's Work: An Autobiography* (New York: Macmillan Company, 1939), 298–99.

56  Fordham, "Subversive Voices," 431, 429.

57  Nerone, "Does Journalism History Matter?," 9.

58  George Gallup and Claude Robinson, "Institute of Public Opinion—Surveys, 1935–8," *Public Opinion Quarterly* 2, no. 3 (1938): 373–98.

59  Sarah Elizabeth Igo, *The Averaged American: Surveys, Citizens, and the Making of a Mass Public* (Cambridge: Harvard University Press, 2007), 21.

60  For a history of the Frankfurt School of social theory, see Martin Jay, *The Dialectical Imagination: A History of the Frankfurt School and the Institute of Social Research, 1923–1950* (Berkeley: University of California Press, 1996).

61  Laura Browder, *Rousing the Nation: Radical Culture in Depression America* (Amherst: University of Massachusetts Press, 1998), 15–67, 68–88, 42, 7, 6. In addition to compelling analyses of Dos Passos, Farrell, and Josephine Herbst, Browder also offers an insightful treatment of the FTP's Living Newspapers as "radical cultural work," 117–55. Horace McCoy, *They Shoot Horses, Don't They?* (Toronto: McClelland & Stewart, 2017).

62  James W. Carey, *Communication as Culture: Essays on Media and Society*, rev. ed. (New York: Routledge, 2008), 5.

63  Richard Schechner, *Between Theater and Anthropology* (Philadelphia: University of Pennsylvania Press, 1985), 36.

64  Stuart Cosgrove, "The Living Newspaper: History, Production and Form" (PhD diss., University of Hull, 1982). Cosgrove subsequently contributed to a coauthored book, republished as Raphael Samuel, Ewan MacColl, and Stuart Cosgrove, *Routledge Revivals: Theatres of the Left, 1880–1935: Workers' Theatre Movements in Britain and America* (1985; New York: Routledge, 2016).

65  Robert Leach, *Makers of Modern Theatre: An Introduction*, 1st ed. (New York: Routledge, 2004), 3.

66  František Deák, "'Blue Blouse' (1923–1928)," *The Drama Review* 17, no. 1 (March 1973): 40; Robert F. Crane, "From Kamchatka to Georgia: The Blue Blouse Movement and Early Soviet Spatial Practice" (PhD diss., University of Pittsburgh, 2013), 11. On other points of contact between European and American Living Newspapers, see Rania Karoula, *The Federal Theatre Project, 1935–1939: Engagement and Experimentation* (Edinburgh: Edinburgh University Press, 2020).

67  Crane, "From Kamchatka to Georgia."

68  Moscow Proletkult, "The Dramatization of a Living Newspaper," trans. Anastasia Lesnikova, *Amateur and Proletarian Theatre in Post-Revolutionary Russia: Primary Sources*, ed. Stefan Aquilina (London: Methuen Drama, 2021), 167, 168.

69  Crane, "From Kamchatka to Georgia," 44.

70  Crane, "From Kamchatka to Georgia," 2, 121.

71  Crane, "From Kamchatka to Georgia," 47.

72  C. D. Innes, *Erwin Piscator's Political Theatre: The Development of Modern German Drama* (Cambridge: Cambridge University Press 1972), 193; Katherine Bliss Eaton, *The Theater of Meyerhold and Brecht,* (Westport, CT: Greenwood Press, 1985), 13.

73  Fredric Jameson, *Brecht and Method* (London: Verso, 2000), 2.

74  Erwin Piscator *The Political Theatre*, trans. Hugh Rorrison (London: Methuen, 1980), 74.

75  Piscator, *The Political Theatre*, 74, 76.

76  Piscator, *The Political Theatre*, 92–94.

77  Bertolt Brecht, *Brecht on Theatre: The Development of an Aesthetic,* ed. John Willett (New York: Hill and Wang, 1964), 30.

78  Brecht, *Brecht on Theatre,* 23, 227.

79  Brecht, *Brecht on Theatre,* 44, 9, 97.

80  Quoted in Lynn Mally, "The Americanization of the Soviet Living Newspaper," *Carl Beck Papers in Russian and East European Studies,* no. 1903 (February 2008): 37.

81  Colin Gardner, "The Losey–Moscow Connection: Experimental Soviet Theatre and the Living Newspaper," *New Theatre Quarterly* 30, no. 3 (August 2014): 249–68.

82  Elmer Rice, *Minority Report: An Autobiography* (New York: Simon & Schuster, 1963), 298, 304.

83  Soyica Colbert, *The African American Theatrical Body: Reception, Performance, and the Stage* (Cambridge: Cambridge University Press, 2011), 62, 49. Colbert offers an incisive analysis of *The Star of Ethiopia* in chapter 2 of her book, "Recuperating Black Diasporic History: W. E. B. Du Bois' *The Star of Ethiopia.*" Colbert shows how the pageant figured Ethiopia as a Black woman whose sacrificial death offers new possibilities for African American subjectivity and belonging (48–90).

84  S. E. Wilmer, *Theatre, Society, and the Nation: Staging American Identities*, Cambridge Studies in American Theatre and Drama (Cambridge: Cambridge University Press, 2002), 105.

85  Mally, "The Americanization of the Soviet Living Newspaper," 11.

86  Michael Denning, *The Cultural Front: The Laboring of American Culture in the Twentieth Century* (London: Verso, 1998), 4.

87  Mally, "The Americanization of the Soviet Living Newspaper," 18–20.

88  Hallie Flanagan, *Arena: The History of the Federal Theatre* (New York: B. Blom, 1965), 70.

89  See Arthur Arent, "*The Technique of the Living Newspaper,*" *Theatre Arts Monthly* (November 1938): 820–25; Watson, "The Living Newspaper"; Flanagan, *Arena.*

90  Gerry Cobb, "'Injunction Granted' in Its Times: A Living Newspaper Reappraised," *New Theatre Quarterly* 6, no. 23 (1990): 280.

91  Morgan Y. Himelstein, *Drama Was a Weapon: The Left-Wing Theatre in New York, 1929–1941* (New Brunswick: Rutgers University Press, 1964); Cosgrove, "The Living Newspaper"; Gerald Rabkin, *Drama and Commitment: Politics in the American Theatre of the Thirties* (Bloomington: Indiana University Press, 1964); Karen Malpede Taylor, *People's Theatre in Amerika* (New York: Drama Book Specialists, 1972); Jay Williams, *Stage Left* (New York: Charles Scribner, 1974).

92  Arnold Goldman, "Life and Death of the Living Newspaper Unit," *Theatre Quarterly* 3, no. 9 (1973): 69–70.

93  Kathryn Flynn and Richard Polese, *The New Deal: A 75th Anniversary Celebration* (Layton, UT: Gibbs Smith, 2008), 76. For Brown's account, see Lorraine Brown, "A Story Yet to Be Told: The Federal Theatre Research Project," *The Black Scholar* 10, no. 10 (August 1979): 70–78.

94  George Kazacoff, *Dangerous Theatre: The Federal Theatre Project as a Forum for New Plays* (Bloomington, IN: Xlibris, Corp., 2011); Sharon Ann Musher, *Democratic Art: The New Deal's Influence on American Culture* (Chicago: University of Chicago Press, 2015); Susan Quinn, *Furious Improvisation: How the WPA and a Cast of Thousands Made High Art Out of Desperate Times,* reprint ed. (New York: Walker Books, 2009); Elizabeth A. Osborne, *Staging the People: Community and Identity in the Federal Theatre Project* (New York: Palgrave Macmillan, 2011); Barry Witham, *The Federal Theatre Project: A Case Study* (Cambridge: Cambridge University Press, 2003); Cecelia Moore, *The Federal Theatre Project in the American South: The Carolina Playmakers and the Quest for American Drama* (Lanham, MD: Lexington Books, 2017); Karoula, *The Federal Theatre Project;* Ann Folino White, *Plowed Under: Food Policy Protests and Performance in New Deal America* (Bloomington: Indiana University Press, 2014), 227–28.

95 Barbara Melosh, *Engendering Culture: Manhood and Womanhood in New Deal Public Art and Theater* (Washington, DC: Smithsonian Institution Press, 1991).

96 Kate Dossett, *Radical Black Theatre in the New Deal* (Chapel Hill: University of North Carolina Press, 2020); Evelyn Quita Craig, *Black Drama of the Federal Theatre Era: Beyond the Formal Horizons* (Amherst: University of Massachusetts Press, 1980); Paul Nadler, "Liberty Censored: Black Living Newspapers of the Federal Theatre Project," *African American Review* 29, no. 4 (Winter 1995): 615; Rena Fraden, *Blueprints for a Black Federal Theatre* (Cambridge: Cambridge University Press, 1996).

97 "Vernacular political theater," Saal writes, as opposed to epic theater, "seeks to stimulate political action by eliciting the audience's identificatory pleasure in the political." Saal, *New Deal Theater, 39.*

98 Browder, *Rousing the Nation,* 7–8; Saal, *New Deal Theater,* 37.

99 Carey, *Communication as Culture,* 20; Benedict Anderson, *Imagined Communities: Reflections on the Origin and Spread of Nationalism* (New York: Verso, 2006); Michael Schudson, *The Power of News* (Cambridge: Harvard University Press, 1982), 14.

100 Richard Schechner, *Between Theater and Anthropology,* 36.

101 Michael Hanchard, "Afro-Modernity: Temporality, Politics, and the African Diaspora," *Public Culture* 11, no. 1 (January 1999): 245–68.

102 Barbie Zelizer, *What Journalism Could Be* (Malden, MA: Polity Press, 2017), 2.

103 Schudson, *The Power of News,* 96; Richard Keeble, "Introduction: On Journalism, Creativity, and the Imagination," in *The Journalistic Imagination: Literary Journalists from Defoe to Capote to Carter,* ed. Richard Keeble and Sharon Wheeler (Oxford: Routledge, 2007), 1–14; G. Stuart Adam, "The Journalistic Imagination," in *Journalism, Communication, and the Law,* ed. G. Stuart Adam (Scarborough, ON: Prentice Hall, 1976), 4, 19.

104 C. Wright Mills, *The Sociological Imagination* (1959; New York: Oxford University Press, 2000), 5.

105 Gallon, *Pleasure in the News,* 14.


CHAPTER ONE: GETTING A FEEL FOR THE OFFICE

1 On "backstage photos" see: Emily Klein, "'Danger: Men Not Working': Constructing Citizenship with Contingent Labor in the Federal Theatre's Living Newspapers," *Women & Performance: A Journal of Feminist Theory* 23, no. 2 (2013): 193–211; Christin Essin, "An Aesthetic of Backstage Labor," *Theatre Topics* 21, no. 1 (March 2011): 33–48.

2 Morris Watson, "Untitled Speaking Notes," box 1, ANG folder, Morris Watson Papers, Ax 774, University of Oregon Libraries Special Collections and University Archives; Ken J. Ward, "'The Vilest Man in the Newspaper Business': F. G. Bonfils's Case against the *Rocky Mountain News,*" *Journalism History* 45, no. 3 (2019): 270–87; Paul Alfred Pratte, *Gods Within the Machine: A History of the American Society of Newspaper Editors, 1923–1993* (Westport, CT: Greenwood Publishing Group, 1995); Bruce J. Evensen, "Journalism's Struggle over Ethics and Professionalism during America's Jazz Age," *Journalism History* 16, no. 3–4 (1989): 54–63. Watson's notes are not dated but refer to *Triple-A Plowed Under* (1936) as a recent production, and likely come from a speaking tour he gave in 1937, "The White Collar Worker Enters the Labor Movement," January 31–February 12, 1937.

3 Watson, "Untitled Speaking Notes."

4 Watson, "Untitled Speaking Notes."

5 I use "repertoire" here in a broad sense that encompasses a theater company's body of work. It is worth noting, however, that in theater and performance studies, repertoire is a dynamic and contested concept. Tracy C. Davis's scholarship on Victorian performance defines repertoire as the systems that make gestures or "performative tropes" intelligible, and also the processes through which they are sustained. Diana Taylor's scholarship on Latin American performance defines repertoire as embodied practices that transmit and sustain knowledge within communities, and especially among colonized groups. Taylor's definition spotlights the often marginalized practices of non-dominant groups; Davis's definition highlights conventions that constitute a mainstream. Tracy C. Davis, "Nineteenth-Century Repertoire," *Nineteenth-Century Theatre*

*and Film* 36, no. 2 (October 2012): 7; Diana Taylor, *The Archive and the Repertoire: Performing Cultural Memory in the Americas* (Durham: Duke University Press, 2003), 19–33.

6   Philip Glende, "Labor Reporting and Its Critics in the CIO Years," *Journalism & Communication Monographs* 22, no. 1 (March 1, 2020): 13. Rewrite staff were those who wrote articles based on notes, reference materials, or phone calls from reporters in the field. See Will Mari, *The American Newsroom: A History, 1920–1960* (Columbia: University of Missouri Press, 2021), 54.

7   Raymond Williams, *Keywords: A Vocabulary of Culture and Society* (New York: Oxford University Press, 1985), 168.

8   Ric Knowles, *Reading the Material Theatre* (Cambridge: Cambridge University Press, 2004); Shannon Jackson, *Social Works: Performing Art, Supporting Publics* (New York: Routledge, 2011).

9   David Welky, *Everything Was Better in America: Print Culture in the Great Depression* (Champaign: University of Illinois Press, 2010), 11.

10  Daniel J. Leab, *A Union of Individuals: The Formation of the American Newspaper Guild* (New York: Columbia University Press, 1970), 28.

11  Welky, *Everything Was Better in America*, 11.

12  Mari, *The American Newsroom*, 72, 91.

13  Fred Carroll, *Race News: Black Journalists and the Fight for Racial Justice in the Twentieth Century* (Champaign: University of Illinois Press, 2017), 19.

14  Mari, *The American Newsroom*, 203, 205.

15  Leab, *A Union of Individuals*, 35.

16  Mari, *The American Newsroom*, 204.

17  Welky, *Everything Was Better in America*, 23. In the end, Hildy makes good on his promise to marry, but until then, he struggles with a compulsion to give up everything that is "good" for him—job security, high pay, and domestic bliss—for his obsession with news. Protagonists like Hildy Johnson were, in David Welky's words, "moral paradoxes" at best: "one part romantic hero and one part ambulance chaser" (23).

18  Mari, *The American Newsroom*, 8.

19  Morris Watson, "The White Collar Worker Enters the Labor Movement: Lecture Delivered by Morris Watson," February 31, 1937, 2.

20  Watson, "The White Collar Worker Enters the Labor Movement," 4.

21  Leab, *A Union of Individuals*, 40–41.

22  Leab, *A Union of Individuals*, 43, 45.

23  Philip M. Glende, "Trouble on the Right, Trouble on the Left: The Early History of the American Newspaper Guild," *Journalism History* 38, no. 3 (October 2012): 144.

24  Leab, *A Union of Individuals*, 102, 206; Glende, "Trouble on the Right," 144. As Mari notes, New York was home to high-profile organizations and figures in journalism history, but was by no means representative of other metropolitan centers, each of which was shaped by distinctive cultural and economic conditions. Mari, *The American Newsroom*, 10.

25  Glende, "Trouble on the Right," 146, 145.

26  Morris Watson, "The AP, the Guild and Me," January 25, 1969, box 2, Biographical Materials folder, Morris Watson Papers.

27  Leab, *A Union of Individuals*, 176–77.

28  Peter H. Irons, *The New Deal Lawyers* (Princeton: Princeton University Press, 1982), 265. Watson writes that he was fired on November 15, 1935, but Irons dates Watson's firing to October 18.

29  Watson, "The AP, the Guild and Me."

30  "Supreme Court Upholds Wagner," *New York Daily News*, April 13, 1937.

31  "Watson to Continue Guild Activities," *Reading (PA) Times*, April 13, 1937.

32  "Morris Watson Quits AP Position," *York (PA) Daily Record*, May 18, 1937.

33  Lorraine Brown, "Federal Theatre: Melodrama, Social Protest, and Genius," *Quarterly Journal of the Library of Congress* 36, no.1 (Winter 1979): 24.

34  Federal Theatre Project, "Untitled, Projects Submitted to FTP," October 23, 1935, RG 69, box 500, National Archives and Records Administration (NARA), Washington, DC.

35  Hallie Flanagan, *Arena: The History of the Federal Theatre* (New York: B. Blom, 1965), 20.

36  Arthur Arent, "'Ethiopia': The First 'Living Newspaper,'" *Educational Theatre Journal* 20, no. 1 (1968): 16.

37 Howard Bay, interview with John O'Connor, transcribed by Rhoda Durkan, February 21, 1976, box 2, folder 13, WPA Oral Histories, George Mason University Special Collections (WPA-GMU), 30.

38 Norman Lloyd, interview with John O'Connor, transcribed by Rhoda Durkan, January 5, 1976, box 7, folder 11, WPA-GMU, 7.

39 On Hale's career, including her theater criticism, see Susan Henry, "Ruth Hale: A 'Passionate Contender' Caught in a 'Curious Collaboration,'" *Journalism History* 28, no. 1 (April 2002): 2–15.

40 "Guild Sponsors Living Newspaper," playbill for *Triple-A Plowed Under* 1.1, March 21, 1936, box 1057, Library of Congress Federal Theatre Project Collection (LOC-FTP).

41 "Untitled Organizational Overview," n.d., Morris Watson Papers.

42 Douglas McDermott rightly argued for the "problem" as the organizing feature of single-issue Living Newspapers. Douglas McDermott, "The Living Newspaper as a Dramatic Form," *Modern Drama* 8, no. 1 (1965): 82–94.

43 On the history of US pageantry, see David Glassberg, *American Historical Pageantry: The Uses of Tradition in the Early Twentieth Century* (Chapel Hill: University of North Carolina Press, 1990); David Krasner, "'The Pageant Is the Thing': Black Nationalism and *The Star of Ethiopia*," in *A Beautiful Pageant: African American Theatre, Drama, and Performance in the Harlem Renaissance, 1910–1927*, ed. David Krasner (New York: Palgrave Macmillan, 2002), 81–94; Naima Prevots, *American Pageantry: A Movement for Art and Democracy* (Ann Arbor: University of Michigan Press, 1990); Shilarna Stokes, "Playing the Crowd: Mass Pageantry in Europe and the United States, 1905–1935" (PhD diss., Columbia University, 2013).

44 Morris Watson, "Draft 'Foreword to Book of "Living Newspaper" Plays,'" March 17, 1937, Morris Watson Papers.

45 Harold Burris-Meyer recalled Rice's commitment to social significance in an interview with Lorraine Brown. Harold Burris-Meyer, interview with Lorraine Brown, transcribed by Rhoda Durkan, March 14, 1977, WPA-GMU, 9–10.

46 In *Arena*, Flanagan recounts how she proposed that the Living Newspaper enlist Rice for the New York directorship. Flanagan, *Arena*, 65.

47 Arent, "Ethiopia," 16.

48 Bahru Zewde, *History of Modern Ethiopia, 1855–1991*, Eastern African Studies (Athens: Ohio University Press, 2002), 151.

49 Nadia Nurhussein, *Black Land: Imperial Ethiopianism and African America* (Princeton: Princeton University Press, 2019), 5.

50 Ivy Wilson, "'ARE YOU MAN ENOUGH?': Imagining Ethiopia and Transnational Black Masculinity," *Callaloo* 33, no. 1 (April 2010): 265–77.

51 Edward Erhagbe and Ehimika Ifidon, "African-Americans and the Italo-Ethiopian Crisis, 1935–1936: The Practical Dimension of Pan-Africanism," *Aethiopica* 11 (April 2012): 68–84.

52 John Munro, "Ethiopia Stretches Forth across the Atlantic: African American Anticolonialism during the Interwar Period," *Left History: An Interdisciplinary Journal of Historical Inquiry and Debate* 13, no. 2 (2008): 47.

53 Carroll, *Race News*, 85.

54 Chiara Grilli, "The Making of the Italian American Colonizer: Colonialism, Race, and the Italo-Ethiopian War," *Interventions* 23, no. 4 (May 19, 2021): 538.

55 Nurhussein, *Black Land*, 121. Representations of Ethiopia circulated earlier, as Nurhussein details, in Jesse A. Shipp and Alex Rogers's *Abyssynia*, starring Bert Williams and George Walker. Nurhussein, *Black Land*, 129–33.

56 For a canonical treatment of the Popular Front, especially in relation to cultural workers, see Michael Denning, *The Cultural Front: The Laboring of American Culture in the Twentieth Century* (London: Verso, 1998).

57 Quoted In Arthur Arent, "Ethiopia," 17.

58 Nurhussein, *Black Land*, 139.

59 Arent, "Ethiopia," 31.

60 Arent, "Ethiopia," 27.

61 Brooks Atkinson, "'Ethiopia,' the First Issue of The Living Newspaper, Which the Federal Theatre Cannot Publish," *New York Times*, January 25, 1936.

62  Nurhussein, *Black Land,* 140.

63  Flanagan, *Arena,* 65. It is possible that Flanagan referred to Shogola Oloba, a group of African expats (living, and not stranded in, the United States) led by Asadata Dafora. Under the leadership of Dafora, who was born in Sierra Leone, Shogola Oloba performed at the Communist Party Bazaar and the New YMCA Little Theatre, as well as premiering a dance-opera called *Kyunkor, or the Witch Woman.* Cary D. Wintz and Paul Finkelman, eds., *Encyclopedia of the Harlem Renaissance* (New York: Routledge, 2004). See also Susan Manning, *Modern Dance, Negro Dance: Race in Motion* (Minneapolis: University of Minnesota Press, 2004), 44–55.

64  Susan Quinn, *Furious Improvisation: How the WPA and a Cast of Thousands Made High Art Out of Desperate Times* (repr., New York: Walker Books, 2009), 67.

65  "Rice Charges WPA Ruins Show It Set Up," *New York Herald Tribune,* January 25, 1936.

66  Atkinson, "Ethiopia."

67  Roi Ottley, "Rice Lost His Job for Battling Bias," *New York Amsterdam News,* February 1, 1936.

68  Heywood Broun to unknown, January 24, 1936, box 27, folder 14, Newspaper Guild of New York Records, Tamiment Library & Robert F. Wagner Labor Archives, New York University (RWL-NYU).

69  Milton Kauffman, "Letter to Federal Theatre Projects of City Projects Council, NYC," January 28, 1936, box 27, folder 14, RWL-NYU.

70  Watson, "Draft 'Foreword to Book of "Living Newspaper" Plays.'"

71  "Untitled Outline of the Living Newspaper," box 1, Living Newspaper—Speeches folder, Morris Watson Papers.

72  Sam Smiley, "Rhetoric on Stage in Living Newspapers," *Quarterly Journal of Speech* 54, no. 1 (February 1, 1968): 29–36.

73  Stokes, "Playing the Crowd." On the history of US pageantry, see Glassberg, *American Historical Pageantry;* Krasner, "The Pageant Is the Thing"; Prevots, *American Pageantry.*

74  "Living Newspaper Goes to Press," playbill for *Triple-A Plowed Under* 1.2, March 21, 1936, box 1057, LOC-FTP.

75  Marlis Schweitzer, "Surviving the City: Press Agents, Publicity Stunts, and the Spectacle of the Urban Female Body," in *Performance and the City,* ed. D. J. Hopkins, Shelley Orr, and Kim Solga (London: Palgrave Macmillan, 2009): 133–51.

76  Transcript of interview with Norman Lloyd, 17.

77  Add Bates, interview with Lorraine Brown, transcribed by Rhoda Durkan, November 30, 1976, WPA-GMU, 5.

78  Stuart Cosgrove, "The Living Newspaper: History, Production and Form" (PhD diss., University of Hull, 1982), 76.

79  Quoted in Cosgrove, "The Living Newspaper," 78.

80  Cosgrove, "The Living Newspaper," 77.

81  Joseph Losey to Morris Watson, July 27, 1936, Living Newspaper—Correspondence folder, Morris Watson Papers.

82  Cosgrove, "The Living Newspaper," 82.

83  Ann Folino White, *Plowed Under: Food Policy Protests and Performance in New Deal America* (Bloomington: Indiana University Press, 2014), 227–28.

84  Glende, "Labor Reporting and Its Critics in the CIO Years," 37, 40.

85  Carole Turbin, "Collars and Consumers: Changing Images of American Manliness and Business," *Enterprise & Society* 1, no. 3 (2000): 514.

86  *OED Online,* s.v. "white-collar."

87  US Congress, House of Representatives, Hearings before a Special Committee on Un-American Activities on H. Res. 282, 75th Cong., 3rd sess.–78th Cong., 2nd sess., *Congressional Record,* vol. 4 (Washington, DC: US Government Printing Office, 1938), 2867.

88  Flanagan, *Arena,* 57, 65.

89  Laurie A. Woodard, "'A Free America for All Peoples . . .': Fredi Washington, the Negro Actors Guild, and the Voice of the People," *Journal of African American History* 105, no. 3 (June 2020): 476.

90  David Bisaha, "Defending the Standard Contract: Unmeasured Work, Class, and Design Professionalism in United Scenic Artists Local 829," *Theatre Survey* 61, no. 2 (March 2020): 232.

91  Sean P. Holmes, *Weavers of Dreams, Unite! Actors' Unionism in Early Twentieth-Century America,* 1st ed. (Urbana: University of Illinois Press, 2013), 120.

92   National Play Bureau, "Bulletin of Procedure—#1," March 18 (no year given), RG 69, box 508, NARA.

93   "Meeting (Minutes): Committee of Organizations Representing the Federal Arts Projects of the WPA with Aubrey Williams and Thad Holt," June 11, 1936, box 1, Living Newspaper—Meetings and Statements, Morris Watson Papers.

94   Watson, "The White Collar Worker Enters the Labor Movement," 1.

95   "Journalism and the Arts in Everyday Life," transcript, *Exploring the Seven Arts*, Federal Radio Theatre, New York, July 7, 1937, 2, 4, 5, box 1, Morris Watson Papers.

96   Transcript of interview with Ethel Aaron Hauser and Philip Barber, February 20, 1976, WPA Oral Histories, box 5, folder 19, George Mason Special Collections, 21. The *Brooklyn Eagle* confirmed that an "improvised celebration" was held at the Ritz Theatre. "Watson Ordered to Resume Work," *Brooklyn Eagle,* April 13, 1937.

97   *Associated Press v. N.L.R.B.,* 301 U.S. 103 (1937).

98   The boxing match allegorized a moment in ANG history when journalist Dean Jennings was forced to resign from the Hearst-owned *San Francisco Call Bulletin* in order to attend an ANG conference. See Patrick Washburn and Michael Sweeney, "Francis Biddle and the Jennings Case in 1934–1935: A Labor Union, the First Amendment, and Government Oversight," in *Journalism's Ethical Progression,* ed. Gwyneth Mellinger and John P. Ferré (Lanham, MD: Lexington Books, 2020), 73–93.

99   Editorial staff of the Living Newspaper under the Supervision of Arthur Arent, *Triple-A Plowed Under: A Living Newspaper, in Federal Theatre Plays,* ed. Pierre de Rohan (New York: Random House, 1938), 20–23.

100  On the Indian Reorganization Act, see Vine Deloria, *The Indian Reorganization Act : Congresses and Bills* (Norman: University of Oklahoma Press, 2002).

101  Loren Kruger, *The National Stage: Theatre and Cultural Legitimation in England, France, and America* (Chicago: University of Chicago Press, 1992).

102  Ethel Aaron to Martin Popper, February 23, 1938, RG 69, box 497, *One-Third of a Nation*—Correspondence folder, NARA.

103  Cosgrove, "The Living Newspaper," 82.

104  Watson, "The AP, the Guild and Me."

105  Quoted in Jane DeHart Mathews, *Federal Theatre, 1935–1939: Plays, Relief, and Politics* (Princeton: Princeton University Press, 2015), 70.

106  "Writing the Living Newspaper," Federal Theatre Project, n.d., 3, 6, 4, LOC-FTP.

107  "Hearings before a Special Committee on Un-American Activities," 2873.

108  Philip Barber, "Interdepartmental Memo to George Kondolf," May 5, 1939, NARA.

109  Ethel Aaron Hauser and Philip Barber, interview with Lorraine Brown, Diane Bowers, transcribed by Rhoda Durkan, WPA-GMU, 2; Joseph Losey to Morris Watson, July 27, 1936, 2, 4, box 1, Living Newspaper—Correspondence folder, Morris Watson Papers.

110  Burris-Meyer, interview, 10.

111  Sharon Ann Musher, *Democratic Art: The New Deal's Influence on American Culture* (Chicago: University of Chicago Press), 115; Howard Pollack, *Marc Blitzstein: His Life, His Work, His World* (Oxford: Oxford University Press, 2012), 206–7.

112  Bay, interview, 4.

113  Hauser and Barber, interview, 19.

CHAPTER TWO: THE COURT OF PUBLIC OPINION

1   Morris Watson, "Foreword to Book of Living Newspaper Plays," 1, March 17, 1937, box 1, Living Newspaper—Article, Radio Programs folder, Morris Watson Papers, Ax 774, University of Oregon Libraries Special Collections and University Archives.

2   Arthur Arent, "'Ethiopia': The First 'Living Newspaper,'" *Educational Theatre Journal* 20, no. 1 (1968): 31.

3   Editorial staff of the Living Newspaper under the Supervision of Arthur Arent, *Triple-A Plowed Under: A Living Newspaper,* in *Federal Theatre Plays,* ed. Pierre de Rohan (New York: Random House, 1938), 57.

4   Stuart Cosgrove, "The Living Newspaper: History, Production and Form" (PhD diss., University of Hull, 1982), 61.

5   A playbill for the Living Newspaper at the Cleveland Repertory Theatre announces "a drama-
    tization of world news events" and lists a series of scenes presenting different headline stories.
    Playbill for "*The Living Newspaper* at the Cleveland Repertory Theatre," Playbills file, box 1095,
    Library of Congress Federal Theatre Collection (LOC-FTP).

6   Arthur Arent, "The Technique of the Living Newspaper," *Theatre Arts* 21 (November 1938):
    821.

7   For a brief treatment, see Stuart Cosgrove, introduction to *"Liberty Deferred" and Other Living
    Newspapers of the 1930s Federal Theatre Project*, ed. Lorraine Brown, Tamara Liller, and Barbara
    Jones Smith (Fairfax, VA: George Mason University Press, 1989), ix–xxv.

8   John Nerone, "The Historical Roots of the Normative Model of Journalism," *Journalism* 14,
    no. 4 (May 1, 2013): 450.

9   Walter Lippmann, *The Phantom Public* (New Brunswick, NJ: Transaction Publishers, 2011),
    3.

10  Lippmann, *The Phantom Public*, 10.

11  In the 1920s and 1930s, voting was mostly restricted, de jure and/or de facto, to white Amer-
    icans. On the relationship between structural inequalities, racism, and civic engagement, see
    for instance Michael Waldman, *The Fight to Vote* (New York: Simon & Schuster, 2016); Jeff
    Manza and Christopher Uggen, *Locked Out: Felon Disenfranchisement and American Democ-
    racy*, 1st ed. (New York: Oxford University Press, 2008); Richard Iton, *Solidarity Blues: Race,
    Culture, and the American Left* (Chapel Hill: University of North Carolina Press, 2000); Vicki
    L. Eaklor, *Queer America: A People's GLBT History of the United States* (New York: New Press,
    2011); Eric S. Yellin, *Racism in the Nation's Service: Government Workers and the Color Line
    in Woodrow Wilson's America* (Chapel Hill: University of North Carolina Press, 2013); Rena
    Fraden, *Blueprints for a Black Federal Theatre* (Cambridge: Cambridge University Press, 1996).

12  "The man who wears the shoe knows best that it pinches and where it pinches, even if the
    expert shoemaker is the best judge of how the trouble is to be remedied." John Dewey, *The
    Public and Its Problems*, 1st ed. (Athens, OH: Swallow Press, 1954), 207.

13  Dewey, *The Public and Its Problems*, 180, 184.

14  Quoted In Anthony Oberschall, "The Historical Roots of Public Opinion Research," in *The
    Sage Handbook of Public Opinion Research* (London: Sage Publications, 2008), 87.

15  Dewey, *The Public and Its Problems*, 183.

16  Christopher B. Balme, *The Theatrical Public Sphere* (Cambridge: Cambridge University Press,
    2014).

17  Hallie Flanagan, *Arena: The History of the Federal Theatre* (New York: B. Blom, 1965), 321.

18  On the figure and significance of the "crowd," as distinct from the "public," in modern social
    and political thought, see Shilarna Stokes, "Playing the Crowd: Mass Pageantry in Europe
    and the United States, 1905–1935" (PhD diss., Columbia University, 2013); Jeffrey T. Schnapp
    and Matthew Tiews, eds., *Crowds* (Stanford: Stanford University Press, 2006).

19  Editorial staff of the Living Newspaper Unit, *1935*, in Brown, Liller, and Smith, *Liberty Deferred*,
    10, hereafter cited parenthetically by page in the text.

20  I take the distinction between chronic time and acute time from John Durham Peters's analysis
    of media that figure time and space. John Durham Peters, "Calendar, Clock, Tower," in *Deus
    in Machina: Religion and Technology in Historical Perspective*, ed. Jeremy Stolow (New York:
    Fordham University Press, 2013), 10.

21  Peters, "Calendar, Clock, Tower," 11.

22  For a history of yellow journalism and its connections to Hearst and Pulitzer, see W. Joseph
    Campbell, *Yellow Journalism: Puncturing the Myths, Defining the Legacies* (New York: Greenwood
    Publishing Group, 2001).

23  Bixby's entrance foreshadows a popular device in the Federal Theatre Project's Living News-
    papers: in *Power*, a spotlight would illuminate the protagonist, Consumer, from the shadows of
    the stage; in *One-Third of a Nation*, discussed in chapter 3, the somewhat pluckier Little Man
    would demand a light to help him enter the stage from the audience. Arthur Arent, *Power*, in
    *Federal Theatre Plays. 1. Triple-A Plowed Under, by the Staff of the Living Newspaper. 2. Power,
    a Living Newspaper, by Arthur Arent. 3. Spirochete, a History, by Arnold Sundgaard*, ed. Pierre
    de Rohan (New York: Random House, 1938); Arthur Arent, *One-Third of a Nation*, in *Federal
    Theatre Plays. 1. Prologue to Glory, by E. P. Conkle. 2. One-Third of a Nation, by Arthur Arent.
    3. Haiti, by William Du Bois*, ed. Pierre de Rohan (New York: Random House, 1938).

24  David Welky, *Everything Was Better in America: Print Culture in the Great Depression* (Champaign: University of Illinois Press, 2010), 29.

25  Welky, *Everything Was Better*, 40.

26  As Colin Gardner notes, "the revue format" offered a "kaleidoscope of front-page issues" that contrasted with the single-issue "chronicle" dramaturgy that dominated the Living Newspaper form. Colin Gardner, "The Losey–Moscow Connection: Experimental Soviet Theatre and the Living Newspaper," *New Theatre Quarterly* 30, no. 3 (August 2014): 256.

27  John Osburn, "The Dramaturgy of the Tabloid: Climax and Novelty in a Theory of Condensed Forms," *Theatre Journal* 46, no. 4 (1994): 521, 507.

28  Gardner, "The Losey–Moscow Connection"; Ilka Saal, *New Deal Theater: The Vernacular Tradition in American Political Theater* (New York: Springer, 2007); Harold Burris-Meyer, interview with Lorraine Brown, transcribed by Rhoda Durkan, March 14, 1977, box 2, folder 13, WPA Oral Histories, George Mason University Special Collections (WPA-GMU), 4.

29  Kendall Thomas, "*Rouge et Noir* Reread: A Popular Constitutional History of the Angelo Herndon Case," *Southern California Law Review,* 65, no. 6 (September 1992): 2628.

30  Michael Warner, *Publics and Counterpublics* (New York: Zone Books, 2002), 66. My use of "interpellation" follows that of the rhetorician Maurice Charland, who draws in turn from Louis Althusser, Edwin Black, and Kenneth Burke. Charland uses "interpellation" to describe the process by which people take on the personae ascribed to them through a particular discourse (such as a speech, founding myth, narrative, or for my purposes, a play). Warner seems to have something similar in mind when he argues that a public "exists by virtue of being addressed" (67). Maurice Charland, "Constitutive Rhetoric: The Case of the Peuple Québécois," *Quarterly Journal of Speech* 73, no. 2 (May 1, 1987): 137–38.

31  Arent, "The Technique of the Living Newspaper," 822.

32  See Jack C. Ellis, *The Documentary Idea: A Critical History of English-Language Documentary Film and Video* (Englewood Cliffs, NJ: Prentice Hall, 1989), 79–81.

33  Elizabeth Osborne offers a comprehensive analysis of the FTP's national reach and regional variations. Elizabeth A. Osborne, *Staging the People: Community and Identity in the Federal Theatre Project* (New York: Palgrave Macmillan, 2011).

34  Brooks Atkinson, "Headlines of 1935 in the Second Issue of the Living Newspaper," *New York Times*, May 14, 1936.

35  "Footlights on a Fortnight," *The New Yorker*, May 23, 1936, 31.

36  "Living Newspaper—1935," *New York Evening Journal*, May 13, 1936.

37  "Living Newspaper—1935."

38  "Wake of the News," *New York Post*, May 18, 1936.

39  Arthur Pollock, "'1935' New Issue of the Federal Theatre's Living Newspaper a Lively Sheet, Opens at the Biltmore Theatre," *Brooklyn Eagle*, May 13, 1936.

40  "Living Newspaper Takes Up '1935,'" *New York Daily News*, May 13, 1936.

41  "The New Play," *New York Sun*, May 13, 1936, transcription in Production Records, box 1047, LOC-FTP.

42  "Events of 1935 Dramatized by WPA Actors," *New York Herald Tribune*, May 13, 1936.

43  Pollock, "'1935' New Issue of the Federal Theatre's Living Newspaper a Lively Sheet."

44  Jury summons print ad for *Injunction Granted!,* Biltmore Theatre, New York, 1936, box 963, folder 4.1.20–4.1.64, LOC-FTP.

CHAPTER THREE: THE LITTLE MAN AND THE LOUDSPEAKER

1  For an analysis of gender's crucial role in the FTP hearings, see Kate Dossett, "Gender and the Dies Committee Hearings on the Federal Theatre Project," *Journal of American Studies* 47, no. 4 (2013): 993–1017.

2  J. Michael Sproule, *Propaganda and Democracy: The American Experience of Media and Mass Persuasion* (Cambridge: Cambridge University Press, 1997), 9.

3  US Congress, House of Representatives, Hearings before a Special Committee on Un-American Activities, on H. Res. 282, 75th Cong., 3rd sess.–78th Cong., 2nd sess., *Congressional Record*, vol. 4 (Washington, DC: US Government Printing Office, 1938), 2850. Harry Hopkins made a similar point but positioned propaganda in service of informed consumption. After *Power*

opened, he stated, "It's propaganda to educate the consumer who's paying for power." Quoted in Rania Karoula, *The Federal Theatre Project, 1935–1939: Engagement and Experimentation* (Edinburgh: Edinburgh University Press, 2020), 76.

4 *Congressional Record*, 2850.

5 *Congressional Record*, 2850.

6 Mark Crispin Miller, introduction to Edward L. Bernays, *Propaganda* (Brooklyn: Ig Publishing, 2005), 9–15.

7 William M. Keith, *Democracy as Discussion: Civic Education and the American Forum Movement* (Lanham, MD: Lexington Books, 2007).

8 John Durham Peters, "Dialogue and Dissemination," in *Speaking into the Air: A History of the Idea of Communication* (Chicago: University of Chicago Press, 1999), 33–62.

9 Loren Kruger, *The National Stage: Theatre and Cultural Legitimation in England, France, and America* (Chicago: University of Chicago Press, 1992), 168.

10 Kate Dossett, *Radical Black Theatre in the New Deal* (Chapel Hill: University of North Carolina Press, 2020), 85.

11 "Meeting (Minutes): Committee of Organizations Representing the Federal Arts Projects of the WPA with Aubrey Williams and Thad Holt," June 11, 1936, box 1, Living Newspaper— Meetings and Statements, Morris Watson Papers, Ax 774, University of Oregon Libraries Special Collections and University Archives.

12 Ad for *Power* at the Alcazar Theater, San Francisco, 1937, Playbills file, box 1096, Library of Congress Federal Theatre Collection (LOC-FTP).

13 Playbill for *One-Third of a Nation* at the Walnut Street Theatre, Philadelphia, October 1938, Playbills file, box 1096, LOC-FTP.

14 Sidney Whipple, "Problems of Slums Presented in Play," *New York World-Telegram*, January 18, 1938.

15 "The Living Newspaper," *Literary Digest*, May 8, 1936, Playbills file, box 1096, LOC-FTP.

16 Brooks Atkinson, "Living Newspaper of the Federal Theatre Reports the Housing Situation," *New York Times*, January 18, 1938; Arthur Pollock, "'1935' New Issue of the Federal Theatre's Living Newspaper a Lively Sheet, Opens at the Biltmore Theatre," *Brooklyn Eagle*, May 13, 1936.

17 Vanessa Beasley and Deborah Smith-Howell, "No Ordinary Rhetorical President: FDR's Speechmaking and Leadership, 1933–1945," in *American Rhetoric in the New Deal Era, 1932–1945: A Rhetorical History of the United States*, vol. 7, ed. Thomas Benson (East Lansing: Michigan State University Press, 2006), 12; Cara Finnegan, "FSA Photography and New Deal Visual Culture," in Benson, *American Rhetoric in the New Deal Era*, 117; Mary E. Stuckey, "FDR, the Rhetoric of Vision, and the Creation of a National Synoptic State," *Quarterly Journal of Speech* 98, no. 3 (August 1, 2012): 304, 306, 310.

18 Franklin Delano Roosevelt, "The Second Inaugural Address, 20 January 1937," in *Public Papers and Addresses of Franklin D. Roosevelt*, vol. 6 (New York: Macmillan, 1938), 4–5.

19 NYLN, "Playbill for 'One-Third of a Nation,' V.3," 1938, 1, box 1051, LOC-FTP.

20 Howard Bay, interview with John O'Connor, transcribed by Rhoda Durkan, February 21, 1976, box 2, folder 13, WPA Oral Histories, George Mason University Special Collections (WPA-GMU), 2, 1.

21 Arthur Arent, *One-Third of a Nation*, in *Federal Theatre Plays. 1. Prologue to Glory, by E. P. Conkle. 2. One-Third of a Nation, by Arthur Arent. 3. Haiti, by William Du Bois*, ed. Pierre de Rohan (New York: Random House, 1938), 13, hereafter cited parenthetically by page in the text.

22 Arthur Arent, "The Technique of the Living Newspaper," *Theatre Arts* 21 (November 1938), 824.

23 Michael Schudson, *The Power of News* (Cambridge: Harvard University Press, 1982), 91.

24 Arent, "*Technique*," 824.

25 Ken Jaworowski, "'One-Third of a Nation' at Metropolitan Playhouse—Review," *New York Times*, May 1, 2011.

26 David Hendy, "Radio Technology," in *The International Encyclopedia of Communication*, ed. Wolfgang Donsbach (Malden, MA: Blackwell, 2008), 4107–11.

27 Cornelia Epping-Jäger, "Voice Politics: Establishing the 'Loud/Speaker' in the Political Communication of National Socialism," in *Media, Culture, and Mediality: New Insights into the Current State of Research*, ed. Ludwig Jäger, Erika Linz, and Irmela Schneider (Bielefeld: transcript Verlag, 2010), 166, 176.

28 Ronda L. Sewald, "Forced Listening: The Contested Use of Loudspeakers for Commercial and Political Messages in the Public Soundscape," *American Quarterly* 63, no. 3 (September 2011): 772.

29 Timothy D. Taylor, Mark Katz, and Tony Grajeda, *Music, Sound, and Technology in America: A Documentary History of Early Phonograph, Cinema, and Radio* (Durham: Duke University Press, 2012), 231.

30 Harold Burris-Meyer, interview with Lorraine Brown, transcribed by Rhoda Durkan, March 14, 1977, box 2, folder 13, WPA-GMU, 3, 6, 8.

31 Brooks Atkinson, "The Saga of the Slums," *New York Times*, January 30, 1938.

32 Taylor, Katz, and Grajeda, *Music, Sound, and Technology in America*, 141.

33 Jack C. Ellis and Betsy A. McLane, *A New History of Documentary Film* (New York: Continuum, 2005), 81.

34 Susan Duffy and Bernard K. Duffy, "Theatrical Responses to Technology during the Depression: Three Federal Theatre Project Plays," *Theatre History Studies* 6 (January 1, 1986): 145.

35 Sarah Elizabeth Igo, *The Averaged American: Surveys, Citizens, and the Making of a Mass Public* (Cambridge: Harvard University Press, 2007), 15.

36 Norman Lloyd, interview with John O'Connor, transcribed by Rhoda Durkan, January 5, 1976, box 7, folder 11, WPA-GMU, 8.

37 *OED Online*, s.v. "Little Man."

38 Hans Fallada, *Little Man, What Now?*, trans. Susan Bennett (Brooklyn: Melville House, 2009).

39 *OED Online*, s.v. "news."

40 Michael Schudson, *Discovering the News: A Social History of American Newspapers* (New York: Basic Books, 1981), 91.

41 Sproule, *Propaganda and Democracy*, 105.

42 Barbara Melosh, *Engendering Culture: Manhood and Womanhood in New Deal Public Art and Theater* (Washington, DC: Smithsonian Institution Press, 1991), 98, 4.

43 The performance theorist Andrew Hewitt identifies the act of walking with a choreography of "civilization" cultivated since the Enlightenment. He theorizes "stumbling," by extension, as "the moment of nature's transition into culture," which is to say, a failure of acculturation and thus of legibility. Democratic imaginaries, as Hewitt points out, often entail universal norms of legibility: "social choreography" enacted without stumbles. Viewed as "social choreography," the Little Man's stumble depicts the awkwardness of entering the stage of politics, and even of acting legibly upon it. Andrew Hewitt, *Social Choreography: Ideology as Performance in Dance and Everyday Movement* (Durham: Duke University Press, 2005), 87.

44 Konstantin Rudnitsky, *Russian and Soviet Theatre: Tradition and the Avant-Garde* (London: Thames & Hudson, 2000), 198.

45 Morris Watson, "Writing the Living Newspaper," Report for the National Service Bureau, 12, 13, n.d., box 133, folder FTP 000 225 25.9, LOC-FTP.

46 Rudnitsky, *Russian and Soviet Theatre*; Jacques Rancière, *The Emancipated Spectator* (Brooklyn: Verso Books, 2014). Blitzstein is quoted in Ilka Saal, *New Deal Theater: The Vernacular Tradition in American Political Theater* (New York: Springer, 2007), 114.

47 Kruger, *The National Stage*, 149.

48 Tracy C. Davis, "Theatricality and Civil Society," in *Theatricality*, ed. Thomas Postlewait and Tracy Davis (Cambridge: Cambridge University Press, 2003), 145. "Dedouble" is also a Kreyòl term with distinctive usages in Haitian performance. The performance scholar Mario LaMothe defines "dedouble" as "the Haitian body desiring to unbind itself from prescriptions (fixed time, place, and socio-cultural conventions). It embraces a way of remembering what is *mistik,* dwòl, hidden or suppressed, that which is not easily categorized and thrives in the rich messiness of the quotidian." For LaMothe as for Davis, dedouble/dedoublement encodes a potentially transgressive response to social relations, Mario LaMothe, "Dedouble and Jeanguy

Saintus' Corporeal Gifts," *emisférica* 11, no. 2 (Spring 2015), accessed August 21, 2020, http://archive.hemisphericinstitute.org/hemi/en/emisferica-121-caribbean-rasanblaj/lamothe.

49  See Ronald Carpenter, "Father Charles E. Coughlin: Delivery, Style in Discourse, and Opinion Leadership," in Benson, *American Rhetoric in the New Deal Era: 315–368*; Robert S. Iltis, "Reconsidering the Demagoguery of Huey Long," in Benton, *American Rhetoric in the New Deal Era: 369–419*.

50  My thanks to Aileen Robinson for the insight about the confederate from her scholarship on magic.

51  Lindsay Goss, "Crisis Actors," presentation, Annual Meeting of the American Society for Theatre Research, Arlington, VA, November 8, 2019, 7.

52  Sproule, *Propaganda and Democracy*, 121.

53  Institute for Propaganda Analysis, *How to Detect Propaganda,* vol. 1.2 (New York: Institute for Propaganda Analysis, 1937).

54  Sproule, *Propaganda and Democracy*, 99.

55  Elisabeth Fondren, "'We Are Propagandists for Democracy': The Institute for Propaganda Analysis' Pioneering Media Literacy Efforts to Fight Disinformation (1937–1942)," *American Journalism* 38, no. 3 (July 3, 2021): 265, 266, 273, 274.

56  "New Plays in Manhattan," *Time*, January 21, 1938, 47.

57  Nelson B. Bell, "Civic Theater Hits Bulls-Eye in Novel Play: 'Living Newspaper,'" *Washington Post*, May 23, 1938.

## CHAPTER FOUR: THE KEEPER OF RECORDS

1  Richard Iton, *Solidarity Blues: Race, Culture, and the American Left* (Chapel Hill: University of North Carolina Press, 2000), 130.

2  Rebecca Sklaroff, *Black Culture and the New Deal* (Chapel Hill: University of North Carolina Press, 2014), 23, 22.

3  Rena Fraden, *Blueprints for a Black Federal Theatre* (Cambridge: Cambridge University Press, 1996), 45–46.

4  Kate Dossett, *Radical Black Theatre in the New Deal* (Chapel Hill: University of North Carolina Press, 2020).

5  "Negro Stars Continue in News Drama—One Third of a Nation," *Chicago Defender* (national edition), July 9, 1938.

6  Editorial staff of the Living Newspaper Unit, *Injunction Granted!,* in *Liberty Deferred and Other Living Newspapers of the 1930s* (Fairfax, VA: George Mason University Press, 1989), 80. For an analysis of the FTP's engagement with Native Americans through its "First Americans" radio plays, see Elizabeth A. Osborne, "Imagined Democracy: The Federal Theatre Project Performs (Native) America (1938–39)," in *Experiments in Democracy: Interracial and Cross-Cultural Exchange in American Theatre, 1912–1945,* ed. Cheryl Black and Jonathan Shandell (Carbondale: Southern Illinois University Press, 2016), 172–90.

7  Fred Carroll, *Race News: Black Journalists and the Fight for Racial Justice in the Twentieth Century* (Champaign: University of Illinois Press, 2017), 79.

8  Dossett, *Radical Black Theatre in the New Deal*, 107.

9  Ida B. Wells, "Lynching Our National Crime," presented at the National Negro Conference, New York, June 1, 1909, http://moses.law.umn.edu/darrow/documents/Proceedings%20of%20the%20National%20Negro%20Conference%201909_%20New%20York_%20May%2031%20and%20June_1.pdf.

10  "Sport News and Gossip," *New York Age,* April 16, 1938.

11  Pam Platt, "John Silvera: Giving History a Nudge," *Florida Today,* February 18, 1997.

12  John Silvera, interview with Lorraine Brown, transcribed by Rhoda Durkan, July 11, 1977, box 9, folder 27, WPA Oral Histories, George Mason University Special Collections (WPA-GMU), 2.

13  Dossett, *Radical Black Theatre in the New Deal*, 102.

14  Dossett, *Radical Black Theatre in the New Deal*, 89.

15  Dossett, *Radical Black Theatre in the New Deal*, 102, 106.

16  Henry Louis Gates Jr., *The Signifying Monkey: A Theory of African American Literary Criticism* (New York: Oxford University Press, 2014).

17  Benedict Anderson, *Imagined Communities* (London: Verso Books, 2016).

18  Abram Hill and John D. Silvera, "Liberty Deferred, Draft 2," in *"Liberty Deferred" and Other Living Newspapers of the 1930s Federal Theatre Project*, ed. Lorraine Brown (Fairfax, VA: George Mason University Press, 1989), 1, 3, hereafter cited parenthetically by page in the text.

19  Daphne Brooks, *Bodies in Dissent: Spectacular Performances of Race and Freedom, 1850–1910* (Durham: Duke University Press, 2006), 4.

20  Dossett, *Radical Black Theatre in the New Deal*, 83.

21  Robin Bernstein, *Racial Innocence: Performing American Childhood from Slavery to Civil Rights* (New York: New York University Press, 2011).

22  Gerald Horne, *The Rise and Fall of the Associated Negro Press: Claude Barnett's Pan-African News and the Jim Crow Paradox* (Urbana: University of Illinois Press, 2017), 12.

23  Susan Manning, *Modern Dance, Negro Dance: Race in Motion* (Minneapolis: University of Minnesota Press, 2004), 44, 143.

24  Richard M. Perloff, "The Press and Lynchings of African Americans," *Journal of Black Studies* 30, no. 3 (2000): 326.

25  Kim Gallon, *Pleasure in the News: African American Readership and Sexuality in the Black Press* (Champaign: University of Illinois Press, 2020), 19.

26  Koritha Mitchell, *Living with Lynching: African American Lynching Plays, Performance, and Citizenship, 1890–1930*, 1st ed. (Urbana: University of Illinois Press, 2012).

27  Tina Post, "The Phantom Punch," *The Appendix* 1, no. 2 (April 11, 2013), http://theappendix .net/issues/2013/4/the-phantom-punch; Tina Post, "Joe Louis's Utopic Glitch," in *Race and Performance after Repetition*, ed. Soyica Diggs Colbert, Douglas A. Jones Jr., and Shane Vogel (Durham: Duke University Press, 2020), 103–26.

28  The cultural historian Harvey Young writes powerfully about lynching as spectacle by considering the role of material remains in remembering people who were lynched and those who participated in their lynching. Harvey Young, "The Black Body as Souvenir in American Lynching," *Theatre Journal* 57, no. 4 (2005): 639–57.

29  In Western, colonial imaginaries, African peoples and cultures are "the antithesis of modernity": primitive, pre-modern, untouched by new technologies, and uninvolved in their production. Afro-modernity both negates this idea and critiques its premises in colonialism and slavery. The subjects of Afro-modernity are conscious of history's role in contemporary politics and white supremacy and therefore, in many cases, actively engaged in reconstructing their past. Michael Hanchard, "Afro-Modernity: Temporality, Politics, and the African Diaspora," *Public Culture* 11, no. 1 (January 1999): 247.

30  Dossett, *Radical Black Theatre in the New Deal*.

31  Paul Nadler, "Liberty Censored: Black Living Newspapers of the Federal Theatre Project," *African American Review* 29, no. 4 (Winter 1995): 619.

32  Dossett, *Radical Black Theatre in the New Deal*, 107–8, 101.

33  Morris Surofsky, "Reader Report for 'Liberty Deferred,'" August 20, 1938, box 241, Library of Congress Federal Theatre Collection, emphasis added.

34  Surofsky, "Reader Report."

35  Candis Callison and Mary Lynn Young, *Reckoning: Journalism's Limits and Possibilities* (New York: Oxford University Press, 2020), 24–36; Carroll, *Race News*, 8.

36  Nadler, "Liberty Censored," 620.

37  Nadler, "Liberty Censored," 620, 621; Dossett, *Radical Black Theatre in the New Deal*, 117–18.

38  Nadler, "Liberty Censored," 621.

39  Dossett, *Radical Black Theatre in the New Deal*, 106–8.

40  Dossett, *Radical Black Theatre in the New Deal*.

41  Dan Burley, "'Liberty Deferred' Living Newspaper," *New York Amsterdam News*, December 10, 1938.

42  Arthur Pollock, "'Harriet,' the City Center, and a Play by Abe Hill Called 'Liberty Deferred,'" *Brooklyn Daily Eagle*, October 1, 1944.

43  Platt, "John Silvera."

44  John D. Silvera, "Still in Blackface," *The Crisis* 46 (1939): 76.

45  Silvera, "Still in Blackface," 76.

46  Platt, "John Silvera."

47  Loften Mitchell, *Voices of the Black Theatre* (Clifton, NJ: J. T. White, 1975), 147.

48  *OED Online*, s.v. "relevance."

49  Colbert, Jones, and Vogel, *Race and Performance after Repetition,* 4.


## CONCLUSION: OUTSIDE AND AFTER THE NYLN

1  "Writing the Living Newspaper," Federal Theatre Project, n.d., Library of Congress Federal Theatre Project Collection (LOC-FTP), 3, 6, 4.

2  Philip Barber, "Interdepartmental Memo to George Kondolf," May 5, 1939, National Archives and Records Administration (NARA).

3  "Theatre Arts Committee," *Time,* May 30, 1938, 26.

4  Michael Denning, *The Cultural Front: The Laboring of American Culture in the Twentieth Century* (London: Verso, 1998), 326–27.

5  Emanuel Eisenberg and Jay Williams, *One-Third of a Mitten*, draft, March 30, 1939, Playscripts file, box 729, folder FTP 000 485, LOC-FTP, 1, 4. The kid glove reference might have also been a jab at Hollywood film producer Samuel Goldwyn, who became the "highest-paid glove salesman in the country" before creating Goldwyn Pictures (which would merge with two other companies to become Metro-Goldwyn-Mayer) and Samuel Goldwyn Productions. For more on Goldwyn's career in the glove business, see Carol Easton, *The Search for Sam Goldwyn* (Jackson: University Press of Mississippi, 1975).

6  Eisenberg and Williams, *One-Third of a Mitten,* 5.

7  Hariman calls parody "the essential corrective to inelasticity." Robert Hariman, "Political Parody and Public Culture," *Quarterly Journal of Speech* 94, no. 3 (August 2008), 249–50.

8  Eisenberg and Williams, *One-Third of a Mitten,* 5.

9  Sianne Ngai, "Theory of the Gimmick," *Critical Inquiry* 43, no. 2 (January 2017): 466; Sianne Ngai, *Theory of the Gimmick: Aesthetic Judgment and Capitalist Form* (Cambridge: Harvard University Press, 2020), 52.

10  Howard Bay, interview with John O'Connor, transcribed by Rhoda Durkan, February 21, 1976, box 2, folder 13, WPA Oral Histories, George Mason University Special Collections, 4.

11  Ngai, *Theory of the Gimmick,* 46, 95–99.

12  Ngai, "Theory of the Gimmick," 504, 494.

13  Christopher Balme, *The Theatrical Public Sphere* (Cambridge: Cambridge University Press, 2014), 17.

14  Arnold Goldman, "Life and Death of the Living Newspaper Unit," *Theatre Quarterly* 3, no. 9 (1973): 72, 79.

15  For a discussion of Living Newspapers produced by FTP personnel after 1939, see Douglas McDermott, "The Living Newspaper as a Dramatic Form" (PhD diss., University of Iowa, 1963), 212–51.

16  Elizabeth A. Osborne, "The Promise of the Green New Deal: A 21st-Century Federal Theatre Project," *TDR: The Drama Review* 65, no. 4 (Winter 2021): 11–28.

17  Playbill for *Written Off?,* a staged reading and discussion of *Shelter/Chicago,* Illinois Humanities Council, Claudia Cassidy Theatre, Chicago Cultural Center, April 29, 2014.

18  Vicky Featherstone, artistic director, Royal Court Theatre, London, interview with the author, March 18, 2021.

19  Featherstone interview.

20  Ryan Calais Cameron, "The Blank Space," for *Living Newspaper: A Counter Narrative,* edition 2, online, December 22–28, 2020, Royal Court Theatre.

21  Chris Thorpe, "Always Maybe the Last Time," for *Living Newspaper: A Counter Narrative,* edition 1, online, December 13–20, 2020, Royal Court Theatre.

# INDEX

Page numbers in *italics* indicate figures.